WITHDRAWN

The Secret Life of Pronouns

THE SECRET LIFE OF PRONOUNS

WHAT OUR WORDS SAY ABOUT US

James W. Pennebaker

BLOOMSBURY PRESS

New York   Berlin   London   Sydney

Published by Bloomsbury Press, New York

All papers used by Bloomsbury Press are natural, recyclable products
made from wood grown in well-managed forests. The manufacturing
processes conform to the environmental regulations of the country of origin.

LIBRARY OF CONGRESS CATALOGING-IN-PUBLICATION DATA

Pennebaker, James W.
The secret life of pronouns : what our words say about us /
James W. Pennebaker. —1st U.S. ed.
p. cm.
Includes bibliographical references and index.
ISBN: 978-1-60819-480-3
1. English language—Pronoun. 2. English language—Grammar. I. Title.
PE1261.P46 2011
425'.55—dc22
2011001289

First U.S. edition 2011

7 9 10 8 6

Designed by Sara Stemen
Typeset by Westchester Book Group
Printed in the U.S.A. by Quad/Graphics, Fairfield, Pennsylvania

For you
        and for us
                and where we have been
                          and where we will go.

Contents

Preface

STOP FOR A minute and think about your last conversation, e-mail, or text message. You think you said something about dinner plans, your laundry, a strategy for the next sales meeting. And you probably did. But at the same time, you said much, much more. The precise words you used to communicate your message revealed more about you than you can imagine.

You, a, am, to, I, but, the, for, not . . .

Pronouns, articles, prepositions, and a handful of other small, stealthy words reveal parts of your personality, thinking style, emotional state, and connections with others. These words, typically called function words, account for less than one-tenth of 1 percent of your vocabulary but make up almost 60 percent of the words you use.* Your brain is not wired to notice them but if you pay close attention, you will start to see their subtle power.

Function words behave differently than you might think. For example, the most commonly used word in spoken English, *I*, is used at far higher rates by followers than by leaders, truth-tellers than liars. People who use high rates of articles—*a, an, the*—do better in college than low users. And if you want to find your true love, compare the ways you use function words with that of your prospective partners.

---

* This is the only footnote you will see in this book. For more background on specific topics, check the notes section at the back of the book. A reference section is also included. Online exercises can be found at www.SecretLifeOfPronouns.com.

Although this book focuses on function words, it really isn't about parts of speech at all. Rather, it's about how these words serve as windows into people's personalities and social connections. My training and early research bridged the areas of social, personality, clinical, and health psychology. Only through some accidental discoveries did I even notice the existence of these stealth words.

At first, the study of function words was a side venture. But as I delved more deeply into the topic, I started making some unexpected connections to leadership, mental health, brain function, and other issues. Soon, my students and I were spending time with computer engineers, linguists, FBI agents, lawyers, doctors, and marketing gurus, and with colleagues in history, political science, communications, and even accounting. And, most recently, we have been swept up in the social media frenzy—applying our ideas and methods to Twitter, Facebook, online dating, blogging, instant messaging, e-mail, and even the occasional old-fashioned telephone call.

This book is a little like a travel guide. It is organized around some of my favorite topics in psychology and the social sciences—personality, gender, deception, leadership, love, history, politics, and groups. The goal is to show how the analysis of function words can lead to new insights in each of these topics. At the same time, I want you to appreciate ways of thinking about and analyzing language. No matter what your personal or professional interest, I hope you come to see the world differently and can use this knowledge to better understand yourself and others.

A REVOLUTION IS under way in the analysis of language that will have a profound effect on the social sciences and humanities. The words that people generate in their lifetimes are like fingerprints. Increasingly, these words can be used to establish people's identities and even their backgrounds. Language use, especially the use of function words, can signal people's social networks and the roles they play in their families, in their neighborhoods, and at work. Wherever there is a word trail, a host of new computer-based methods can follow it. Shakespeare, Confucius, authors of ancient religious texts, politicians, and novelists have left behind a mind-boggling number of words that scholars from all disciplines can now study with new eyes and unprecedented tools.

Although the analysis of language is the focus of this book, it is really a work of psychology. Whereas linguists are primarily interested in language for its own sake, I'm interested in what people's words say about their psychological states. Words, then, can be thought of as powerful tools to excavate people's thoughts, feelings, motivations, and connections with others. With advancements in computer technologies, this approach is informing a wide range of scholars across many disciplines—linguists, sociolinguists, English scholars, anthropological linguists, neuroscientists, psycholinguists, developmentalists, computer scientists, computational linguists, and others. Some of the most innovative work is now coming from collaborations between academics of all stripes and companies such as Google.

If you are interested in the topics or approach of this book, there are a handful of very bright thinkers and writers whose work is accessible to a wide audience. Some who have influenced my approach the most include the sociologist Erving Goffman, the linguist George Lakoff, the cognitive scientist Steven Pinker, the sociolinguist Deborah Tannen, and the anthropologist Anna Wierzbicka.

The contributions of many others have directly affected my thinking about the fundamental connections between word use and psychological state. Freud's early work on slips of the tongue marked the first psychological acknowledgment that unintended words that pop out of our mouths can reveal hidden thoughts and feelings. Later psychoanalysts, such as Louis Gottschalk and Walter Weintraub, provided road maps on how to link seemingly innocuous words to deeper motivations and fears that patients were expressing.

Several computer-based text analysis systems presaged my own computer work, especially Philip Stone's General Inquirer program in the 1960s. Any comprehensive story about the early days of text analysis also includes names such as Doug Biber, Herb Clark, Donald Foster, Howard Giles, Rod Hart, Robert Hogenraad, Hans Kordy, Klaus Krippendorf, Colin Martindale, Erhard Mergenthaler, and others.

The people who have influenced me the most, however, have been my students and colleagues over the years. This book reflects the collaborative effort of dozens, even hundreds, of people. Those who have been most central to the current language project include Jenna Baddeley, David Beaver, Roger Booth, Martha Francis, Art Graesser, Carla Groom, Jeff Hancock, Molly Ireland, Ewa Kacewicz, Laura King, Matthias Mehl, Kate Niederhoffer, Keith Petrie, Nairán Ramírez-Esparza, Stephanie Rude, Yitai Seih, Richard Slatcher, Lori Stone Handelman, and Yla Tausczik. Bill Swann, Bob Josephs, and my other colleagues in the psychology department at the University of Texas at Austin have also been important in guiding my work.

This book would not have been possible without funding from the National Science Foundation, Army Research Institute, National Institutes of Health, and College of Liberal Arts at the University of Texas. I'm especially grateful for the support of my book whisperer, Marc Aronson, agent, Deirdre Mullane, and editors at Bloomsbury Press, Peter Ginna and Pete Beatty.

Three people have influenced this book more than any. Cindy Chung has been at the heart of the language research with me for many years. Her ideas, feedback, and humor have made the journey a pure pleasure. Sam Gosling, my colleague and co-conspirator, has pressed me to think more broadly about personality and social processes. Finally, my wife, Ruth, has inspired, guided, and nudged me to think about stories, social relationships, and the real world in new ways every day. Her delicate fingerprints are on every page of this book.

CHAPTER 1

Discovering the Secret Life of the Most Forgettable Words

Good morning everyone! Have a fabulous day! Xoxo Paris :)
> —PARIS HILTON, media personality

went to the mountains above Beirut yesterday to meet with Walid Jumblatt—the leader of the Druze—fascinating experience.
> —JOHN MCCAIN, U.S. Senator

Hanging out with friends—"pom" martinis-getting ready to watch xmas special. 10 eastern 9 central. Going caroling afterward!
> —OPRAH WINFREY, media mogul and television host

time to drink a bottle of wine and sketch for the new tour. st.louis was brilliant. there's eyeliner on my knee, and blood on my elbow. shady
> —LADY GAGA, singer and songwriter

OVER 100,000 YEARS ago, our ancestors began talking. About 5,000 years ago, humans started writing. In the last 150 years, we adopted everything from the telegraph, radio, and television to e-mail, text messages, blogs, and other social media. The ways we connect with one another may have changed but we still are compelled to communicate our ideas, experiences, and emotions to those around us.

Beginning in 2006, we began to use Twitter. Anyone with a Twitter account can broadcast brief updates, or "tweets," that can be instantly read by almost anyone. On a minute-by-minute basis, you can know what your friends or even world-famous celebrities are thinking. Many readers may wonder why people would want to do this. However, once you immerse yourself in the Twitter world, you can begin to appreciate some of its appeal.

Look back at the four tweets that begin this chapter. On a certain level, these tweets are no different from everyday communication. One can imagine overhearing similar things from someone at the next table in a restaurant. What are the different people telling others? Paris Hilton is simply calling out a greeting. John McCain is describing meeting an important person in Lebanon. Oprah Winfrey tells us about her plans for the evening. Lady Gaga wants us to know that she is getting into the spirit of her new tour.

But there is more in these tweets than their authors appreciate. Each entry is like a fingerprint. For example, if this were a multiple-choice test and people were asked to match the tweet with the author, most would make a perfect score on the test. Even if you had never heard of any of the authors, the mere label of "media personality," "U.S. senator," etc. would provide enough information to make educated guesses about who tweeted what.

The tweets also provide insights into each person's thinking and personality. Hilton is relentlessly upbeat with her exclamation points and emoticons. McCain works to impress his readers with his big words and worldliness. Winfrey, the consummate salesperson, "drops" what time the Christmas special (which is actually *her* Christmas special) will be aired. And Lady Gaga conveys that she is a bit wild but also thoughtful and, judging by her use of pronouns, somewhat prone to depression.

If we started analyzing more tweets from each of these people, we would begin to get a much richer sense of their motivations, fears, emotions, and the ways they connect with others and themselves. Each person uses words in a unique way. Some people, like Lady Gaga, tend to be highly personal in the ways they communicate—they are self-reflective in their use of words such as *I* and *me*. Others, like John McCain, reveal that they have a great deal of trouble in connecting to others. In fact, if you would like to try out a quick personality analysis tool based on peoples' Twitter feeds, try out the experimental website that my colleagues and I created, www.analyzewords.com.

Often, some of the most revealing words that we use are the shortest and most forgettable. Pronouns (such as *I, you, we,* and *they*), articles (*a, an, the*), prepositions (e.g., *to, for, over*), and other stealth words broadcast the kind of people we are. And this is the story of this book.

It has been a long road from our ancestors' uttering their first sentences to Paris Hilton's tweeting her greetings. Due in large part to the current technological revolution, we now have the tools to analyze tweets and Facebook updates, e-mails, old-fashioned letters and books, and the words from everyday life. For the first time, we are able to use computers to determine how everyday words can reflect our social and psychological states.

Who, for example, would have ever predicted that the high school student who uses too many verbs in her college admissions essay is likely to make lower grades in college? Or that the poet who overuses the word *I* in his poetry is at higher risk of suicide? Or that a certain world leader's use of pronouns could reliably presage whether he'd lead his country into war? By looking more carefully at the ways people convey their thoughts in language we can begin to get a sense of their personalities, emotions, and connections with others.

WHEN SOCIAL PSYCHOLOGY AND LANGUAGE MEET

Before describing the secret life of words, it may be helpful to say a bit about the author. That would be me. I'm a social psychologist whose interest in words came about almost accidentally. As you will see, the focus of this book is really on people rather than language per se. Words and language are, of course, fascinating topics. Through the eyes of a social psychologist, words are even more intriguing as clues to the inner workings of people.

By way of background, my early career dealt with health, emotions, and the nature of traumatic experiences. In the early 1980s, I stumbled on a finding that fascinated me. People who reported having a terrible traumatic experience *and* who kept the experience a secret had far more health problems than people who openly talked about their traumas. Why would keeping a secret be so toxic? More importantly, if you asked people to disclose emotionally powerful secrets, would their health improve? The answer, my students and I soon discovered, was yes.

We began running experiments where people were asked to write about traumatic experiences for fifteen to twenty minutes a day for three or four consecutive days. Compared to people who were told to write about nonemotional topics, those who wrote about trauma evidenced improved physical health. Later studies found that emotional writing boosted immune function, brought about drops in blood pressure, and reduced feelings of depression and elevated daily moods. Now, over twenty-five years after the first writing experiment, more than two hundred similar writing studies have been conducted all over the world. While the effects are often modest, the mere act of translating emotional upheavals into words is consistently associated with improvements in physical and mental health.

IN SEARCH OF A THEORY TO EXPLAIN
THE POWER OF WRITING

Why does writing work? Some scientists suggest that repeatedly confronting painful emotions eventually lessens their impact—we adapt to them. Another group points to the unhealthy effects of rumination and unfinished business. Many people who have a traumatic experience keep replaying the events in their minds in a futile attempt to make sense of their suffering. The never-ending thoughts about their emotional upheavals can disrupt their sleep and make it impossible to focus on their jobs and their relationships. Writing about the trauma, according to this view, allows people to find meaning or understanding in these events and helps to resolve their emotional turmoil.

The answer isn't simple. I'm now convinced that when people write about traumatic events, several healthy changes occur simultaneously, including changes in people's thinking patterns, emotional responses, brain activity, sleep and health behaviors, and so forth. Discovering why writing is effective for one person may not explain why it works for someone else.

What the early writing researchers failed to consider was that people were using words to describe their personal upheavals. Perhaps the key to expressive writing was buried in what people actually say in their essays. The stories people wrote were powerful and oftentimes haunting. In almost every project, participants wrote about physical, sexual, and emotional abuse, divorce, drug and alcohol problems, suicides, terrible accidents, and feelings of failure, humiliation, and suffering. Not only was there a wide range of powerful stories but the ways people wrote about them differed widely. Some people used humor, others were full of rage, yet other stories were written in a cold, detached, and matter-of-fact way.

If a group of clinical psychologists or just regular people read these essays, could they decipher what dimensions of writing predicted improved physical health? We tried this and the answer was no. The stories were too complicated and even the most conscientious readers couldn't agree about which elements of people's heartbreaking stories were most meaningful. Some other approach was needed to unlock the reason behind the effectiveness of expressive writing.

THE COMPUTER REVOLUTION AND THE BIRTH OF LIWC

It was 1991 and the revolution in computer technology was well under way. There had been some major breakthroughs in the computerized analysis of language in research that had been done at Princeton, Harvard, and MIT in the 1960s and 1970s. Surely, with this new technology, I could get a computer program that could analyze my trauma essays. No judges, no heartache. I could get some answers with the press of a button.

Unfortunately, no simple computer programs were available at the time. "How hard could it be to write such a program?" I asked myself. By a happy coincidence, a new graduate student who had been a professional programmer had just joined my research team. "Martha," I casually told her, "I've got a great idea for a new program that should only take about three weeks to develop." Martha E. Francis turned out to be a creative programmer with a flair for social psychology, though she had no idea what she was getting into. Although the guts of the program were written very quickly, the "three-week project" took on a life of its own. In three years, we finally rolled out the first version of a computer program we called Linguistic Inquiry and Word Count, or LIWC (pronounced "Luke").

The idea behind LIWC was that the words people used—whether in a trauma essay or everyday speech—would reflect their feelings and that by the simple process of counting these words we could gain insights into their emotional states. We assumed that angry people would use anger-related words; sad people would use sadness words. In writing about a trauma, the emotional states of our participants should be reflected in their selection of emotionally relevant words.

So, in developing the LIWC program, we created a series of word dictionaries designed to capture different psychological concepts. For example, we built an anger dictionary, now made up of over 180 words, that comprised numerous words related to anger, such as *hate, rage, kill, slash, revenge*, etc. We also included word stems such as *kill* so that any word that starts with the letters K-I-L-L, such as *killer, killing, kills*, and *killed*, would be counted as well. We then went on to build dictionaries for sadness, anxiety, positive emotions, and other mood states.

The trauma essays differed in multiple dimensions beyond their emotional tone. To cast a fairly broad net we developed other lexicons that measured the occurrence of other types of words, such as the use of different types of pronouns (e.g., first-person singular—such as *I, me,* and *my*), articles (*a, an, the*), different types of thinking-related words that signal cause-effect thinking (*cause, because, reason, rationale*), and so forth. Before we knew it, we had created almost eighty different dictionaries that we felt would include nearly all of the types of words people commonly use in everyday language.

The reason it took almost three years to get LIWC running was because of the painstaking process of building each dictionary. We employed an army of students who evaluated every word that was part of any dictionary. For example, should the word *frustration* be included in the anger dictionary? Panels of student judges had to all agree that it was related to anger (in this case, it was).

Thanks to Martha's programming skills and the thousands of hours spent by our student judges, LIWC was eventually ready to go. The final program instantly analyzed computer-based text or document files and calculated the percentage of words associated with each dictionary. The most recent version of LIWC can analyze thousands of individual digital files in a matter of seconds. Although our initial studies all focused on trauma essays, we eventually moved to poems, novels, blogs, Twitter feeds, letters, IMs, transcripts of conversations, and any other documents that contain words.

To appreciate how a word-counting program works, let's look at the first two sentences of Lewis Carroll's *Alice's Adventures in Wonderland*:

> Alice was beginning to get very tired of sitting by her sister on the bank, and of having nothing to do: once or twice she had peeped into the book her sister was reading, but it had no pictures or conversations in it, "and what is the use of a book," thought Alice "without pictures or conversation?"
>
> So she was considering in her own mind (as well as she could, for the hot day made her feel very sleepy and stupid), whether the pleasure of making a daisy-chain would be worth the trouble of getting up and picking the daisies, when suddenly a White Rabbit with pink eyes ran close by her.

LIWC would begin its analysis by first counting all the words in the text, which, in this case, is 113. It would then look at each word separately to determine if it was included in any of the existing dictionaries. So, for example, LIWC would first see the word *Alice* but would find no such word in any of its dictionaries. It would then move to the word *was*. Voilà! The word *was* would be in several dictionaries, including the verb dictionary, the auxiliary-verb dictionary, and the past-tense verb dictionary. The count for each of those dictionaries would now be 1. As LIWC proceeded in its task, it would then locate the next word, *beginning*, in the time dictionary; *to* in the preposition dictionary; and so forth. Finally, after evaluating all 113 words in the text and assigning each of them to the relevant dictionaries, LIWC would then calculate the percentage of total words that are linked to each dictionary. So, for example, in this passage, about 7 percent of all the words are personal pronouns, 9 percent are articles, and 3.6 percent are words related to emotion.

In analyzing a text, LIWC had many advantages over my troublesome human experts. Programs such as LIWC are 100 percent reliable in that you get the same results every time you run the program on a particular text. They are very fast, able to analyze the collected works of Shakespeare in under twenty seconds. And the results from the analysis of one person's text can be directly compared with those of anyone else's.

Despite these admirable features, word counting programs are also remarkably stupid. They can't detect irony or sarcasm and are singularly lacking in a sense of humor. Particularly damning is that they fail to capture the context of language. One word, for example, can have very different meanings depending on how it is used.

Consider the word *mad*. The LIWC program counts *mad* in its anger and negative-emotion dictionaries. If someone said, "I'm mad at you for kissing my new boyfriend," LIWC's interpretation of *mad* as an anger word would no doubt be correct. But if the same person said, "I'm mad about my new boyfriend," LIWC would be mistaken to sort *mad* according to its given definitions. In this case, *mad* means not angry but "crazily happy." Or, returning to Alice in Wonderland, the Mad Tea Party was not a hostile affair. Rather, *mad* in this context simply means "peculiar" or "insane."

LIWC, like almost all word-counting systems, makes lots of errors. It is a probabilistic system. Sometimes it classifies correctly and sometimes it doesn't. We have now run enough studies to determine that statistically it is usually correct, and the good news is that the more words there are available to analyze, the more precise the system. Another bit of good news is that researchers are developing smarter word-count programs that will eventually take into account syntax, grammar, and context in general.

Given the current state of the art, it is little wonder that serious linguists and literary scholars find word-counting programs somewhat distasteful. The thing is, linguists care about language and literary scholars care about literature. And, in my own begrudging way, I care about these things too. But what I'm really interested in is the relationship between word use and people's psychological states. Can we identify features of language that reveal how people are thinking? And, if so, can we use this information to change their thinking in a beneficial way?

IDENTIFYING HEALTHY WRITING
WITH A COMPUTER PROGRAM

The entire purpose of developing LIWC was to see if the ways people wrote about their traumatic experiences could predict later improvements in their health. Put another way, could we use LIWC to identify healthy writing?

During LIWC's development, several expressive writing studies had been conducted that could answer this question. In my lab, three had been conducted with college students. Others had been run by colleagues who had relied on more diverse samples, including a study of maximum-security prisoners, a group of New Zealand medical students, and a cohort of senior engineers recently laid off from their jobs. Now that we had essays from a wide range of people across six different studies, we could get our computer program to find which word categories were associated with healthy writing. Three important find-ings emerged.

THE IMPORTANCE OF POSITIVE EMOTIONS

A rough measure of people's emotional state can be found by counting words in their trauma essays that signify positive emotion (e.g., *love, care, happy*) and negative emotion (e.g., *sad, pain, anger*). The results from the six writing studies were somewhat unexpected. Overall, the more people used positive emotions while writing about emotional up-heavals, the more their physical and mental health improved in the weeks and months after the experiment.

Negative emotion words showed a different pattern. People whose physical health improved the most from writing used a moderate num-ber of negative emotion words. That is, people who expressed negative emotion language at very high rates did not benefit from writing—almost as if they were awash in their unhappiness. By the same token, those who used very few negative emotion words did not benefit—perhaps a sign that they were not acknowledging the emotional impact of their topic. The emotional findings, then, suggest that to gain the most benefit from writing about life's traumas, acknowledge the nega-tive but celebrate the positive.

THE IMPORTANCE OF CONSTRUCTING A STORY

One of the exciting aspects of the LIWC program was that we were able to identify word categories that reflected the degree to which people were actively thinking. Two of the cognitive dimensions included insight or self-reflection words (such as *think, realize, believe*) and an-other made up of causal words (such as *because, effect, rationale*). The people whose health improved the most started out using fairly low rates of cognitive words but increased in their use over the four days of writing. It wasn't the level of cognitive words that was important but the increase from the first to last day. In some ways, use of insight and causal words was necessary for people to construct a coherent story of their trauma. On the first writing session, people would often spill out their experience in a disorganized way. However, as they wrote about it day after day, they began to make sense of it. This greater understanding was partially reflected in the ways they used cognitive words.

These findings suggested that *having* a coherent story to explain a painful experience was not necessarily as useful as *constructing* a coherent story. This helped to explain a personal observation that had bothered me for years. When the first writing studies were published, my work was often featured in the media. At cocktail parties or informal gatherings, I sometimes found myself to be a trauma magnet. People who knew about my research would gravitate to me in order to tell me all about their horrific life experiences. Many of them also were in very poor physical health. At first, I thought that their talking about their stories would be good for them. However, I'd see the same people at another gathering months later and they would often tell me exactly the same stories and their health would be unchanged.

The word count research revealed the problem. The people telling their traumatic stories were essentially telling the same stories over and over. There was no change to the stories, no growth, no increase in understanding. Repeating the same story in the same way is not unlike ruminative thinking—a classic symptom of depression.

There is an important lesson here. If haunted by an emotional upheaval in your life, try writing about it or sharing the experience with others. However, if you catch yourself telling exactly the same story over and over in order to get past your distress, rethink your strategy. Try writing or talking about your trauma in a completely different way. How would a more detached narrator describe what happened? What other ways of explaining the event might exist? If you're successful, research studies suggest that you will sleep better, experience better physical health, and notice yourself feeling happier and less overcome by your upheaval.

THE IMPORTANCE OF CHANGING PERSPECTIVES

Thanks to the LIWC program, we found that three aspects of emotional writing predicted improvements in people's physical and mental health: accentuating the positive parts of an upheaval, acknowledging the negative parts, and constructing a story over the days of writing. More complex analyses soon revealed another dimension of word use that no one had seen before.

In the 1990s, a group of researchers at the University of Colorado introduced a computer program called Latent Semantic Analysis (or LSA) that could track patterns of word use both within and across different essays. The beauty of LSA was that it could mathematically compare how similar any two writing samples were. On the surface, then, we could determine if people who wrote about the same topics from day to day might benefit more than those who wrote about different topics. It was a grand idea, but try as we might, we couldn't find any good evidence to support it.

One of my graduate students, Sherlock Campbell, had spent almost a year getting the LSA program to work. The more he and I thought about the LSA project, the more we realized that we had been thinking about language the wrong way. Instead of analyzing the content of what people were writing, why not analyze their language style? To do this, we needed to turn the LSA program on its head. Instead of analyzing the content of the essays by focusing on nouns, regular verbs, and adjectives, we asked the program to focus on the words that revealed writing style. Writing style, we were learning, was generally revealed through function words, including pronouns, prepositions, articles, and a small number of similar short but common words.

The results were breathtaking. (OK, if you are not a computational linguist, "breathtaking" may be a bit of an overstatement. You had to be there.) The more people changed in the ways they used function words from writing to writing, the more their health later improved. As we started to focus on different classes of function words, one particular group of culprits stood out as more important than the others: personal pronouns. More specifically, the more people changed in their use of first-person singular pronouns (e.g., *I, me, my*) compared with other pronouns (e.g., *we, you, she, they*), the better their health later became. The effects were large and held up for study after study.

After spending over a year on the computer program, Sherlock was thrilled. He took great pride in noting that we had discovered the "secret life of pronouns." And he deserves the credit for the title of this book.

The findings may sound esoteric but in real life they aren't. The writings of those whose health improved showed a high rate of the use of I-words on one occasion and then high rates of the use of other pronouns on the next occasion, and then switching back and forth in subsequent writings. In other words, healthy people say something about their own thoughts and feelings in one instance and then explore what is happening with other people before writing about themselves again.

This perspective switching is actually quite common in psychotherapy. If a man visits his therapist and begins repeatedly complaining about his wife's behavior, what she says, how aloof she is, and so forth, the therapist will likely stop the client after several minutes and say, "You've been talking about your wife at length but you haven't said anything about yourself. How do *you* feel when this happens?" Similarly, if another client—a woman in this case—with marital problems sees her therapist and spends most of her time talking about her own thoughts, feelings, and behaviors without ever talking about her spouse, the therapist will probably redirect the conversation in a similar way by asking, "You've told me a lot about your own feelings when this happens—how do you think your husband feels about this?" Perhaps like good therapy, healthy writing may involve looking at a problem from multiple perspectives.

WORDS AS MIRRORS, WORDS AS TOOLS

Stand back for a minute and consider the meaning of all of our findings regarding expressive writing. Writing about emotional upheavals can improve people's mental and physical health. Not all people benefit from this exercise however. Those who do benefit tend to write differently from those who don't. Healthy writing involves positive emotion words, a moderate use of negative emotion words, increasing use of cognitive words, and changes in pronoun use. Translating these effects into everyday language: People who benefit from writing express more optimism, acknowledge negative events, are constructing a meaningful story of their experience, and have the ability to change perspectives as they write.

Most surprising, though, was that these discoveries were reflected through people's use of a small number of almost-invisible stealth words. The stealth words, which had been there all along, reflected critical changes in the ways people were thinking.

These language findings are certainly interesting, but can we put them to good use? If we bring people into the lab and encourage them to use positive emotion words, increase their use of cognitive words, and oscillate in their use of personal pronouns while they write, will their health improve? In other words, do words *reflect* a psychological state or do they *cause* it?

Over the years, several studies have been conducted to try to answer this question. In one elaborate experiment, Cheryl Hughes, a former student of mine at Southern Methodist University, gave different students lists of words that she asked them to use in their expressive writing. Some received lists of positive emotion words, others received negative emotion words, some were given cognitive word lists and others weren't. While she succeeded in manipulating the words people used in the predicted directions, the writing had no effect on health. Other clever attempts have been made to get people to change the rates at which they use cognitive words or to change the types of pronouns from writing to writing while addressing emotional topics. The current evidence is convincing: Word use generally *reflects* psychological state rather than influences or causes it.

That words we use mirror our thoughts and feelings is not a startling revelation. But the findings point to ways we can now use word analyses to change people's thinking. Recall that healthy writing is characterized by an increasing use of words such as *because, cause, effect, reason*, and related cognitive words. Simply requiring people to use the words at higher rates over the course of writing has no meaningful effects—the writers are simply focusing on words and not their underlying purpose. However, if we encourage people to write about a trauma and to work to construct a meaningful story, their writing takes on a more dynamic tone. They begin to stand back and look at their trauma with a broader perspective. The cognitive work they put into the story results in a better product and one that is more likely to allow them to get through their trauma.

The analysis of words tells us how people are thinking and, at the same time, gives us a way to guide their thinking in the future. Words can be both mirrors and tools.

AS INTERESTING AS our findings about expressive writing were, they are, by now, but a footnote to the many ways that we've come to use LIWC. When Martha Francis and I first developed the program, our goals were modest: identify healthy writing by looking at words. But our timing was propitious. Without computer technology and the availability of large text databases, linguists might have studied the words and psychologists or physicians might have studied health, but no one would have naturally put the two together.

Now anyone can access millions of words from thousands of people in no time at all. As someone who loves to play with numbers and statistics, I had discovered the perfect playground in LIWC. Late at night I would often find myself analyzing text files just to see who used what kinds of language. For example, most of the expressive writing studies included both women and men. Were there any differences between the sexes in the way people used language? Yes, there were differences—big differences—but they didn't make any sense. So I did what anyone does when trying to sort out a problem late at night: I just ignored it. But then I would run another batch of text files the next day and find the same odd word differences between men and women. I won't tell you the findings now because it would ruin the thrill of chapter 3, but trust me, the effects are big, unpredictable, and, once you think about them, make perfect sense.

As I played with more and more data sets, recurring word patterns kept popping up. Not only were there differences in the ways women and men used words but there were big differences as a function of people's age. And social class. And emotional state, level of honesty, personality type, degree of formality, leadership ability, quality of relationships, and on and on. Word use was associated with almost every dimension of social psychology that I had ever studied. Particularly intriguing was that most of the word differences were associated with the most common and forgettable words in the English language.

Thirty years ago, had someone said that one of the high points of my professional life would be discovering the secret life of pronouns, I'm pretty sure I would have changed careers. Now I'm convinced that by understanding how and when we use these function words, we get a much better sense of the social and psychological processes affecting all of our behaviors, from our relationships with friends and family members to our ability to communicate effectively with people in business and the larger world.

If a friend's language changes unexpectedly, we may be able to determine if he or she is depressed, angry, or deceptive. If you are an archivist or investigator, your ability to decode function words can help in identifying the true author of a text or the possible motive behind the writing of the text.

Most interesting for me, however, is that the analysis of the words we use in speaking and writing can be extraordinarily useful in helping us to understand ourselves. In the chapters that follow, you will see many examples where I have analyzed my own e-mail, letters of recommendation, and daily speech patterns in talking with friends and family members. By looking closely at words, I've discovered ways of improving my relationships with my family and friends, of being a better teacher, and of becoming a better leader. While I didn't fundamentally change the way I spoke or wrote, these word analyses pointed to some of my natural shortcomings, which I have worked to improve.

Finally, this book is a travelogue of the journey my students, colleagues, and I have been taking as we've been studying the ways we all use language. The values guiding most of this research have been curiosity and playfulness. If you are a serious linguist, this book may disappoint or infuriate you. If you love words for their own sake, I may not share your reverence. (Indeed, after I published a paper showing that suicidal poets used pronouns differently from nonsuicidal poets, a slightly inebriated poet threatened me with a butter knife at a party in my own home.) Ultimately, I'm interested in psychology and social behavior. Words, in my world, are a window into the inner workings of people, a fascinating and revealing way to think about language and its links to the world around us all.

CHAPTER 2

Ignoring the Content,
Celebrating the Style

A LL WORDS ARE not equal. In any given sentence, some words provide basic content and meaning whereas others serve quieter support functions. Ironically, the quiet words can say more about a person than the more meaningful ones. A central theme of this book is that the content of speech can be distinguished from the style of speech. Further, words that reflect language style can reveal aspects of people's personality, social connections, and psychological states.

This chapter lays out the overall logic of word analysis. It serves as the foundation for the rest of the book. If you simply want to see how different types of words reflect personality, deception, and psychological state, feel free to skip this chapter. You may well regret it. But then you will never know.

IT'S HELPFUL TO start with a simple exercise to give you a feeling about the ways different words work. Look closely at the picture on the next page. Who are the people? What is happening? What are their thoughts, feelings, and concerns?

How would you write or talk about this drawing? Stop for a second and describe the picture to yourself. You might even jot down your description on a piece of paper so that you can refer back to your writing throughout the chapter.

In fact, thousands of people have written about this picture as part of various psychology experiments. The kinds of stories that people tell vary widely. Some view the people as two women, others as one or two men. Some cast the two as part of a story dealing with good

versus evil, wisdom versus youth, or just a family relationship between people of different generations.

Despite the differences in stories and themes, the ways people write their stories are even more striking. As an example, read the first sentences that three college students wrote in describing the picture:

PERSON 1: In the aforementioned picture an elderly woman is about to speak to a middle aged woman who looks condescending and calculating.
PERSON 2: I see an old woman looking back on her years remembering how it was to be beautiful and young.
PERSON 3: The old woman is a witch or something. She looks kinda like she is coaxing the young one to do something.

Now look more closely at each person's writing. Can you get a sense of who each of these three people is? Who would you like to get coffee with? Which one do you trust the most? What factors influenced your answers? Although all three students saw the same drawing, they interpreted it differently. More important, however, is how they used words to describe their impressions. Even in these brief sentences, you get a sense of who these students are. The first person appears stiff and distant, relying on large words in a self-conscious way. The second has a more personal and warmer touch. The third person sounds more casual than the other two and seems not to be taking the assignment as seriously.

All three people have stamped part of their personality into their writing style. Through their largely unconscious use of words, we can begin to get a sense of who they are, how they think about others and about themselves. We can do a reasonably good job in predicting that person 1 is a male and the other two are females. He probably has a higher grade average than the other two, although his social life is likely suffering. Person 2 is the one most likely to be depressed. Person 3 is probably not doing well in school—and may well be spending too much time with friends and drinking too much.

These are more than educated guesses. They are based on evidence that the words people use in their daily lives can tell us a great deal about their personality, age, sex, social class, stress levels, biological activity, and social relationships. Words leave behind clues of a person. By analyzing these clues, we get a glimpse of each author's personal world.

What could someone tell about you based on the words you used to describe the picture? How do we know that person 1 is a socially isolated male and person 2 is a depressive female? The secret is in distinguishing between *what* people are saying versus *how* they are saying it. Looking back at the three statements, the content of the writing is certainly different, but more striking is the way they are expressing themselves. There is a meaningful difference, then, between language content and language style.

IT AIN'T WHAT YOU SAY, IT'S THE WAY YOU SAY IT

What accounts for style? Gordon Allport, a founder of modern-day personality psychology, asked this question in trying to define the essential differences among people. He noted that people revealed themselves in almost everything they did. Some walk quickly and don't move their arms; others seem to skip by bouncing on the balls of their feet; yet others amble, careen, or trudge along. Walking styles, he argued, are one way that people differ. But they also differ in the ways they dress, eat, and peel an orange. Style may not tell us much about where a person is walking, how hungry they are, or their preferences for fruit, but it is a meaningful window into people's personality, attitudes, and social worlds.

Language style is no exception. How people speak or write reveals meaningful clues to personality. The challenge is in determining what accounts for style. Interestingly, linguists, high school English teachers, and Mother Nature have provided us with some hints about words that reflect style versus content.

Content words are words that have a culturally shared meaning in labeling an object or action. For our purposes, content words include:

Nouns e.g., *table, uncle, justice, Fido*

Regular and action verbs e.g., *to love, to walk, to hide*

Most modifiers e.g., adjectives (*blue, fast, mouthwatering*) and adverbs (*sadly, hungrily*)

Content words are absolutely necessary to convey an idea to someone else. Consider the three people who wrote briefly in response to the picture.

PERSON 1: In the aforementioned **picture** an **elderly woman** is about to **speak** to a **middle aged woman** who **looks condescending** and **calculating.**

PERSON 2: I **see** an **old woman looking** back on her **years remembering** how it was to be **beautiful** and **young.**

PERSON 3: The **old woman** is a **witch** or something. She **looks** kinda like she is **coaxing** the **young** one to do something.

Imagine you are talking with someone whose English is very poor. That person is trying to describe the picture. All you can understand are the content words that are highlighted. The fact is, you can get a good sense of what the speaker is trying to say by just hearing the content-related words. That's good. Content words should convey content. Admittedly, this wouldn't be a very satisfying interaction but you would be fairly certain what was going on in the speaker's mind.

Style (or function) words are words that connect, shape, and organize content words. Although this definition is a bit slippery, most style words fall into a general class of words variously referred to as function words, stealth words, or even junk words. A good way to think about style words is that, by themselves, they really don't have any meaning to anyone. For example, a content word like *table* can trigger an image in everyone's mind—the same with words like *walking, blue,* and *bug.* Now try to imagine *that* or *because* or *really* or *the* or even *my.* We might use words like this in most sentences but they are fairly useless on their own.

Most function words include:

CATEGORY	EXAMPLES
Pronouns	*I, she, it*
Articles	*a, an, the*
Prepositions	*up, with, in, for*
Auxiliary verbs	*is, don't, have*
Negations	*no, not, never*
Conjunctions	*but, and, because*
Quantifiers	*few, some, most*
Common adverbs	*very, really*

To appreciate the significance of these often-misunderstood words, let's return to our three people describing the picture.

> PERSON 1: **In the aforementioned** picture **an** elderly woman **is about to** speak **to a** middle aged woman **who** looks condescending **and** calculating.
>
> PERSON 2: **I** see **an** old woman looking **back on her** years remembering **how it was to be** beautiful **and** young.
>
> PERSON 3: **The** old woman **is a** witch **or something**. **She** looks **kinda like she is** coaxing **the** young **one to do something**.

Now imagine that someone was only able to speak to you using the highlighted style words while trying to describe the picture. You would have absolutely no idea what the person was talking about.

Why make such a big deal about style words? Because pronouns, prepositions, and other function words are the keys to the soul. OK, maybe that's a bit of an overstatement, but bear with me. Stealth words are:

- used at very high rates
- short and hard to detect
- processed in the brain differently than content words
- very, very social

Each of these features helps to explain why function words are psychologically important and, at the same time, why so few people have examined them closely. Stealth words, then, really are quite stylish. It's about time that these forgettable, throwaway little words get their due.

FUNCTION WORDS IN EVERYDAY LANGUAGE: THEY'RE EVERYWHERE

In 1863, four months after the devastating Battle of Gettysburg, Abraham Lincoln delivered one of the most significant speeches in American history. Overlooking the battlefield where 7,500 soldiers died, Lincoln's brief speech helped to reframe the Civil War. Read his speech quickly so that you can form an impression of what's being said.

> Four score and seven years ago our fathers brought forth, upon this continent, a new nation, conceived in Liberty, and dedicated to the proposition that all men are created equal.
>
> Now we are engaged in a great civil war, testing whether that nation, or any nation so conceived, and so dedicated, can long endure. We are met here on a great battlefield of that war. We have come to dedicate a portion of it as a final resting place for those who here gave their lives that that nation might live. It is altogether fitting and proper that we should do this.
>
> But in a larger sense we can not dedicate—we can not consecrate—we can not hallow this ground. The brave men, living and dead, who struggled, here, have consecrated it far above our poor power to add or detract. The world will little note, nor long remember, what we say here, but can never forget what they did here.
>
> It is for us, the living, rather to be dedicated here to the unfinished work which they have, thus far, so nobly carried on. It is rather for us to be here dedicated to the great task remaining before us—that from these honored dead we take increased devotion to that cause for which they here gave the last full measure of devotion—that we here highly resolve that these dead shall not have died in vain; that this nation shall have a new birth of freedom; and that this government of the people, by the people, for the people, shall not perish from the earth.

Now, close your eyes and reflect on the content of the speech. Which words occurred most frequently? In your mind, try to recall which words Lincoln used the most in penning such a powerful speech. I'm serious. Shut your eyes and make a list in your mind of the most frequently used words in this speech.

OK, you can open your eyes. Most unsuspecting people who are asked to do this will think the most common words are *nation, war, men,* and possibly *dead*. You probably won't be surprised to learn that function words are far more frequent than any content words. In this particular speech, the most commonly used word was *that*, which was used twelve times and accounted for 4.5 percent of all the words in the speech. Other frequently used words: *the* (4.1 percent), *we* (3.7 percent), *here* (3.5 percent), *to* (3.0 percent), *a* (2.6 percent), *and* (2.2 percent), *can, for, have, it, not, of, this* (1.9 percent each). In fact, these fourteen little words account for almost 37 percent of all the words Lincoln used in this beautifully crafted speech. Only one content word is in the top fifteen, *nation*, which was used only 1.9 percent of the time. It is remarkable that such a great speech can be largely composed of small, insignificant words.

A very small number of stealth words account for most of the words we hear, read, and say. Over the last twenty years, my colleagues and I have amassed a very large collection of text files that includes thousands upon thousands of natural conversations, books, Internet blogs, music lyrics, Wikipedia entries, etc., representing billions of words. Although there are some variations in word use depending on what people are writing or saying, it is striking to see how common function words are in all types of text.

Spend a minute inspecting the word table on the next page. This is a list of the twenty most commonly used words in English based on our large language bank. Across both written and spoken text, for example, the word *I* accounts for 3.6 percent of all words that are used. If you consider these twenty words together, they represent almost 30 percent of all words that people use, read, and hear.

Notice that all of the words in the table are quite short and are made up exclusively of pronouns, prepositions, conjunctions, articles, and auxiliary verbs. If we extended the list to all of the common stealth or function words in English, the list would include around 450 words. Indeed, these 450 words account for over half (55 percent) of all the words we use.

**THE MOST FREQUENTLY USED WORDS ACROSS
BOTH SPOKEN AND WRITTEN TEXTS**

RANK	WORD	PERCENTAGE OF ALL WORDS
1	I	3.64
2	the	3.48
3	and	2.92
4	to	2.91
5	a	1.94
6	of	1.83
7	that	1.48
8	in	1.29
9	it	1.19
10	my	1.08
11	is	1.06
12	you	1.05
13	was	1.01
14	for	0.80
15	have	0.70
16	with	0.67
17	he	0.66
18	me	0.64
19	on	0.63
20	but	0.62

To put this in perspective, the average English speaker has an impressive vocabulary of perhaps one hundred thousand words. This means that only a trivial percentage of the words we know are associated with linguistic style—about 0.04 percent of all words. The other 99.96 percent of our vocabulary is made up of content words. This split is comparable in other languages—German, Spanish, Turkish, Arabic, Korean, and others we have studied. In all languages, a small number of function words are used at dizzying rates compared to a large number of content words that are used at very low rates.

Briefly consider the implications of these numbers. If you want to learn a new language such as German or Finnish, you can pick up almost half the language in an afternoon. Most anyone can master the top one hundred stealth words with minimal training. By early evening, you could sit down with any German newspaper or Finnish philosophy text and identify half of the words that were used. The only downside is that you would have absolutely no idea what you were reading.

FUNCTION WORDS: THEY'RE SHORT AND ALMOST INVISIBLE

Look back at the top twenty function words. You will notice that seventeen of the twenty words are three letters or fewer in length. The most common words in every language tend to be short and are usually a single, easy-to-pronounce syllable.

Not only are stealth words short, they are hard to perceive. One reason we have trouble spotting the high usage of function words in the Lincoln speech is that our brains naturally slide over them. We automatically focus on content-related words instead. The invisibility is also evident in the ways we remember words. Think, for example, of the last conversation you had with someone. Can you recall any specific words that the other person spoke? In all likelihood, you remember only the content words.

Perhaps the strongest test of invisibility is in actively trying to listen to people's use of style versus content words. Sit by a television or radio or simply begin listening to people speaking around you. Consciously try to attend to style-related words. You will note that they are spoken extremely quickly—lingering, on average, for less than two-tenths of a second. In fact, this speed is often used in psychology experiments to present words or pictures that are just barely perceptible. Assuming you are able to pay attention to these words for a few minutes, you will find that you lose track of what the content of the conversation is. It is almost impossible to attend to function words on their own.

THE AMAZING CASE OF JOHN KERRY
AND HIS INVISIBLE PRONOUNS

In the 2004 presidential campaign, Democrat John Kerry was running for president against the incumbent George W. Bush. In the months running up to the election, Bush's popularity ratings were suffering and Kerry posed a serious threat. A recurring problem with Kerry, however, was that he came across as aloof and somewhat arrogant. When he spoke, his body language was rigid and standoffish. His speeches and interviews tended to sound wooden and inauthentic.

According to a *New York Times* article, in an attempt to appear more warm, Kerry's advisers were working with him to use we-words (e.g., *we, us, our*) more and I-words less. On reading the article, it was clear that Kerry was in trouble.

As will be detailed later, use of I-words is associated with being honest and personal, and when politicians use them, we-words sound cold, rigid, and emotionally distant. At the time, Kerry was already using we-words at twice the rate of Bush and I-words at half Bush's rate. Kerry's advisers, who were some of the smartest people in the country, failed to understand how invisible stealth words worked.

This should be an important lesson. Function words are almost impossible to hear and your stereotypes about how they work may well be wrong.

Another surprising aspect of stealth words is that they are very hard to master after about age twelve. Learning another language as an adult is usually quite difficult. However, most people can quickly learn the words for objects, numbers, and colors. They can also memorize the words *for, in, above, with,* and related words. But mastering the use of most common function words in an ongoing conversation is far more difficult. In fact, you can usually tell if someone is not a native English speaker by looking at their writing. Their errors will likely be in their use of style words rather than any nouns or regular verbs.

STYLE WORDS AND THE BRAIN

The distinction between style and content words can also be seen in people who suffer from brain damage. Occasionally, a person will have a stroke or other brain injury that affects a highly specific location on the left side of the brain. If it is in one area, the person can lose the ability to use content words but still retain the ability to use function words. Strokes in other areas can produce the opposite results.

The two brain areas of interest—Broca's area and Wernicke's area—are usually located on the outer surface of the left side of the brain, called the cerebral cortex.

Broca's area, named after the nineteenth-century French surgeon Paul Broca, is located in the frontal lobe. In the 1860s, Broca published a series of articles reporting that damage to Broca's area was often associated with patients speaking in a painfully slow and disconnected way. More striking, however, is that they often were unable to use function words effectively. As an example, if a Broca's patient were asked to describe the picture at the beginning of the chapter, he or she might say, "Girl . . . ummm . . . woman . . . ahh . . . picture, uhhh . . . old. OK. Old woman." Often, Broca patients are socially awkward and frustrated by their inability to communicate with others.

The discovery of Broca's area became more significant several years later when Carl Wernicke published his observations about another

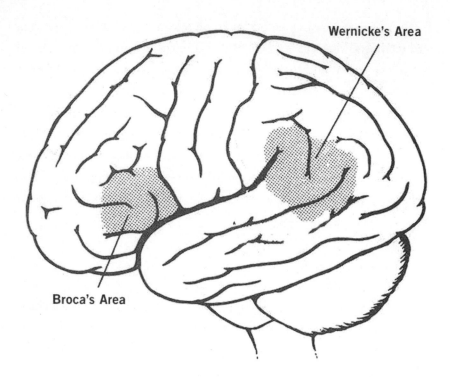

Wernicke's Area

Broca's Area

brain area in the temporal lobe of the brain now called Wernicke's area. Damage to this area resulted in a completely different set of symptoms. Specifically, Wernicke damage often results in people's inability to use nouns and regular verbs while, at the same time, they freely use function words. A Wernicke patient who is asked to describe the same picture might say something like, "Well, right here is one of them and I think she's next to that one. So if I see over there you'll see her too. Let's see. I'm thinking of her now. She's over there."

To say that Broca's area controls style words and Wernicke's controls content words is a gross oversimplification. Nevertheless, it points to the fact that the distinction between content and style words is occurring at a fairly basic level in the brain.

Particularly noteworthy is that Broca's area—the region linked to function words—is in the frontal lobe of the brain. The frontal lobe controls a number of skills, many of them social. For example, dozens of studies have demonstrated how frontal areas are linked to abilities to express and conceal emotions. Other frontal areas are associated with the ability to read other people's facial expressions. A number of promising studies now suggest that many of our abilities to control our emotions and to establish social relations with others are related to frontal lobe activity.

Perhaps the most dramatic example of frontal lobe damage and changes in social behavior and personality was the case of Phineas Gage. Gage was an explosives expert for a railroad in the mid-1800s. By all accounts, he was a careful, conscientious, and serious individual. One summer day, he was tamping down some blasting powder in preparation for an explosion to clear some rocks. He accidentally created a spark with his long tamping rod that ignited the powder, causing the rod to shoot upward, where it neatly tore a hole through his skull and destroyed much of his frontal lobe. To everyone's amazement, Gage wasn't killed and he returned to good health within a few weeks. That is, except for the hole in the front of his head. Over the next months, Phineas Gage's personality changed dramatically. He went from reserved to loud, from conscientious to impulsive, from respectful to obscene, and from sober to, well, not sober. He was a completely different person and never returned to his old personality.

In the early 1900s, Ivan Pavlov noted the same thing in his research with dogs. Pavlov, who won one of the first Nobel Prizes, is best remembered for his experiments where a dog could be trained to salivate when a bell rang. In a failed attempt to find the location of classical conditioning in the brain, Pavlov surgically disrupted different parts of dogs' brains. He reported that only damage to the frontal lobe affected the animal's personality. Although the dogs with frontal lobe injury still remembered things from before the surgery, they were simply different dogs.

If the frontal lobe is closely linked to personality and social behaviors, it is not surprising that any language areas in the frontal lobe— such as Broca's area—would also be related to personality and social behaviors.

FUNCTION WORDS ARE VERY VERY SOCIAL

Brain research points to the inescapable conclusion that function words are related to our social worlds. In fact, stealth words by their very nature are social.

Imagine you are walking down the street on a windy afternoon and a piece of paper lands on the ground in front of you. There is a hand-written note on the paper that says:

> **He is around but I don't know where.**
> **I will be back here very soon. Don't do it!**

The note is grammatically correct and is understandable in a certain sense. Is something important about to happen? Certainly there is an urgency. But, really, we have no idea what this person is talking about. Every word in the note is a function word. Who and where is "he"? When is "will be" and "soon"? Who is "I"? Where is "here"? What shouldn't the person do? Now that you think about it, this note makes absolutely no sense.

In a normal conversation, we automatically know what all the function words refer to based on who we are speaking to, where we are, and what we have already been talking about. Whoever wrote the note had a shared understanding with its intended recipient about the who, where, and when. Maybe the note was typed by some guy named Bob to be read by Julia. A few minutes earlier, they might have had the following discussion:

BOB (ON CELL PHONE TALKING TO JULIA): Julia, you caught me at a crazy time. I've got to buy a stapler but I'll leave a note on the door if I'm not here when you arrive.

JULIA: Great. I need to have the accountant sign my expense form. Do you know where he is?

BOB: I'll see if he's in . . .

JULIA: Did I tell you that I'm thinking of smoking again? I always feel more alert and happy when I smoke. I know it annoys you.

BOB: Are you nuts? Let's talk about this. Gotta go. See you later.

All of a sudden, we know that "He is around" = the accountant is somewhere in the building, "I" = Bob, "will be back very soon" = Bob will be back at work within maybe thirty minutes of when the note was written, "Don't do it" = Julia really shouldn't start smoking again.

What's interesting is that this note has real meaning only for Bob and Julia on a specific day in a specific location. If Julia finds the note in a week it will no longer make sense. Any stranger who happens on the note will not have the keys to unlock the meanings of all of these function words.

Function words require social skills to use properly. The speaker assumes that the listener knows who everyone is. The listener must be paying attention and know the speaker to follow the conversation. So the mere ability to understand a simple conversation chock-full of function words demands social knowledge.

The same is true for articles, prepositions, and all other stealth words. Consider these slightly different sentences:

"I can't believe that he gave her the ring."
"I can't believe that he gave her a ring."

The difference between "the" ring and "a" ring is subtle but significant. If the word *the* is present, it means that the speaker is referring to a specific ring that the listener has some knowledge of. The sentence with "a" ring, in contrast, suggests something very different about the evolving relationship between "him" and "her." More important, "a" ring tells us that the speaker and listener do not have a shared knowledge of the particular ring that was given.

All function words work similarly in that they are tied to the personal relationship between the speaker and listener. Even the author of a book and the book's reader must enter into a shared social world. If I now make reference to the earlier paragraph about Julia's smoking, you instantly know what *I, now, to, the, earlier,* and *about* refer to. Had that same phrase been written three pages ago, no one would have been able to figure it out. All function words, such as *before, over,* and *to,* require a basic awareness of the speaker's location in time and space. The ability to use them, then, is a marker of basic social skills. On the other hand, talking about nouns and verbs demands the ability to understand culturally shared categories and definitions.

What's so amazing is that our brains are able to decide which function words to use almost instantaneously. Assuming you are a native English speaker, no one has ever sat down with you and explained the difference between using *a* and *the*. If we are talking with someone we have never met and casually mention a particular window in the room, two minutes later both of us will know which window when it is referred to as "the window." Similarly, when we later refer to it as being clean, we will remember that "it" = the window.

Function words also reflect and color subtle ways we think about objects and events in our lives. With prepositions and other function words, as with articles and pronouns, we are able to make linguistic shifts as quickly as we can speak. It's hard to imagine stopping a conversation in midsentence to decide whether you should say "I went *to* my friend's house" versus "I went *over to* my friend's house" versus "I went *by* my friend's house." The differences among *to, over to,* and *by* are almost imperceptible to the listener but they all have a slightly different meaning about the trip or the friend or the friend's house.

As a final note, we are not capable of easily controlling how and when we use function words. They are hard for us to perceive in others and to control in ourselves. They are processed in our brains extremely quickly and efficiently. All the time, our brain is remembering recent references to a person or object so that we can use the right pronouns and articles in the next sentence.

BEYOND ENGLISH: FUNCTION WORDS
AS CULTURAL CLUES

Every language must be able to distinguish between "a table" and "the table," between "she" and "he," and between "going to a store" and "going by a store." In some languages these distinctions are signaled by separate function words and in others, they are added to a surrounding noun or verb. The ways that function words are used differ by culture and often tell us something about the culture itself.

In our research on function words, my students, colleagues, and I have developed the LIWC computer program for use with a number of languages, including Spanish, German, Arabic, Italian, French, Russian, Dutch, Chinese, and others. So far, virtually all the language links to social and psychological phenomena we have found in English have generalized to other languages. In developing cross-language text analysis programs, we come across unique issues every time we begin exploring a new language.

Pronoun Dropping

In some languages, separate words for pronouns are rarely used. In Spanish, for example, *estoy triste* literally means "am sad." The word "I" is not needed since the personal pronoun is implicit in the verb conjugation. Of course, a speaker could say "Yo estoy triste," which would be the equivalent of "*I* am sad," with a strong emphasis on the word *I*. As discussed in the emotion chapter, when English speakers are depressed, they tend to use the word *I* more in everyday language—apparently because they are paying more attention to themselves. Spanish speakers, when they are depressed, greatly increase in their use of the first-person singular pronoun, *yo*.

Why do some cultures drop personal pronouns and others don't? One argument is that languages from more tightly knit collectivist cultures tend to drop pronouns, whereas the more individualist societies retain them.

Status Markers in Language

Most languages are constructed to identify who in a conversation has greater status or respect. In Old English, our linguistic ancestors distinguished between *you* and *thou*. By the late eighteenth century, the formal and informal distinction was disappearing. Most European languages still use formal and informal versions of the pronoun *you*, although the distinction is becoming less common. Other languages, such as Japanese, signal relative status in the conjugation of verbs and other words. Indeed, it is almost impossible to say "I spoke with you about the car" without signaling the relative status of the speaker and addressee.

Direct Versus Indirect Knowledge

Some languages, such as Turkish, require you to provide evidence for any statement you make. If I said to you "It was very hot in Austin yesterday" in English, you would likely shrug your shoulders and assume that I'm telling you the truth. In Turkish, however, you would use different forms of the verb "was" to denote whether I personally experienced the hot weather or am simply relaying this information from some other source.

Social Knowledge Lost in Translation

In a striking series of studies, Stanford's Lera Boroditsky has demonstrated how the language you are speaking at the time dictates how you remember pictures or events. A bilingual Japanese-English speaker would likely remember the relative status of three other people if introduced to them in Japanese rather than in English. A bilingual Turkish-English speaker will remember my talking about Austin's weather differently if we spoke in Turkish compared to English.

Indeed, when anything is translated from one language into another, parts simply disappear or are created. If I have to translate "thank you very much" into Spanish, I will have to make an educated guess whether to make it a formal or an informal *you*. And when the same phrase is translated back into English, the formality information is stripped away.

Interestingly, nouns and regular verbs generally translate across languages fairly smoothly. It is the function words that can cause the biggest problems.

LANGUAGE STYLE AND PSYCHOLOGY: MAKING THE LEAP TO THE NEXT LEVEL

Function words are everywhere. We use and are exposed to them all the time. They are virtually impossible to hear and to manipulate. And many of these stealth words say something about the speaker, the listener, and their relationship. But this book really isn't about function words per se. If you are talking with a friend and mention "a chair" versus "the chair" versus "that chair," it really says very little about you. However, what if we count your use of articles over the course of a day or week? What if we find that there are some people out there who use *a* and *the* at very high rates and another group that tends to not use articles at all?

In fact, there *are* people who use articles at very high rates and others who rarely use them. Across hundreds of thousands of language samples from books to blogs to everyday informal conversation, men consistently use articles at higher rates than women. And, even taking people's sex into account, high article users tend to be more organized and emotionally stable. Indeed, men and women who habitually use *a* and *the* at higher rates tend to be more conscientious, more politically conservative, and older.

And now things start to get interesting. Using articles in daily speech doesn't make a person a well-adjusted, older conservative politician like John McCain (who, in fact, used articles at high rates compared to his opponents in the 2008 presidential election campaign). Rather, the use of articles can begin to tell us about the ways people think, feel, and connect with others in their worlds. And the same is true for pronouns, prepositions, and virtually all function words.

This is the heart of my story. By listening to, counting, and analyzing stealth words, we can learn about people in ways that even they
may not appreciate or comprehend. At the same time, the ways people
use stealth words can subtly affect how we perceive them and their
messages. Before starting our journey on stealth words and the human
condition, you might need a brief road map to jog your memory about
what different function words mean. At the end of the book, a short
word-spotting guide is available. As you study your own language or
the words of others, you can refer back to the guide as needed to better
understand what the words mean.

CHAPTER 3

The Words of Sex, Age, and Power

T HERE IS NO better way to start a discussion of language and differences among people than with gender. Do men and women use words differently? As you may suspect, the answer is yes. Now that this has been established, take the following test.

In daily conversations, e-mails, informal talks, blogs, and even most formal writing, who uses the following parts of speech more, men or women?

For each of the questions, circle the correct answer:

1. First-person singular (e.g., *I, me, my*):
   a. women use more
   b. men use more
   c. no difference between women and men

2. First-person plural (e.g., *we, us, our*)
   a. women use more
   b. men use more
   c. no difference between women and men

3. Articles (*a, an, the*)
   a. women use more
   b. men use more
   c. no difference between women and men

4. Positive emotion words (e.g., *love, fun, good*)
   a. women use more
   b. men use more
   c. no difference between women and men

5.   Cognitive words (e.g., *think, reason, believe*)

   a. women use more

   b. men use more

   c. no difference between women and men

6.   Social words (e.g., *they, friend, parent*)

   a. women use more

   b. men use more

   c. no difference between women and men

This should be a very easy test for everyone. A day doesn't go by where we don't hear thousands of words from both men and women. In fact, we have all been deluged with words from people of both sexes our entire lives. Who could possibly miss these questions?

As it turns out, most people do. This includes the leading scholars in many top departments of psychology and linguistics around the world. Your high school English teachers would have done no better. How about you? The answers are: 1. a; 2. c; 3. b; 4. c; 5. a; 6. a. Women use first-person singular, cognitive, and social words more; men use articles more; and there are no meaningful differences between men and women for first-person plural or positive emotion words. If you are like most people, you probably got the social words question right and missed most of the others.

Before going farther, it might be helpful to review the test answer key:

1. *Women use first-person singular pronouns, or I-words, more than men.* People's pronouns track their focus of attention. If someone is anxious, self-conscious, in pain, or depressed, they pay more attention to themselves. Research suggests that women, on average, are more self-aware and self-focused than are men. The differences in the use of I-words between women and men are not subtle. In natural conversations, blogs, and speeches, women use I-words at much higher rates.

2. *Men and women use first-person plural words, or we-words,*

at the same rate. The use of *we* highlights one of the most enigmatic function words in our vocabulary. The natural assumption is that when speakers use *we*, they are referring to themselves and their close friends. There are even famous psychology studies where people see the word *we* flashed on a screen and it makes them feel all warm and fuzzy and more connected to others.

We, as it turns out, is really two very different words. Yes, there is the warm and fuzzy we—"my wife and I," "my dog and me," "my family." You can feel the welcoming arms of the *w* and *e* embrace us. So, yes, there is that tight sense of group identity that goes with *we* some of the time.

Another *we*, however, is the cooler, distanced, and largely impersonal *we*. My graduate students know this *we*. It's when I say, "You know, we really need to analyze that data." My son rarely feels warm about his father when I say, "We need to take out the trash." As it happens, I have no intention of actually analyzing that data. Nor am I proposing to my son that we take a family outing to the trash bin. In many situations, people use the word *we* when they mean *you*. It serves as a polite form to order others around.

A variation on the cool we-meaning-you is the royal *we*. "We are not amused," Queen Victoria is supposed to have said, meaning that the queen herself was not amused. Soon after the birth of her first grandchild, England's prime minister Margaret Thatcher announced to the press, "We have become a grandmother." Royalty, office holders, and senior administrators occasionally slip in the royal *we* when they should really be using the word *I*.

Finally, there is the purely ambiguous *we* that is particularly loved by politicians. *We need change in this country and we deserve it! Our taxes are too high and we need to do something about it!* I sometimes sit around with my students trying to deconstruct political speeches in order to figure out who the "we" is. Sometimes, the politician means "you," sometimes "I," sometimes "you and I," and sometimes "everyone on earth who agrees with me."

The reason *we* is such a fun word is that half of the time it is used as a way to bring the speaker closer to others and the other half of the time to deflect responsibility away from the speaker. And indeed, there are sex differences. Women tend to use the warm *we* and men are more drawn to the distanced *we*. On average, however, men and women end up using we-words at about the same rates.

3. *Men use articles* (a, an, the) *more than do women.* Except for people who read the last chapter closely, hardly anyone would know the answer to this one. Articles? Who cares about articles? I do, for one. And I personally want you to care because they are very important words. Articles are used with nouns—especially concrete, highly specific nouns. A person who uses an article is talking about a particular object or thing. Guys talk about objects and things more than women do. They talk about the broken carburetor, the wife, and a steak on the grill for the dinner. We'll return to this shameless generalization in a minute.

4. *No differences in the use of positive emotion words.* Although women use slightly more negative emotion words in everyday conversation than do men, the two sexes use positive emotion words at the same high rate.

5. *Women use more cognitive words than men.* Cognitive words are words that reflect different ways of thinking and include words that tap insight (*understand, know, think*), causal thinking (*because, reason, rationale*), and related dimensions. That women use more of these words is a slap in the face of Aristotle, who believed that women were less rational than men and incapable of philosophical thought. But there is a simple explanation. It all comes into focus with social words.

6. *Women use social words at far higher rates than men.* Social words refer to any words that are related to other human beings. Surely you got this one correct. Women do, indeed, think more and talk more about other people.

The various sex differences in word use actually make a coherent story. When women and men get together, what do they talk about? Women disproportionately talk about other people and men talk about, well, carburetors and other objects and things. Ultimately, which topics—other people versus carburetors—are more complex and require more cognitive work in explaining? Human relationships are not rocket science—they are far, far more complicated. We can get our top scientists together and send people to the moon. Two speakers—male or female—can troubleshoot a carburetor in under an hour. But even the most creative and diligent scientists, much less two interested speakers, are unable to understand, explain, or agree on why actress Jennifer Lopez is attracted to the men she is or how long she will remain married to her current husband.

PREPARATION FOR THE NEXT TEST: OTHER WORD CATEGORIES THAT DISTINGUISH BETWEEN MEN AND WOMEN

The sex-differences test you just took is only the beginning. Men and women differ in a variety of other language dimensions that will be discussed throughout the book. In case there is another gender-language exam, it is important to appreciate that men and women also differ in the following ways:

MEN USE MORE	WOMEN USE MORE
Big words	Personal pronouns
Nouns	Verbs (including auxiliary verbs)
Prepositions	Negative emotion (especially anxiety)
Numbers	Negations (*no, not, never*)
Words per sentence	Certainty words (*always, absolutely*)
Swear words	Hedge phrases ("I think," "I believe")

These additional language differences buttress what has already been noted. Males categorize their worlds by counting, naming, and organizing the objects they confront. Women, in addition to personalizing their topics, talk in a more dynamic way, focusing on how their topics change. Discussions of change require more verbs.

Finally, one of the most studied dimensions of women's language concerns hedge phrases, or hedges. Hedges typically start a sentence in the form of a phrase such as "I think that" or "It seems to me" or "I don't know but . . ." Consider the meaning of the two following answers to the question

> What's the weather like outside?
> I think it's cold.
> It's cold.

The answer "I think it's cold," as opposed to "It's cold," tells more than the outside temperature. The "I think" phrase is implicitly acknowledging, "Although there are different views on this—and you may indeed come to a different conclusion—my own personal belief is that it might be cold outside. I could be wrong, of course, and if you have a different sense of the weather, I won't be offended." To say "I think," then, implies that there are multiple perspectives and, at the same time, announces that the estimation of coldness is ultimately an opinion rather than a fact. To say "It's cold" is to say the weather outside is cold. An indisputable fact. End of discussion.

Consistent with the greater social interests of women, it is not surprising that they are more likely to use hedges than are men. Interestingly, women are just as likely to use hedges when talking with other women as when talking with men.

GENDER, STEREOTYPES, AND COMPUTERS

There is nothing inherently mysterious about the language of women and men. Nevertheless, most of us have been blind to these sex differences our entire lives. I'm no different. Soon after developing the computerized word counting program LIWC, I started analyzing dozens, then hundreds, then thousands of essays, blogs, and other text samples from men and women. One of the first analyses revealed the pattern of effects you have just read about. When I first found that women used I-words more than men, I just ignored the results. Had to be a fluke. Another study, same effects. Another fluke, I thought. It probably took a dozen analyses with very large samples to slap me awake.

The stereotypes we hold about women and men are deeply ingrained. Even within the scientific community, the study of gender differences in language is highly politicized. One group of scientists passionately believes that men and women are essentially the same; another believes that they are profoundly different. Yet others simply don't want to think about it. But the stereotypes persist. Some believe that women are more emotional and men are more logical or that women talk about others and men talk about themselves. Yet others are convinced that women simply say twice as many words every day as men. Even though most of these beliefs have been debunked by good scientific studies, it is hard to let go of them.

Beginning in the late 1960s and early 1970s, the women's movement awakened the culture to the fact that women and men were not treated equally. A Berkeley linguist, Robin Lakoff, published a stunning book in 1975, *Language and Woman's Place*, that pointed out how women and men talked differently. Lakoff argued that men used the language of power and rudeness, while women's speech tended to be quieter, passive, and excessively polite. In the decades that followed, several studies supported Lakoff's observations. By the early 1990s, Deborah Tannen, a linguist at Georgetown University, attracted international notice with her book *You Just Don't Understand*. Her book, which was on the *New York Times* bestseller list for over four years, argued that men and women often talk past each other without appreciating that the other sex is almost another culture. Women, for example, are highly attentive to the thoughts and feelings of others; men are less so. Women view men's speaking styles as blunt and uncaring; men view women's as indirect and obscure.

Sociolinguists such as Lakoff and Tannen focus on broad social dimensions such as gender, race, social class, and power. Their approach is qualitative, involving recording and analyzing conversations on a case-by-case basis. It is slow, painstaking work. Over the course of a year, a good sociolinguist may analyze only a few interactions. Whereas the qualitative approach is powerful at getting an in-depth understanding of a small group of interactions, the methods are not designed to get an accurate picture of an entire society or culture. This is where computer-based text analysis methods can help. By analyzing the blogs of hundreds of thousands of people, for example, the computer-based methods can quickly determine the nature of gender differences as a function of age, class, native language, region, and other domains. In other words, a relatively slow but careful qualitative approach can give us an in-depth view of a small group of people; a computer-based quantitative approach provides a broader social and cultural perspective. The two methods, then, complement each other in ways that the two research camps often fail to appreciate.

HOW BIG ARE GENDER DIFFERENCES IN LANGUAGE?

Although men and women use words differently, the differences can often be subtle. In one large study of over fourteen thousand language samples, we found that about 14.2 percent of women's words were personal pronouns compared with only 12.7 percent for men. From a statistical perspective, this is a *huge* difference. The kind of whopping statistical effect that brings tears of joy to a scientist's eyes (or at least mine).

But a tear-inducing statistical effect does not always translate into an everyday meaningful effect. Let's say we find a slow-talking person who speaks at the rate of a hundred words per minute. In any given minute, an average woman should say 14.2 personal pronouns and the average male 12.7. That is, the woman will mention about one and a half pronouns more than the man every minute. These numbers add up over the course of the day. For example, the average man and woman each say about sixteen thousand words a day. In the course of a year, women will say about eighty-five thousand more pronouns than will men. It boggles the mind. But does it matter? Although women are uttering almost 12 percent more pronouns than men, our brains are not constructed to pick up the difference. The average person can't consciously detect a 12 percent difference and can't even see the difference in written text. If you are intent on stealth word detection, you need to either count the words by hand or use a computer to do the dirty work.

Although we might not be very good at perceiving the differences in language between men and women, how well do computers do at distinguishing the writing of women from men? Let's say we saved the text of well over 100,000 blog posts from, oh, I don't know, 19,320 blog authors who identified themselves by their sex. Imagine that we then trained our computer program to sort the blogs by function-word use into male bloggers versus female bloggers. As you might have guessed, we have done just this. Overall, the computer correctly classifies the sex of the author 72 percent of the time (50 percent is chance). If we also look at the *content* (in addition to the style) of what people are writing, our accuracy increases slightly to about 76 percent. Note that these guesses are far superior to human guesses, which are in the 55–65 percent accuracy range.

All of these statistics tell us that, on average, women and men use words differently. The differences are subtle and not easily picked up by the human ear. And, of course, it is even more complicated than I've suggested. All people change their language depending on the situations that they are in. In formal settings, for example, people tend to use far fewer pronouns, more articles, and fewer social words—meaning most of us speak like prototypical men. When hanging around with our family in a relaxed setting, we all talk more like women. In short, the gender effects that exist in language reflect, to some degree, gender.

But the context of speaking probably accounts for even more of our language choices.

AN EAR FOR GENDER: PLAYWRIGHTS AND SCREENWRITERS

As a reader, you probably have a certain fondness for the written word. You can easily spot a passage that is well written versus one that is poorly written. As a teacher, I have long wondered what it takes for someone to become a good writer. Better yet, how does one become a great writer? In his delightful book *On Writing*, novelist Stephen King argues that with practice and hard work, it is possible for a competent writer to become a good writer. However, no amount of work or training can elevate a good writer to a great one. A great writer, in King's mind, is a different breed.

A common theme in the writing literature is that a great writer has an uncanny ear for words. The ability to capture dialogue is akin to having perfect pitch for music. World-class dialogue writers seem to intuitively know how words are used by a wide range of characters. Think of some of the leading dialogue writers in plays and movies: Arthur Miller's stark language in *Death of a Salesman*, Joseph Mankiewicz's *All About Eve*, and most anything by William Shakespeare, Tom Stoppard, Woody Allen, Tony Kushner, and Nora Ephron.

A few years ago, I gave a talk on gender and language and someone asked if playwrights and screenwriters naturally knew how women and men spoke. My wife happens to be a superb professional writer and I thought back to her work and announced with certainty: yes. There were no studies to my knowledge but I would bet a reasonable amount of money that the people who are particularly good at dialogue innately use words that are appropriate for the sex of their characters. The expert had spoken.

That night in my hotel room I checked my computer to see if I had some plays or movie scripts to analyze. I did: Shakespeare's *Romeo and Juliet* and Nora Ephron's *Sleepless in Seattle*. Both works had a major male and female protagonist—one script written by a man, the other by a woman. A few hundred keystrokes later, I had an answer. Both Mr. Romeo and Ms. Juliet talk like men, and both Ephron's main characters talk a lot like women. In Aldous Huxley's words, this was the slaying of a beautiful hypothesis by an ugly fact. But maybe these two authors or scripts were a fluke.

A few days later, I met with one of my graduate students, Molly Ireland. Although Molly knew a lot about psychology, her undergraduate training in literature and philosophy gave her a particularly broad perspective on plays and movies. She eagerly took on a large-scale project that involved analyzing over 110 scripts from more than 70 different playwrights and screenwriters. Such a project could answer several questions. Do writers differ in their abilities to capture the language of women and men? Does capturing the voice of the sexes vary depending on the specific play or movie? That is, one could imagine that a writer might have a sensitive leading man talk like a woman in one movie and like a macho man in another.

Fortunately, we have conducted several studies over the years where we have asked hundreds of people to wear a tape recorder as they go about their daily lives. We have also collected language samples from interviews, lab studies, and other sources. These transcripts have given us a base of thousands of conversations of men and women. Using these data, we can compare the ways that real males and females talk with the ways that leading characters in literature talk.

The results were fascinating. To make the results a bit simpler, Molly and I converted the statistics to a nine-point masculinity-femininity language scale. A score of 1 means that the lead character is speaking like a super-male. You know how super-males talk—lots of articles and prepositions, very few pronouns, social words, or cognitive words. A score of 9 means that the character talks like a super-female—essentially the opposite pattern of the super-male. And a score of 5 means the character's language is not sex linked.

The Masculinity-Femininity Language Scores of the Lead Female and Male Characters

1	2	3	4	5	6	7	8	9
STRONG MASCULINE				**NEITHER**			**STRONG FEMININE**	
LANGUAGE			**MASCULINE NOR FEMININE**				**LANGUAGE**	

WHERE WOMEN TALK LIKE WOMEN AND MEN TALK LIKE MEN

WRITER	SCRIPT(S)	LEAD FEMALES	LEAD MALES
Joan Tewkesbury	*Nashville*	9	4
Spike Lee	*Do the Right Thing*	8	5
David Lynch	*Blue Velvet, Mulholland Drive*	6	4
Sam Shepard	*Buried Child, Mad Dog Blues*	6	4
Thornton Wilder	*Our Town*	6	1

WHERE BOTH WOMEN AND MEN TALK LIKE WOMEN

WRITER	SCRIPT(S)	LEAD FEMALES	LEAD MALES
Nora Ephron	*You've Got Mail, Sleepless in Seattle*	9	6
Gertrude Stein	*Brewsie and Willie, Three Sisters Who Are Not Sisters*	9	8
Sofia Coppola	*Lost in Translation*	7	8
Woody Allen	*Hannah and Her Sisters*	6	7
Callie Khouri	*Thelma and Louise*	6	8

WHERE BOTH MEN AND WOMEN TALK LIKE MEN

Quentin Tarantino	*Pulp Fiction*	**2**	*4*
William Shakespeare	*Romeo and Juliet, Titus Andronicus*	**3**	*3*
Lona Williams	*Drop Dead Gorgeous*	**3**	*3*
Cameron Crowe	*Almost Famous, Jerry McGuire*	**4**	*3*
Courtney Hunt	*Frozen River*	**5**	*3*

Note: Numbers between 1 and 4 in bold indicate a more masculine language and numbers between 6 and 9 in italics suggest a more feminine language.

Each of the tables gives a sense of the ways different authors portray their main characters. Thornton Wilder, in *Our Town*, tracks the lives of several characters, including Emily Webb. We see Emily as an eager high school student who later falls in love with George. After dying in childbirth, Emily appears one final time in the graveyard after she has just gone back in time and watched a scene from her childhood. When she returns to her seat in the cemetery in the final scene, she talks with some of the other dead souls about the shock of watching her early family life.

> EMILY: I didn't realize. So all that was going on and we never noticed. Take me back—up the hill—to my grave. But first: Wait! One more look . . . Do any human beings ever realize life while they live it?—every, every minute?
>
> STAGE MANAGER: No. The saints and poets, maybe—they do some. . . .
>
> EMILY: Oh, Mr. Stimson, I should have listened to them.

SIMON STIMSON: Yes, now you know. Now you know! That's what it was to be alive. To move about in a cloud of ignorance; to go up and down trampling on the feelings of those . . . of those about you. To spend and waste time as though you had a million years. To be always at the mercy of one self-centered passion, or another. Now you know—that's the happy existence you wanted to go back to. Ignorance and blindness. . . .

EMILY: They don't understand, do they?

MRS. JULIA GIBBS: No, dear. They don't understand.

. . .

STAGE MANAGER: Most everybody's asleep in Grover's Corners. There are a few lights on: Shorty Hawkins, down at the depot, has just watched the Albany train go by. And at the livery stable somebody's setting up late and talking. —Yes, it's clearing up. There are the stars—doing their old, old crisscross journeys in the sky. Scholars haven't settled the matter yet, but they seem to think there are no living beings up there. Just chalk . . . or fire. Only this one is straining away, straining away all the time to make something of itself. The strain's so bad that every sixteen hours everybody lies down and gets a rest. Hm . . . Eleven o'clock in Grover's Corners. —You get a good rest, too. Good night.

If you haven't seen or read *Our Town* in a while, it is a remarkable piece of work. Even in this brief scene, the women—Emily and her mother-in-law Julia Gibbs—focus on their own feelings and those of others. The men, Simon Stimson and the stage manager, use virtually no pronouns and describe the world in nice objective manly ways. Wilder's men do indeed talk like prototypical men and his women talk like prototypical women.

Compare Wilder's writing with Callie Khouri's screenplay *Thelma and Louise*. Through a series of haunting misadventures, the two main characters, Thelma and Louise, find themselves running from the law after shooting a would-be rapist. The primary investigator, Hal, talks with Louise by phone and pleads for her to give herself up:

LOUISE: Would you believe me if I told you this whole thing is an accident?

HAL: I do believe you. That's what I want everybody to believe. Trouble is, it doesn't look like an accident and you're not here to tell me about it . . . I need you to help me here. . . . You want to come on in?

LOUISE: I don't think so.

HAL: Then I'm sorry. We're gonna have to charge you with murder. Now, do you want to come out of this alive?

LOUISE: You know, certain words and phrases just keep floating through my mind, things like incarceration, cavity search, life imprisonment, death by electrocution, that sort of thing. So, come out alive? I don't know. Let us think about that.

HAL: Louise, I'll do anything. I know what's makin' you run. I know what happened to you in Texas.

What makes Khouri's men so interesting is that they actually speak more like women than do the women. Hal's frequent use of pronouns and low use of articles points to his deep interest in other people as opposed to concrete objects. Another important feature of the movie is that all the men—including the role played by Brad Pitt—have a feminine speaking style. At the same time, none would be considered remotely effeminate in their actions.

Just the opposite pattern can be seen in Quentin Tarantino's script *Pulp Fiction*. Perhaps the most traditionally feminine character in the movie is the young French woman, Fabian, who is involved with Butch (played by Bruce Willis). Despite her girl-like appearance and child-like voice, Fabian's words are decidedly masculine. In this scene, Butch has just returned from throwing a boxing match and accidentally killing his opponent (life is not easy for any Tarantino character). Fabian is not aware of what has happened and announces that she has decided that she would like to have a potbelly.

FABIAN: A pot belly. Pot bellies are sexy.

BUTCH: Well you should be happy, 'cause you do.

FABIAN: Shut up, Fatso! I don't have a pot! I have a bit of a tummy, like Madonna when she did "Lucky Star," it's not the same thing.

BUTCH: I didn't realize there was a difference between a tummy and a pot belly.

FABIAN: The difference is huge.

BUTCH: You want me to have a pot?

FABIAN: No. Pot bellies make a man look either oafish, or like a gorilla. But on a woman, a pot belly is very sexy. The rest of you is normal. Normal face, normal legs, normal hips, normal ass, but with a big, perfectly round pot belly. If I had one, I'd wear a tee-shirt two sizes too small to accentuate it.

BUTCH: You think guys would find that attractive?

FABIAN: I don't give a damn what men find attractive. It's unfortunate what we find pleasing to the touch and pleasing to the eye is seldom the same.

That Quentin Tarantino's characters use the language of males might not be too shocking for serious moviegoers. But what about the Bard himself, William Shakespeare? In perhaps the most famous scene of *Romeo and Juliet*, the young lovers proclaim:

ROMEO: What light through yonder window breaks? It is the East, and Juliet is the sun! Arise, fair sun, and kill the envious moon, Who is already sick and pale with grief That thou her maid are far more fair than she. Be not her maid, since she is envious. Her vestal livery is but sick and green, And none but fools do wear it. Cast it off. It is my lady; O, it is my love! O that she knew she were! She speaks, yet she says nothing. What of that? Her eye discourses; I will answer it. I am too bold; 'tis not to me she speaks. Two of the fairest stars in all the heaven, Having some business, do entreat her eyes To twinkle in their spheres till they return. What if her eyes were there, they in her head? The brightness of her cheek would shame those stars As daylight does a lamp; her eyes in heaven Would through the airy region stream so bright That birds would sing and think it were not night. See how she leans her cheek upon her hand! O that I were a glove upon that hand, That I might touch that cheek! . . .

JULIET: O Romeo, Romeo! Wherefore art thou Romeo? Deny thy father and refuse thy name; Or, if thou wilt not, be but sworn my love, And I'll no longer be a Capulet. . . .'Tis but your name that is my enemy. Thou art thyself, though not a Montague. What's Montague? it is nor hand, nor foot, Nor arm, nor face. O, be some other name Belonging to a man. What's in a name? That which we call a rose By any other word would smell as sweet. So Romeo would, were he not Romeo called, Retain that dear perfection which he owes Without that title. Romeo, doff thy name; And for thy name, which is no part of thee, Take all myself.

We can feel the yearning and innocence of Romeo and Juliet, the lightness and openness. A cursory reading would never reveal that both—especially Juliet—are expressing themselves the ways that males tend to do. Both use I-words at low levels, use a below-average number of personal pronouns in general, and have above-average article usage, especially for such a personal and intimate setting.

Shakespeare and Tarantino are males and write like males. Their male and female characters use function words the ways males do. The two writers may share the same stealth word usage, but they clearly differ in the content and breadth of what they write. Shakespeare is of interest because he brilliantly conveys real-life themes and concerns women have. But his use of function words, much like Tarantino's, suggests that he fails at getting inside the minds of women.

Do these things matter from the audience's perspective? Yes, but in a subtle way. Recall Deborah Tannen's analogy of sex differences being akin to cultural differences. Most of us can read, say, Dostoyevsky's *Crime and Punishment* and come away with an appreciation of Raskolnikov's tortured thoughts of murdering the pawnbroker. We can do this even without speaking Russian or knowing nineteenth-century St. Petersburg culture. Of course, the St. Petersburg native reading Dostoyevsky's work in 1866 would undoubtedly possess a more intimate understanding of the book than would twenty-first-century native English speakers. By the same token, a woman scriptwriter's depiction of a man's way of speaking may mischaracterize the ways males actually speak, but if the content is compelling, we will probably not notice it.

SEX DIFFERENCES IN LANGUAGE: THE POSSIBLE ROLE OF TESTOSTERONE

Women and men use language differently, tend to talk about different topics, and ultimately may represent two subcultures of humans. Clearly, girls and boys are socialized differently, which may account for many of the language differences. Is it also possible that our interests may be influenced by our hormones? And if our interests are hormone related, perhaps our hormones may guide our everyday language use.

Beyond the anatomical differences of women and men, the two sexes have strikingly different hormonal profiles. Compared to men, women have very high levels of estrogen—a family of hormones that regulate the menstrual cycle, the development of female sex organs, breasts, and pubic hair, as well as aid in the ability to become pregnant. For men, the hormone testosterone is associated with the development of male sex organs and secondary sex characteristics such as facial hair. Women also secrete testosterone but at much lower levels than men, just as men have low levels of estrogen.

For a variety of reasons, both men and women occasionally undergo testosterone therapy, whereby they are given periodic injections of the hormone. What would happen to their language during times when their testosterone levels were high versus when they were low? Through an odd series of events, I was able to answer the question.

Around the year 2000, I was contacted by Professor James Dabbs, a world-renowned expert on the psychological correlates of testosterone. A tall, distinguished southerner with a polite, regal bearing, Jim had measured testosterone levels of murderers, lawyers, actors, priests, academics, and others—always with a twinkle in his eye. Much of his work examined the links between aggressive behaviors and testosterone levels. (During one serious conference on hormones and behavior, Jim started his talk by looking around the packed lecture hall and snorting, "There's not enough testosterone in this entire room to rob a single liquor store.")

Jim had received a letter from a biological female who was undergoing therapy to become male, a female-to-male (FTM) sex change, or, more accurately, gender reassignment. The person, GH, was twenty-eight years old and had been involved in gender reassignment for three years. In addition to a double mastectomy, GH received injections of testosterone every two to four weeks. GH had read about Jim's research and wanted to know if he would like to study GH's diaries, which he (GH) had been keeping for several years. Knowing that I studied language, Jim felt I could examine the effects of testosterone on function words.

GH was articulate and a prolific writer. He provided my research team with two years of his diaries along with a detailed record of his testosterone injections. While we were transcribing GH's diaries, I was invited to give a series of talks in Boston. One night, I found myself in a bar talking to a gentleman who happened to be an anthropologist. In the midst of our conversation, I mentioned the GH project. My new anthropologist friend was silent for a minute and finally said that he, too, was taking testosterone injections on the advice of his physician. He was sixty years old and had been taking testosterone for four years in an attempt to restore his upper-body strength. "Really?" I asked innocently. "Do you have a record of your injections?" Yes. "By any chance do you keep a diary?" No, but he was willing to let me analyze all of his outgoing e-mails for the previous year.

The analyses were straightforward. For both GH and the anthropologist, the words that they wrote each day were analyzed using the LIWC computer program. The word categories were then compared against the number of days since each person's last testosterone injection. The idea was that as time passed since the last injection, each person's testosterone levels would drop.

The similarity of effects for the two people was striking and the overall results promising. Whether their testosterone went up or down, no predictable changes were seen in their use of articles, prepositions, nouns, verbs, and negative emotion words. However, there was one fascinating and reliable difference—in social pronouns (including words like *we*, *us*, *he*, *she*, *they*, and *them*). As testosterone levels dropped, they used more social pronouns. Think what this means: Both GH and the anthropologist inject themselves with testosterone and they now focus on tasks, goals, events, and the occasional object—but not people. And then, as the days wear on, they awake each morning and notice that there are other human beings around. And these human beings are interesting and worth talking about and talking to. And then, a few weeks later and another injection, and voilà! They're cured. No more worrying about others.

This study gives us a glimpse of how testosterone may psychologically affect people. Prior to receiving their results, I asked both participants how they felt that testosterone affected their language. GH was certain that the injections gave him more energy, made his mood more positive, and stimulated more thoughts of sex, aggression, sports, and traditional masculine things. The anthropologist, on the other hand, was adamant that testosterone had absolutely no psychological effect on him whatsoever. Both were wrong.

What does a study like this tell us about sex differences and the biology of function words? Only a little, I'm afraid. Injections of testosterone did not change GH's sex or the anthropologist's masculinity. There is no evidence that this hormonal assault had any effects on the ways either person understood, thought about, or categorized their world. It is significant, for example, that not a hint of changes in articles, nouns, verbs, cognitive words, or prepositions occurred. Finally, this was a study on only two people in unusual circumstances, meaning we should be cautious in generalizing the findings.

On a broader level, however, the testosterone study, along with the various gender-language projects, tells us a little about the ways men and women see and understand their worlds. Men are less interested in thinking and talking about other people than are women. The effects may be influenced by testosterone, but quite frankly, the testosterone findings are too preliminary to make grand pronouncements just yet.

That there are differences in social interests between women and men isn't exactly news. However, the fact that men consistently use more articles, nouns, and prepositions *is* news. OK, maybe it's not going to be on CNN's *Headline News*. But it is news because these language differences signal that men tend to talk and think about concrete objects and things in highly specific ways. They are naturally categorizing things. Further, the use of prepositions signals that the categorization process is being done in hierarchical and spatial ways. Think about when we use prepositions:

> The keys to the trunk of the car from Maria are next to the lamp under the picture of the boat painted by your mother.

The words *to, of, from, next to, under, of,* and *by* specify which and whose keys and exactly where they are in space. There is a hierarchical structure in the sense that these are not just any keys. Rather, they are part of the category of trunks, which are part of the category of cars from Maria. Similarly, the location of the keys is specified in both horizontal (next to) and vertical (under) planes. Statistically, it is much more likely that a sentence such as this would be uttered by a man than a woman. It's not that the man has a penchant for prepositions and nouns—rather a man naturally categorizes and assigns objects to spatial locations at rates higher than women.

WORDS OF WISDOM: LANGUAGE USE OVER THE LIFE SPAN

In most large surveys, researchers ask three questions: sex, age, and social class. Social class, which we will discuss soon, is usually asked indirectly with questions linked to race, education, or income. Why do survey makers want to know your sex, age, and social class if studying your political attitudes or buying behaviors? Because these three variables predict a stunning amount about people. If I know your sex, age, and social class, I can make surprisingly accurate guesses about your movie and music preferences, your religious and political views, your physical and mental health, and even your life expectancy.

These three demographic factors are also linked to language use. In many ways, the connections between language and age are more interesting than the connections to gender. If you are born a woman, the odds are very, very high that you will remain a woman your entire life. However, if you are born a baby, the odds are astronomically high that you won't remain one very long.

That our language—more specifically our use of function words—changes over the life span is, in some ways, surprising. But less so if you consider how our goals and life situations evolve, as do our bodies. As we get older, we change in the ways we orient to our friends and family, sex, money, health, death, and dozens of other life concerns.

Our personalities shift as well. Studies with thousands of people indicate that how we feel about ourselves is generally quite positive up until about age twelve. From about thirteen to twenty, our self-esteem levels drop to some of the lowest levels in our lives. Thereafter, to around the age of seventy, most people's self-esteem gradually increases. In fact, by around the age of sixty-five, many of us feel as good about ourselves as when we were nine years old—which is as good as it ever gets. And then, self-esteem tends to drop during the last few years of life. Other studies, based on 5,400 pairs of twins, find that as people get older, they become less outgoing, more emotionally stable, and a bit more impulsive.

The personality research is at odds with the bleak stereotypes of older people as being lonely, selfish, rigid, and bitter. Some of the more promising research that combats these stereotypes is being conducted by Laura Carstensen and her colleagues at Stanford University. She finds that as people age, emotion becomes a more important part of life. With greater attention to emotional states, people learn to regulate their emotions more effectively, resulting in greater happiness and fewer negative feelings. Although people over the age of seventy tend to have fewer friends, their social networks become stronger.

A fitting observation by the main character, Lloyd, in the Farrelly brothers' classic film *Dumb and Dumber* says it all. After asking an elderly woman to guard his possessions for a few minutes, Lloyd remarks, "Thanks. Hey, I guess they're right. Senior citizens, although slow and dangerous behind the wheel, can still serve a purpose. I'll be right back. Don't you go dying on me!" The elderly woman cheerfully snatches everything Lloyd owns.

How does language change as people age? We have tested this in several ways. The first was to go back to the giant blog project where we analyzed the collected posts of over nineteen thousand bloggers. The blog site that we "harvested" in 2004 was made up of people who were, on average, about twenty years old. We split the sample into three age groups: adolescent (ages thirteen to seventeen), young adult (ages twenty-three to twenty-seven), and adult (ages thirty-three to forty-seven). Despite the restricted age range, the three groups used emotion and function words very differently. Teens used personal pronouns (*I*, *you*), short words, and auxiliary verbs at very high rates. The older the people became, the more they used bigger words, prepositions, and articles.

We also conducted a systematic analysis on people who took part in one of several dozen expressive writing studies. As you recall from the first chapter, I've long been involved in studies where we ask people to write about deeply personal and oftentimes traumatic experiences. Over the years, researchers from labs around the world have sent me the writing samples from studies they have conducted. For the aging project, I teamed up with Lori Stone Handelman, a brilliant graduate student who later became a highly respected book editor in New York. Lori and I analyzed data from over 3,200 people who participated in one of 45 writing studies from 17 different universities. Although the average person in the studies was about twenty-four years old, the ages ranged from eight to eighty years old.

As you might imagine, people wrote about a wide array of topics—from sexual abuse and drug addiction to the death of a pet to not making the high school football team or cheerleading squad. Many of the essays were heartbreaking. For most, there was the sense that people put their soul into writing their stories.

Computer analyses of the texts yielded large and sometimes unexpected findings. When writing about emotional topics, the younger and older participants used strikingly different words.

Perhaps more impressive was the emotional tone of the young versus older writers. Consistent with the survey research, older people

YOUNGER WRITERS	OLDER WRITERS
Personal pronouns (especially *I*)	Articles, nouns, prepositions
Time references	Big words
Past-tense verbs	Future-tense verbs
	Cognitive words (insight words)

used more positive emotion words and younger people expressed more negative feelings. The differences became apparent by the age of forty but exploded among the oldest age group.

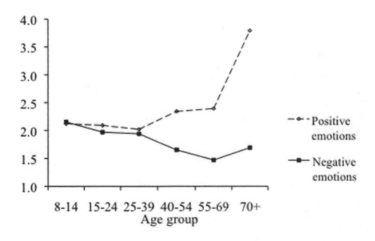

What makes these findings so intriguing is that all people were asked to write about some of the most troubling experiences of their entire lives. Younger people could dredge up an impressive number of dark words to express their pain. As writers got older and older, their negative emotion vocabulary diminished and their positive emotion word count skyrocketed. As you can see on the next page, the very youngest writer in this sample, who was eight years old, had a very different approach to the subject of his emotional story (Randy) than the oldest participant, who was dealing with cancer:

Eight-year old elementary school student: My enemy is Randy he makes me mad. Outside he calls me names, he ignores me, he does not stop bothering me, so I call him names when he starts. He does not stop so I start and get him back he makes me mad so I make him mad so I try to ignore him but he keeps making me mad . . . My mom says he is a bad influence.

Eighty-year old retiree. I am 80 years old, but I try to keep busy and go about life as though there is no ending. Sure I am not as fast or move as quick as I once did, but I do not feel it was the fault of the cancer and I try to do the best I can with what I've got. When negative thoughts try to creep in my thoughts I immediately try to replace them with positive thoughts of how lucky I am to still be here. For the 38 treatments I drove the car myself every morning alone and had a good chance of meditation and this is where I found my positive attitude from seeing the beauty of nature and changing of the seasons.

Would you rather be eighty years old or eight? After reading these essays, the answer is not as simple as you might have thought. You get a greater appreciation of Laura Carstensen's argument that the older we get, the better we are able to regulate our emotions. At the same time, aging allows us to look at the world in a more detached way.

One concern that many life-span scientists have is that differences in language between, say, a group of seventy-year-olds and a group of forty-year-olds may not reflect the effects of age. Rather, all the seventy-year-olds have gone through shared life experiences that the forty-year-olds haven't. For example, in some of the studies that were run in the early 1990s, all those who were in their seventies had grown up without television and had lived through World War II. Those in their forties generally had lived with television all their lives and were part of the baby boom generation. Maybe seventy-year-olds are just happy because they didn't have television growing up. Probably not, however.

One way that we bypassed this problem was to study the collected works of ten novelists, poets, and playwrights over the last four centuries who wrote extensively over the course of their lives. With this group of authors, we simply tracked their language use as they got older. Overall, eight of the ten authors showed the same age-related language patterns that we found in our other projects (the two exceptions were Louisa May Alcott and Charles Dickens).

A nice example is from the writings of the British novelist Jane Austen. Austen was born in 1775 and died at the age of forty-two. Her first work was written when she was twelve and she continued writing until her death. Her original manuscripts, including short novels, letters, and poems, were later published in a book called *Juvenilia*; her last book, *Sanditon*, was not quite finished when she died. Compare the first paragraphs of her first and last novels.

Jack and Alice: A Novel (from *Juvenilia*)
Mr Johnson was once upon a time about 53; in a twelve-month afterwards he was 54, which so much delighted him that he was determined to celebrate his next Birth day by giving a Masquerade to his Children and Friends. Accordingly on the Day he attained his 55th year tickets were dispatched to all his Neighbours to that purpose. His acquaintance indeed in that part of the World were not very numerous as they consisted only of Lady Williams, Mr and Mrs Jones, Charles Adams and the 3 Miss Simpsons, who composed the neighbourhood of Pammydiddle and formed the Masquerade.

Sanditon
A Gentleman & Lady travelling from Tunbridge towards that part of the Sussex Coast which lies between Hastings & E. Bourne, being induced by Business to quit the high road, & attempt a very

rough Lane, were overturned in toiling up its long ascent half rock, half sand. - - - The accident happened just beyond the only Gentleman's House near the Lane - - - a House, which their Driver on being first required to take that direction, had conceived to be necessarily their object, & had with most unwilling Looks been constrained to pass by.

Even at the age of twelve (and she may have been as old as fifteen), Austen was precocious. Nevertheless, the writing samples betray clues of the author's age. In *Sanditon*, Austen uses far more prepositions, nouns, and cognitive words (e.g., *induced, quit, overturned, constrained*). The young Austen uses more personal pronouns and references to time (e.g., *time, month, day*). Although the young Austen uses an inordinate number of large words for a person of any age, it's clear that her thinking is far less complex than the older Austen's.

Austen's age-related language changes map those of the poets Wordsworth, Yeats, Robert Graves, and Edna St. Vincent Millay, as well as fellow novelist George Eliot and playwright Joanna Baillie. Shakespeare's profile is a bit complicated but even he shows the same general patterns.

One final note of interest about the language of age and sex: You may have noticed that older people often use function words like men and younger people tend to use them like women. This isn't some kind of statistical fluke. These patterns hold up across cultures, languages, and centuries. Interestingly, it's not that women start to talk like men and men just stay the same. Rather, men and women usually have parallel changes. For example, at ages eight to fourteen, about 19 percent of girls' words are pronouns, compared with 17 percent for boys. By the time they reach seventy, the rates drop to 15 percent for women and 12 percent for men.

We will return to the possible reasons for these patterns after discussing social class differences, which, as you will see, overlap with some sex and age effects.

SOCIAL CLASS AND LANGUAGE

From the very beginning of my education, I was always taught that in the United States we do not have social classes. England and India did, of course. But not the U.S. In graduate school in social psychology, there were often discussions of racial differences and inequality in the United States but never anything about social class. That's right, the U.S. didn't have social classes. By the time I was a young faculty member studying physical health, most conferences I attended in the U.S. would include presentations demonstrating large racial differences in blood pressure and other diseases, smoking and obesity and other health behaviors, and life expectancy. Nothing about social class. Well, you know why.

By the early 1990s, I was attending more and more international conferences. If the speakers were from Europe, their graphs and tables always included class information but not race. The Americans were just the opposite. By the mid-1990s, however, something shifted. Statisticians started remarking that the effects of social class in the United States were often stronger than the effects of race. Indeed, in the last decade, a dizzying number of studies have shown powerful effects of class on smoking, drinking, depression, obesity, and every physical and mental health problem you can imagine.

Social class is generally measured by years of education that people have completed and their yearly income. You might think that lower social class is associated with health problems because poorer people don't have access to health care. In fact, the exact same social class effects are found in Sweden and other countries where health care is universal. Social class is linked to almost everything we do—the foods we buy, the movies we see, the people we vote for, and the ways we raise our children. And, predictably, the ways we use function words.

Over the last forty years, a smattering of studies have pointed to social class differences in language development, vocabulary, and even language patterns in the home. None to my knowledge have examined language differences among large samples of adults. Recently, my colleagues David Beaver, a linguist, and Gary Lavergne, a researcher in the University of Texas at Austin (UT-Austin) Office of Admissions, and I teamed up to study the admissions essays that high school students write in order to gain access to college. UT-Austin is a selective undergraduate institution and recruits about seven thousand top students each year. In addition to writing two essays, applicants must also complete a large number of surveys in order to be considered for admission. Among other things, students are asked to supply information about their families' social class—including education of parents and estimated parental income. Examining the data for four consecutive years allowed us to study the social class–language connection with over twenty-five thousand students.

The table on the next page should be somewhat familiar. Students coming from higher social classes tended to use bigger words, more articles (and nouns), and more prepositions. Students from lower social classes tended to be more personal in their admissions essays, using more pronouns, auxiliary verbs, present-tense verbs, and cognitive mechanism words (many of which are associated with hedges).

Statistically, these are very large effects. The patterns are identical for males and females, and younger and older applicants. Also, these are all smart and motivated students. Why are there social class differences in function word use? Clearly, something about the students' upbringing and life experiences is influencing their word choices.

One promising idea is that there are differences in language use within families of differing social classes from the beginning. There is some preliminary research to support this idea. Perhaps the most cited and overinterpreted study was one done by Betty Hart and Todd Risley in the mid-1980s. In their study, thirteen professional families, twenty-three working-class families, and six families on welfare were tape-recorded in their midwestern homes for an hour once a month for over two years. When the study started, most of the children were under a year old. The tape recordings were carefully transcribed and all the words of the children and adults were counted.

**PERCENTAGE OF WORDS USED BY COLLEGE STUDENT APPLICANTS
ACCORDING TO SOCIAL CLASS**

	LOWER MIDDLE	MIDDLE	UPPER MIDDLE
High social class use			
Big words	18.7	19.8	20.6
Articles	6.49	6.85	7.05
Prepositions	14.5	14.8	14.9
Lower social class use			
Personal pronouns	11.6	10.9	10.6
First-person singular pronouns	8.31	7.98	7.78
Impersonal pronouns	5.41	5.03	4.78
Auxiliary verbs	9.18	8.54	8.10
Present-tense verbs	6.64	5.94	5.56
Cognitive mechanism words	17.9	17.6	17.3
Number of students	4,878	12,885	6,328

The authors discovered that children in the poorest families were exposed to fewer than half as many words as those from the professional families. Those in the working-class families were in between. By the end of the study, children in the professional families had vocabularies (based on the recordings) that were twice as large as those of the welfare families' children. On the surface, this was an impressive study. However, even the authors agree that the results should be interpreted with caution. For example, there were only six families in the lowest social class group. In addition, all the professional families had at least one parent who was a faculty member and almost all were white. In all likelihood, the professional families felt quite comfortable having students in their house every month recording what they said. The welfare families, on the other hand, were all African-American and likely had a very different view of the study than those in the professional families. For example, the lower-class families may well have been more suspicious of the experimenters and may have avoided talking on the recording days.

It is likely that the verbal experiences of children brought up in lower-class families are different from those brought up in wealthier, more highly educated families. Why this might result in different patterns of function word usage may be related to issues of power and status.

SPEAKING OF SEX, AGE, AND SOCIAL CLASS:
THE SOUND OF POWER

In this chapter, two groups of words repeatedly emerge. The first, which we will call the *noun cluster*, includes articles, nouns, prepositions, and big words. The second will be referred to as the *pronoun-verb cluster*. It is composed of personal and impersonal pronouns (especially first-person singular), auxiliary verbs, and certain cognitive words frequently linked to hedge phrases. Men, older people, and higher social classes all use noun clusters at high rates; women, younger people, and lower social classes use pronoun-verb clusters at high rates. Most simple hypotheses to explain these differences fall apart at some point. For example, one might argue that people who are more verbal might be drawn to, say, pronoun-verb words. This might be true for women and older people but not lower social classes. Perhaps those high in noun clusters simply read more and are exposed to more words—again, this might work for older people and higher social classes but not men.

The simplest explanation is that people higher in power and status are drawn to noun clusters and people lower in power and status rely on pronouns and verbs. For the sake of argument, why would those with more authority use more noun-related words? And, equally important, why would lower levels of power be associated with the use of more verbs and pronouns?

One solution is to consider what power and status buy. Adam Galinsky, a researcher in the Kellogg School of Management at Northwestern University, has conducted a number of studies where people either think they have power in a group or think they don't. If they believe they control their fate, they are much more likely to make decisions on their own and ignore others' ideas. Those with less power are easily swayed by others. In short, if you don't have power in a situation, it is in your best interests to pay attention to others. But if you are the boss, you should pay close attention to the task at hand.

As noted in the last chapter, when people are task focused, they don't pay attention to themselves. Most tasks, in fact, require a clear awareness of the objects, events, and concrete features that are necessary to accomplish the task goals. Much like the two people with the artificially high testosterone levels, task-focused people are able to make decisions without human relationships getting in the way.

While signaling less status, the use of pronouns and verbs also suggests that speakers are more socially oriented. Most pronouns are, by definition, social. Words such as *we, you, she,* and *they* tell us that the speaker is aware of and thinking about other human beings. First-person singular pronouns are a bit different in that they signal self-attention. Indeed, in later chapters, we summarize evidence suggesting that humans (and nonhuman mammals) tend to pay more attention to themselves in settings where they are subordinate to more powerful others. Why verbs in general and auxiliary verbs in particular may signal lower power is not entirely clear. Auxiliary verbs (such as *is, have, do*) are generally part of a passive way of speaking: "He was hit by the ball" as opposed to the more active "The ball hit him."

The similarity in word use across age, sex, and social class is only a small part of the puzzle of function words and social psychology. Being a woman or a man, young or old, rich or poor is only a small part of our identities. We have just glimpsed the language of who we are. In the next chapter, we dig more deeply into the individual psychology of each of us.

CHAPTER 4

Personality: Finding the Person Within

W HO ARE YOU? You, yes, you—the one reading these words right now—are the sum of your traits, values, stories, skills, job, friends, relationships, material possessions, and, of course, the words you use. Stop for a second and think how you would describe yourself to a stranger. Be careful, however. In this chapter, you will see how your choice of function words reveals more than you might guess.

Most online dating services encourage their members to write something revealing about themselves on their websites. As it happens, my students and I have collected a few thousand such self-descriptions in our research. Some examples:

> I'm a nice person. Very down to earth. Drama-free. Hard worker. Caring. Honest. Sympathetic. Supportive. Intuitive. Inquisitive. Curious. I'm not superficial. I don't keep superficial relationships. Got great friends and a good life.
>
> —Juan, 27-year-old male

> I have a great build. I am a good cook, have a fantastic job, home owner, exceptional morals, good decision maker, non smoker, no baggage and marriage minded. I love biking, kayaking, swimming, jet skis, hiking, snowboarding, rollerblading, horseback riding. I also have a great interest in music, movies, plays, comedy clubs etc.
>
> —Marcus, 39-year-old male

Father of two girls. I have a house, truck, dogs, kids. like to be outside and love football and my girls.

—Tony, 31-year-old male

                ❀   ❀   ❀

I am a romantic, enthusiastic, passionate and fun-loving woman. Immensely important to me are family, friends, kindness, integrity and especially laughter. I balance my dedication to my work with my spiritual life through daily meditations and a healthy lifestyle. I celebrate every day.

—Margaret, 53-year-old female

I consider myself a very eclectic individual. I can have fun almost anywhere and will try anything once . . . (except maybe country line dancing). I've had some unique experiences in my life and will continue to explore what life has to offer. I dig antiques, knitting and crocheting, and my 13 year old car that I refuse to let go despite the fact that my window is temperamental and only rolls down when it feels like it and I have to tape some wires together for my brake lights to work. I'm a makeup artist so naturally there's a girly girl side to me.

—Gigi, 31-year-old female

The people who know me best consider me to be a warm-hearted, generous friend, independent, resourceful, but a bit stubborn at times.

—Mirah, 34-year-old female

Reading personal ads is a little like watching parts of movies. Each description tells a story about the writer both in *what* is said and in *how* it is said. For example, compare the first three men. Juan, the twenty-seven-year-old, describes himself in traditional personality dimensions that are inherently social—honest, sympathetic, supportive. And then he ends with a factual statement that he has great friends. The thirty-nine-year-old Marcus describes himself by his actions and possessions. There is no sense of his emotions or connections with others. But he does have a great build. The description by the thirty-one-year-old Tony is oddly poignant. In a handful of words, he conveys a socially isolated life with his few possessions, his dogs, but, most important, his daughters.

The ads from the three women are equally revealing. Margaret, the fifty-three-year-old woman, says less about her personality traits than about the central values that guide her. Gigi is a storyteller. You know on your first date that she will talk about some of her unique experiences. Even the eccentric story of her malfunctioning car window is part of who she is. And the last woman, Mirah, may not even trust her own views of herself and so tells the readers what other people think of her personality. Even though all of the men and women on these dating sites are consciously marketing themselves, we still snatch a glimpse of who they are.

In addition to revealing something of each person's identity, the different ads point to the strikingly different ways that people think about personality. The very essence of some people can be their possessions, their occupations, their skills, their traits or dominant characteristics, their values, or their stories.

If you look back at the six personal ads, you will see large disparities in the function words that each person uses. The usual sex differences emerge—women use far more pronouns (especially I-words), auxiliary verbs, and cognitive words. Men use more articles and nouns. But there are large differences even within the men's and women's descriptions. For almost every function and emotion word category, each person has a unique pattern of word use. It is these different patterns that provide insights into their worlds.

In all likelihood, those who posted the ads went on dates. They probably shared more about who they were and, in return, expected their dates to divulge information about themselves as well. During the dates, they undoubtedly talked about their daily lives, the recent weather, food, clothes, or other topics that grabbed their attention. Similar discussions can happen on job interviews, when meeting an office mate for the first time, or simply talking to someone at a party. We directly and indirectly share and seek information about personality all the time. One might think, then, that modern-day psychology would have some fast and efficient ways to categorize people's stories about themselves. One would be wrong.

Studying people's personalities by listening to what they say is enormously difficult. Everyone's stories are different in substance and style. In online dating, some write for pages, others include only a sentence or two. How can you compare one person who just lists his occupation and possessions with another who lays out his life goals? How does one even go about organizing and categorizing people's self-descriptions? Historically, researchers have hired an army of raters to read each self-descriptive essay and then make judgments about the essay writers' personality, writing style, goals, and interests. The process is slow, unreliable, and very expensive.

Recently, however, my colleagues and others have begun to apply some promising computer solutions to analyzing open-ended personality descriptions. As you might guess, different patterns of function words reveal important parts of people's personalities and the ways they think.

FINDING PERSONALITY IN FUNCTION WORDS

In the early 1980s, a young graduate student in the linguistics department at the University of Southern California decided to investigate how different literary genres varied in their respective use of language. For example, do literary novels, nonfiction books, plays, mysteries, and even romance novels differ in the ways their authors employ words, grammar, and syntax? The student, Douglas Biber, happened on a statistical method not common in linguistics at the time, called factor analysis (more on that in a moment), and ultimately produced a seminal book titled *Variation Across Speech and Writing* that answered this question. English scholars, of course, had long been able to tell the difference between a mystery and romance novel—the plots were different. But Biber's computer-based method suggested that romance novels were more personal, as measured by pronoun use, and relied more on present-tense verbs than mysteries and other genres. In fact, he found that virtually every genre had its own unique linguistic profile.

I came across Biber's book in the mid-1990s and was fascinated by this thinking. Although he focused on ways to distinguish great and not-so-great literature by analyzing parts of speech, there was no reason that someone couldn't distinguish people in the same way by looking at their writing. About this time, I teamed up with a former colleague of mine, Laura King, from the University of Missouri, who is among the most creative personality psychologists in the world. Whereas Biber analyzed words in books to distinguish genres of literature, Laura and I wondered if we could use people's everyday writing to distinguish genres of people. That is, do different writing styles reflect different personalities?

The first step was to get hundreds, even thousands of writing samples from people who were all writing on the same general topic. By good fortune, I routinely teach a large introductory psychology class every year. At the beginning of each semester, my students are introduced to the nature of consciousness and thinking. One of the pioneers of modern-day psychology, William James, wrote extensively in 1890 about the nature of thought—likening it to a stream. One thought or feeling naturally leads to another, which then leads to another. Each thought or sensation stimulates the next, which may be completely unrelated to a thought that appeared a minute earlier or might occur a minute later. Further, as James noted, as our minds float down the stream of consciousness we can be aware of only a single thought at a time.

Since James, many researchers have experimented with stream of consciousness by having people either talk or write continuously about their thoughts as they occur. For many years now, I have required my students to track their thoughts in writing for twenty minutes to give them a better understanding of William James and the nature of consciousness. Although the exercise is required and students submit their writing online, their writing is not graded. We now have almost eight thousand essays that students have given us permission to use for research.

To appreciate stream-of-consciousness writing, imagine how you might write if you were tracking your own thoughts and feelings. The instructions are simple—simply write continuously about your thoughts and feelings as they occur to you. Don't stop, just write. Here are two fairly standard examples from college students:

> The refrigerator is making this funny noise. People are walking down the hall talking loudly. Someone is playing their music very loudly. My stomach is growling. I think I want a snack. My head is itching. My mouth is dry. I want something to drink. I need some more bottled water in my room. I need to repaint my finger nails. The color is chipping off. My ring on my finger needs to be sized, it is too big for me.

Or another:

> I am not feeling well. I wonder if Nick got home safely. Maybe I will call him and see if he's okay. I'm nervous about the psychology test. I should have read the chapters tonight but I am sick. I miss home. I miss my family and my dogs. Buzz is so cute and Red always barks but I still love her. I hope I'm not sick when I have to take this test on Thursday.

In both of these examples, people are writing in the here and now. That is, they report their experiences in the immediate present without much structure or analysis. We often refer to this type of thinking as an example of *immediacy*. We all think like this occasionally. And there are times we even talk like this—perhaps when tired or simply chatting mindlessly with a close friend—using small words, the present tense, and high rates of personal pronouns, especially I-words.

Across hundreds of essays, we separated out the various classes of function words, including personal pronouns, articles, prepositions, conjunctions, and auxiliary verbs. We then used a statistical method called factor analysis to see what clumps of function words emerged. With the stream-of-consciousness essays, three factors appeared that pointed to very different writing styles: *formal, analytic*, and *narrative*. In fact, no matter which texts we analyze, we generally find the same dimensions within almost any genre of writing, including similar types of literature, song lyrics, college admissions essays, or suicide notes.

FORMAL THINKING

The most consistent function word factor that always emerges, *formality*, often appears stiff, sometimes humorless, with a touch of arrogance. Formal thinking can be thought of as the opposite of immediacy. Highly formal (or low-immediacy) thinking and writing typically include big words and high rates of articles, nouns, numbers, and prepositions. At the same time, formal writing has very few I-words, verbs (especially present-tense verbs), discrepancy words (e.g., *would, should, could*), and common adverbs (*really, very, so*). Here is an example of someone who the computer identified as very high in formal thinking:

> I hear the sound of sandals scuffing the ground. Vague sounds of the television and radio blend into an almost incoherent hum and beat. A monolog comes onto the television in the living room. Hum -the sound of the TruAir air purifier catches my attention amidst the bath of sounds in the apartment room. . . . Cosmic riddles come to my mind, why does the universe have entropy?

Compared to the examples of immediacy, the high-formality writer is much more intellectual and a bit distant. There is a sense that he is putting on a serious performance. Interestingly, Biber's first factor in his genre analysis was also formality. Academic writing and general nonfiction tend to be highly formal compared with romance novels, which are high in immediacy.

Formality in writing and speaking is related to a number of important issues. Those highest in formal thinking tend to be more concerned with status and power and are less self-reflective. Compared to the less formal writers, they drink and smoke less, are more mentally healthy, but also tend to be less honest with themselves and others. As people age, their writing and speaking styles shift from more immediate to more formal. In other words, the first dimension of stealth words has tremendous social and psychological implications.

ANALYTIC THINKING

The factor of analytic thinking identifies people who work to understand their world. The hallmark of analyzing is making distinctions. These distinctions could be between what people did and what they didn't do, which part of the test they passed and which part they failed. Words that contribute to analytic thinking include exclusives (*but, without, except*), negations (*no, not, never*), causal words (*because, reason, effect*), insight words (*realize, know, meaning*), tentative words (*maybe, perhaps*), certainty (*absolutely, always*), and quantifiers (*some, many, greater*). An example of high analytic thinking:

> I always knew everyone's different but I guess since I was with a
> few friends I don't usually hang out with was why this came to my
> mind. It's weird how some things are so common and simple for
> someone but complicated and strange for another. Who knows why
> I think the way that I do but it usually seems to be different than
> most people I have met. Some people really need attention and
> they'll do whatever it is to get it. I'm not sure if they should be
> blamed because it's probably the only way they know how to act.

The woman who wrote this essay is subtly trying to parse the world. Even though she is not a good writer, she attempts to understand what makes one group of people different from others. The analytic thinking factor reflects cognitive complexity. People who make distinctions in speaking and writing make higher grades in college, tend to be more honest, and are more open to new experiences. They also read more and have more complex views of themselves than those who are low in analytic thinking.

NARRATIVE THINKING

Some people are natural storytellers. They can't control themselves. From a simple language perspective, the function words that generally reveal storytelling involve people (which means the use of personal pronouns of all types—especially third-person pronouns), past-tense verbs, and conjunctions (especially inclusive words such as *with, and, together*). Here is a lovely example:

> Okay, so my friend Chris came to visit town for the football game this weekend. She decided that she wanted to have a GOOOOD time so we went out on Friday night, and she got wasted off her ass . . . . . She was throwing up at parties and in bathrooms of EVERY place we went! We got kicked out of Waffle House . . . . . KICKED OUT! I mean seriously, who gets kicked out of Waffle House . . . . It was crazy.

Kicked out of Waffle House? Crazy indeed. Even though the writing assignment is for people to track their thoughts and feelings as they occur, at least 20 percent of the writers can't help but tell a story of some kind. In fact, people who score high on the narrative thinking factor tend to have better social skills, more friends, and rate themselves as more outgoing.

Briefly consider what these findings mean. By statistically clumping people's function words into meaningful categories, we are seeing how they think, how they organize their worlds, and how they relate to other people. Their almost-invisible function words are revealing the very essence of who they are.

As Laura King and I delved into the study of thinking styles, we found that people are surprisingly consistent in their thinking and writing styles. For example, the ways students wrote in the stream-of-consciousness exercise was related to the ways they wrote when writing a paper on the ways the nervous system worked. Other studies suggest that your thinking styles when you are young will remain with you most of your life. In fact, if you have ever happened across a school paper or diary entry you wrote when you were a young teenager, you will likely see that your writing and thinking styles have not changed that dramatically. In other words, people's language styles are part of who they are.

People also fluctuate in their thinking styles depending on who they are with, what they are doing, and how they feel about themselves. As will be discussed in later chapters, someone who is in the middle of a depression may slide from high to very low levels of formal thinking. And a person attempting to make an important life decision may evidence signs of increased analytic thinking in her or his e-mail, blogs, or natural conversations.

Finally, we can study anyone's writing or speaking style and begin to get a better sense of who they are. As an example, look back at the various personal ads at the beginning of the chapter. Armed with your knowledge of ways of thinking, you can spot who is the highest in formal thinking (Marcus and Mirah), analytic thinking (Juan and Mirah), and narrative thinking (Margaret and Gigi). These analyses are based on very few words and should be interpreted with caution; the more words that can be collected, the more trustworthy the conclusions. When we return to the study of love and relationships (chapter 8), you will be able to see how we can match thinking styles and predict which relationships are more likely to last based on a pair's writing or speaking style.

THE MAGIC OF FACTOR ANALYSIS

Some people who read this book won't particularly like graphs or tables, and certainly not statistics. Even if you have a deep-seated aversion to statistics, you might find this box interesting. Fascinating, really.

Factor analysis is based on the idea of correlation. A simple correlation is a statistic that can tell us how any two variables are related to each other, or covary. The more nervous people report being, the more guilty they usually feel. Ratings of nervousness and guilt naturally covary. We know this by measuring ratings of nervousness and guilt on questionnaires and then correlating people's responses to these two items. The resulting statistic, the correlation coefficient, tells us how closely the two concepts are mathematically linked.

Factor analysis is a more elaborate correlation method. Instead of just correlating two variables, it relies on correlations of large groups of variables. So, imagine that we give people a questionnaire that asks them to rate the degree to which they feel nervous, guilty, afraid, sad, enthusiastic, energetic, and joyful. We would probably find two clumps of correlations here. Ratings of nervous, guilty, afraid, and sad would all be closely linked to each other. A person feeling nervous would likely feel guilty, afraid, and sad. A second clump would include the items enthusiastic, energetic, and joyful. A factor analysis would determine how the original seven questionnaire items naturally broke into broader factors. In this case, the factor analysis would reveal that there were two distinct clumps of variables—negative emotion states and positive emotion states.

Factor analysis is wonderful because it helps researchers boil down a large group of variables into more manageable overarching factors. Biber, for example, relied on dozens of language dimensions that linguists care about—proper nouns, noun phrases, gerunds, possessive pronouns. By running factor analyses on the use of these language dimensions across over four hundred books and articles, he was able to reduce the dozens of language dimensions to only about seven dimensions. His relatively simple factors were able to discriminate the literary genres he studied. As described below, factor analysis is a grand method for the analysis of personality as well.

FINDING PERSONALITY IN PICTURES

One of my colleagues, Sam Gosling, is a groundbreaking personality researcher who studies what he calls "behavioral residue." He tries to guess people's personalities by looking at their offices, bedrooms, web pages, book collections, and music collections. He finds that people leave bits of their personalities wherever they go. The rigid, conscientious person typically has a neat office and bedroom and elegantly organized music collection. The same person may even have a detailed system to save e-mails.

The words we write and speak can also be thought of as a form of behavioral residue. Function words are good indicators of the broad ways that people connect to others, think about their worlds, and even think about themselves. By the same token, content words can yield valuable clues to people as well. Why does one of your friends always talk about his cats and another feels compelled to mention her new diet? The content of a conversation reveals what issues are important to people, including their values, their goals, and, at the broadest level, their personality.

The content of speech reveals what people are paying attention to. A few years ago before studying language, I became interested in how people naturally looked at their worlds. Do people differ in the ways they pay attention to their environment as they walk around? To what degree do we all see the same objects and events in different ways? As part of a little experiment, I fitted a small video camera inside a baseball cap. Several of my students agreed to be guinea pigs in my project. All were given the same instructions:

After you have put on your camera-hat, walk down the stairs at the end of the hall and leave the building. Walk the two blocks to the main shopping district close to campus. Go into the drugstore on the corner and buy a pack of gum. Leave the store and walk back to the lab taking a particular backstreet to the Psychology Building. Be your usual self and ignore your hat.

The entire excursion took about ten minutes for each of the five students and me. Everyone followed instructions and the scenery along the route was virtually identical. But as we watched the videos, all of us were amazed at how each of us looked around as we walked. One student with rather low self-esteem looked at the ground most of the time, rarely looking at anyone's face as they came along. Two younger students carefully checked out anyone of the opposite sex. Another person froze in front of the gum display comparing the relative prices of the different brands. I was particularly struck by the video of one of the very tall males who was a foot taller than I am. He scanned over the top of everyone's heads and saw the world in ways I never imagined.

Most of my students could guess which video segment was filmed by which person simply because they knew each other's interests, values, personalities, and, in one case, height. Each person tended to look at objects, people, and the world in different ways. Their brains processed their walks differently because each person took in different information. Had I interviewed each student in detail about their walk to the drugstore, they would have used different content words to describe it. I suspect that had we analyzed their content words, we would have discovered something about who they were—just as we would have with their use of function words.

SEEING YOURSELF THROUGH A BOTTLE

A couple of years after the camera-hat exercise, I was in a conversation with one of my beginning graduate students, Cindy Chung. Cindy, a native Canadian, had spent her entire life in Toronto. She had just moved to Texas and was finding the state a bit different from any place she had ever seen or imagined. Perhaps because of the brutally hot weather at the time, she felt the need to carry around a bottle of water everywhere. I think she believed that a blinding sandstorm could blow in at any time and it was important to be prepared. As we spoke about the nature of language and perception, we each made reference to the different ways people might see her water bottle. Somehow the water bottle became the focus of the discussion. In fact, we took a picture of the bottle and had other people tell us about it.

Cindy's actual water bottle:

Since that discussion in 2002, thousands of people have seen this bottle and have taken part in a brief five-minute bottle exercise. If you would like to try out the bottle experiment, go to www.SecretLifeOf Pronouns.com and click on the link "Perceptual Style: You are what you see." In fact, I would urge you to try it out before reading any farther. We'll wait here. If you didn't go to the website, the instructions are straightforward: *For the next 5 minutes, write what you see in the picture as if you were describing it to someone who hadn't seen it. Write contin-*

uously. Below the picture is a writing area along with a small timer that tells you when the five minutes have elapsed. Go ahead and look at the picture and imagine what you would write over the next five minutes.

The ways people write about the bottle vary a great deal. Some excerpts:

> This is a clear plastic bottle looking similar to a water bottle it has a white cap on the bottle there is a red label and I can see the first two letters are I believe OZ the last 2 letters are KA. The label is red with a picture above the lettering. There is also a blue box with small text that is hard to read. Ingredients and company information is in small yellow type . . .
>
> —61-year-old woman

> It is a little plastic bottle of water with a red emblem on it. Its top is white. There is some water in the bottle. Maybe in one third of the bottle there is water. The light comes from the right so the shadow of the bottle lies to the left of the bottle. Some parts of the bottle are shining because of the light . . .
>
> —25-year-old woman

> This is a clear, colorless water bottle. It is about 8 inches tall, and small enough that you could put your hand around it, and still have a finger left over. It has a white screw on cap that keeps the water fresh until you open it, and it also keeps the water from spilling out, so you can close it between sips. . . . It's also empty. It has no water in it, so I hope you're not thirsty. But that also makes it light weight, so it's easy to carry. It's also easy to knock it over when it's empty.
>
> —60-year-old man

Each of the people emphasizes different aspects of the bottle. The first person focuses almost exclusively on the words and lettering. The second person describes the shadow that the bottle casts. The third person conveys the sensations of holding the bottle and drinking from it, feelings of thirst, its lightness.

The bottle project influenced the way I think about personality. As more and more people described the bottle, Cindy and I started to analyze their descriptions in new ways. Initially, of course, we linked people's function words with what we knew of their personality. For example, the more people used pronouns (as in "I hope you're not thirsty"), the more sociable they reported being. I-words were used slightly more by people who were insecure, anxious, or depressed. People displaying markers of formal thinking used high rates of articles and prepositions in their descriptions and tended to be older, more organized, and conscientious.

But something was missing in these analyses. Go back and look at the examples. Yes, the three people use function words differently but what is more striking is *what* each pays attention to. Why does one person notice the colors and another imagines what the bottle would feel like in his hand? How people naturally describe an object tells us a little about the ways they think and perceive. For example, when I did this task on my own, it never occurred to me to describe how the bottle would feel.

We needed a more efficient way to analyze how people were seeing and experiencing the picture. A few weeks later, Cindy stopped me in the hall with a solution. It was simple and ingenious. The technique, which eventually became known as the Meaning Extraction Method, relied on the most common content words in all the bottle essays we received.

To understand how the technique works, look again at the three bottle texts. As you would predict, the most common words are function words: *the, it, is, a, of.* In addition, there is a much smaller number of content words. Although the three texts consist of a total 110 different words, within the 40 most frequently used words, there are 14 content words: *water, bottle, red, small, white, cap, clear, easy, empty, label, left, letters, light,* and *plastic.* If there were, say, almost 1,500 complete essays that people had written about the bottle, there would be far more content words. In fact, we found that 1,500 essays produced over 200,000 total words, but only about 175 content words were used frequently.

Now imagine that we go into each of the 1,500 essays and determine how often each person uses each of the 175 common content words. Next, we determine how these content words naturally clump together. If you think this sounds suspiciously like factor analysis, you would be correct. Factor analysis, as you recall, can mathematically determine which groups of content words are used together by the various authors of the bottle texts. We discovered that a person who uses the word *yellow* in an essay is also a person who tends to use other color words—*blue, green, white*—as well as words like *sky, mountain, banner,* and *label*. When you look at this clump of words, you realize immediately that these are all words people typically use together when describing the label on the bottle.

Another word clump includes words like *cylinder, shape, cone, top, tall, wide,* and other words related to the bottle's shape. Yet another theme that pops out includes words like *light, gray, shadow, reflection, background, wall,* and *table*: a background/lighting theme. There is even a theme that identifies people who are obsessed with whether the cap's seal has been broken and how it would feel to hold or drink from the bottle—much like the third essay above.

If you are not an expert in computers and factor analysis, you are probably thinking, "Duh! Why do you need a computer program to tell if someone is talking about colors versus shapes? It's obvious." Trust me, it isn't obvious to a computer. The Meaning Extraction Method is almost magical—it can automatically pull out the themes that exist in a large number of similar text files. The computer—rather than human beings—can detect the underlying themes in people's writings.

From a psychological perspective, it allows us to see what kind of people emphasize which themes in their writing. Even at the most superficial level, the results tell us that there are some people who focus on colors and others who don't. Another group writes about the words and lettering—and others don't.

We have also explored the behaviors of people who emphasize different themes of the bottle. The most interesting are those who write about the lighting and shadow cast on the left side of the bottle. Among college students, those who write about the shadow tend to be more thoughtful and artistic and less concerned about appearances. They make higher grades, go to more art shows, and play more computer games. They also are less likely to drink heavily, to make to-do lists, to vacuum, to fix things when they break, to take baths (although, fortunately, they shower as much as others), and to blow-dry their hair.

Other patterns emerge as well. Those who emphasize the words on the label are more likely to be female and to read more. Those interested in the texture and the feeling of the bottle tend to report more physical symptoms of all types. And the students who write about the surface of the bottle seem to erect a barrier between themselves and others. They report being less agreeable, avoid having heart-to-heart talks with others, and, if they have a major upheaval, prefer not to talk with others about it.

Who would have thought that describing something as inconsequential as a bottle of water could reveal so much? Although promising, the patterns of effects are not very strong—although they are statistically trustworthy. In other words, it would be foolhardy to ask our friends to describe the bottle and then rush out and buy some of them a blow dryer if they mention the shadow in the picture. Instead, think of these findings as a hint of what is available to us in analyzing language. Imagine what we might see if we ask people to describe more complex things.

SEEING YOURSELF BY SEEING OTHERS

I love the bottle test. Buoyed by the findings, my students and I tried another picture. This time, we wanted a more complex and socially relevant stimulus. A regular picture of real people was needed. To find

one, I rummaged through my desk drawers looking for pictures. Presto—I discovered a photo of two very dear friends at an outdoor party my wife and I had had several years earlier. With their permission, I started using this picture in several studies.

Before going into the findings of the Garden Party Project, look at the picture above. Spend a few minutes writing down how you would describe it to another person who couldn't actually see it. If you decide not to write your description, at least do the project in your mind and remember what you focus on.

Perhaps more than anyone, this picture fascinated one of my graduate students, Kate Niederhoffer. Kate's research interests spanned traditional social psychology and the world of business and marketing. She looked at the picture and wondered if the ways people described it could predict their buying patterns. More broadly, she wanted to know if people's daily behaviors were reflected in the ways they looked at the world. Kate, who now helps run a marketing company that uses text analysis, set up a website where hundreds of people from all walks of life described the picture and also completed an exhaustive questionnaire about their daily behaviors. (A short version of the questionnaire, the LIFE scale, can be completed at www.SecretLifeOfPronouns/LIFE.)

Hundreds of people ended up describing the backyard party picture. The types of descriptions varied tremendously. Some examples:

> This is the woman's house. She is happily married. Right now this guy is telling her a story or a dirty joke because the woman is obviously surprised by what he is saying. She is drinking home made iced tea. These two people are not married to each other but both of them are married.
>
> —22-year-old female, recently engaged to be married

> The lady just came from inside the house after pouring herself some beer from a freshly tapped keg. She has already had a lot to drink making her actions seem artificial. The man looks like he is more interested in grabbing the beer from her hand rather then meeting her. The man wants to grab the beer from her hand and take off.
>
> —19-year-old male who reported drinking alcohol excessively

> There are two people talking in the backyard of a house where a barbecue party is being held. She is wearing a long sleeve, denim, button-up shirt (probably from the Gap), tucked in, with the sleeves rolled up twice onto her forearm. She has medium brown hair that is tastefully cut (with layers) to just under her chin. She also has on a black (Gucci?) belt and a red bracelet on her right wrist.
>
> —25-year-old female who spends over $500 per month on her wardrobe

> The two people in this picture are engaged in a deep discussion about politics. The woman is expressing her surprise that the man is a Republican. She is shocked at the logic of his argument . . . The man is demonstrating (with his hands) that he appreciates the ideal

of "smaller government" that he feels is best attributed to the Republican party.

　　　　　　　　—21-year-old female who is active in politics

The Meaning Extraction Method pulled out a number of consistent themes from people's writing. Common ones included the social connection between the two people (are they dating, married; what has he just said), an analysis of their clothes (from simple descriptions to fashion observations), accessories (their watches, his glasses, her lipstick), what the woman is drinking (alcohol, tea, is she drunk?), the yard (flowers, trees, the trampoline), the house (window, siding, roof), and more about the two of them (her facial expression, their races and ages). As with the bottle experiment, each of these themes was actually a clump of related words.

As you can see, the themes people wrote about were indeed related to their own lives. People in dating relationships, especially women, wrote about the couple's likely relationship and often commented on the wedding rings they apparently are wearing. Participants who reported spending a great deal of money on their own clothes and clothing accessories were much more likely to write about the couple's clothes and accessories. Gardeners commented on the flowers and trees. And the more people admitted to drinking alcohol excessively, the more likely they were to infer the woman was drinking beer and was a bit tipsy.

That word use can predict buying behavior is not news to Google and other search engine companies. If you use a product like Gmail and receive an e-mail from a friend about his having Raisin Bran for breakfast, you might notice that a number of discreet ads appear on your e-mail page about fruit snacks, Mango Fruit Chillers, or a drug to reduce cholesterol. Today I received an e-mail from a family member whose forty-year-old friend has been irrational and moody and was asking my advice on what to do. The ads that popped up included "Treat Teen Acne," "The Best Book for Teens," and "Have a New

Baby?" Apparently, some of the words—perhaps words like *irrational* and *moody*—are statistically associated with teenagers and having a new baby.

PROJECTIVE TESTS

Using pictures of the bottle and the garden party is a variation on a much older idea in psychology. Sigmund Freud, Carl Jung, and especially Freud's daughter Anna Freud claimed that people naturally project their own thoughts and feelings onto other people and objects. Someone who may be angry at themselves for missing an appointment may run across an old friend and comment, "What's going on? You seem to be a little angry about something." Through the defense mechanism of projection, the individuals may not recognize anger in themselves but see it everywhere else.

In the early 1920s, a young German psychoanalyst, Hermann Rorschach, expanded on this idea. He developed a method in which people looked at ambiguous pictures of inkblots and then described what they saw. The Rorschach test was based on the idea that people's deepest emotions and concerns would be projected onto the inkblots. For example, a person who lived in constant fear of an abusive parent might see one of the inkblots as a ferocious bear, whereas another person in a happier family might see the same inkblot as a butterfly. Since Rorschach's early work, thousands of therapists have relied on the Rorschach test to explore people's psychological states. Many researchers question the Rorschach because people's responses are not reliable and vary a great deal depending on the therapist who administers the test. I can't help wondering if the method might be improved by administering and scoring the Rorschach by a computer.

In the 1930s, another projective test—the Thematic Apperception Test, or TAT—was created by Henry Murray and Christiana Morgan at Harvard. Instead of requiring people to blurt out the first thing they saw in inkblots, the TAT encouraged people to make up stories based on a series of ambiguous drawings. The stories that come from the

pictures were said to reflect a variety of underlying psychological issues in the participants' lives. The drawing above is one of the standard TAT stimuli. People are typically asked to look at the picture for a few seconds and then describe what they think is occurring in the scene.

Try it yourself. If you would like to take this test before it is discussed below, go to www.SecretLifeOfPronouns/TAT. In the online version, you will receive computerized feedback based on an experimental method we are developing. Even if you don't go to the website, look at the picture and make up a brief story that describes what is happening. What is each person thinking and doing? What has happened in the past and what will likely happen in the future?

One application of the TAT has been to examine basic psychological needs. Influenced by Murray, David McClelland developed a model that assumed we are all driven by three basic needs: a need for achievement, a need for power, and a need for affiliation. Using different

TAT pictures, McClelland determined the strengths of each of the needs in influencing behavior. The picture you just saw is relevant to all three needs but was initially selected for assessing the needs for achievement and power. The online experimental test of the TAT has attracted thousands of people from around the world. Here are two responses to the drawing:

> This is a story of the clash between Shirley, the conservative supervisor, and her new employee who has been with the firm for just a short time. Shirley is not happy with the enthusiasm that Sonia puts into her work as it tends to show her up and that is not a situation she enjoys as a supervisor . . . Shirley's body is not relaxed showing where her concentration lies, not on the experiment but on the person she has come to despise because of the threat she is to her entrenched position. Sonia successfully completes her task . . . and she is rewarded with a position of experimental scientist in a new department . . . Shirley has never been recognized for the . . . loyal person that she has proved to be over the years with the organization.
>
> —64-year-old male

> Julie woke up early this morning knowing that it would be a hard day at the lab. Her mother was the one in charge and she was very strict, old fashioned, and thought that none of Julie's ideas were ever worth her time . . . After a few moments of mixing chemicals . . . the beaker melted and the chemicals started foaming up all over the place, ruining everything they touched. Her mother screamed at her . . . but this time Julie was done taking that crap from her mom . . . She finally decided to tell her mom how she had felt all these years. Strangely enough, she listened . . . They both were relieved to finally talk things out and have a chance of having a good relationship.
>
> —17-year-old female

There is a certain transparency in these and most TAT stories. The first story suggests someone who may feel threatened by younger people at his job and has a sense of powerlessness. In McClelland's words, the story hints at an inhibited need for power. In fact, one way to detect inhibited power motivation according to McClelland is to see how frequently the person uses negation words such as *no, not, never.* The sixty-four-year-old gentleman who wrote the essay used *not* or *never* five times—which is quite impressive. Is it possible that the story reflects some of the same experiences that he is having in his life?

And, by the same token, do you think the seventeen-year-old female who wrote the second essay may be having some conflict with her own mother? Just a wild guess, of course. The second essay indicates that the writer is high in her need for affiliation and moderate in her needs for achievement and power.

The scoring methods for knowing people's needs are a bit complicated. Historically, essays such as these were read phrase by phrase and scored by professionally trained raters. More recently, computer programs have been developed that systematically look for words that suggest needs for achievement (e.g., *win, lose, succeed, fail, try*), power (e.g., *threat, boss, employee, lead, follow, master, submissive*), and affiliation (e.g., *love, friend, lonely*). Note that words that are opposite in meaning, such as *win* and *lose*, can both reflect the same need. People who are obsessed with achieving may alternately aspire to success and, at the same time, fear failure. People who are low on a need for achievement simply don't think along the success-failure dimension.

Research on needs for achievement, affiliation, and power has yielded important findings. Those with an inhibited need for power, for example, have been found to have elevated blood pressure levels. David Winter, one of the leaders in the analysis of need states, has done elegant work on speeches of world leaders and accurately predicted leadership styles, possibility of declaring war, and other behaviors. For example, analyses of the first inaugural addresses by John F. Kennedy and George W. Bush indicated that both were inordinately high in need for power and affiliation. In Winter's view, this can be a toxic combination where a powerful leader is inclined to rely on a tightly knit cohort of friends in making major decisions. In early 2001, after analyzing Bush's first inaugural address, Winter warned that Bush's language was consistent with a pattern of aggressiveness based on a tight group of followers who would be resistant to dissenting opinions.

INFERRING PERSONALITY INSIDE
AND OUTSIDE THE LAB

Methods like the bottle and garden party test as well as the Rorschach and TAT are all aimed at inferring people's behaviors or personalities from the ways they use words. The techniques are generally administered in controlled laboratory settings. People see the same pictures with the same instructions and are asked to write or talk about them in the same ways. When the situation is virtually identical from person to person, any differences we see in language should reflect differences in the people themselves.

One frustration for researchers is that it is not possible to know how their results generalize beyond the artificial constraints of the laboratory. For example, in the bottle study, those who wrote about the bottle's shadow tended to be more artistic, better psychology students, and less obsessed with cleanliness and order. How can this be interpreted? In all likelihood, we have stumbled across a perceptual style that is only apparent when people are interpreting certain visual scenes. In other words, the bottle findings tell us something about how some people naturally detect nuances in the visual properties of objects. It could be something about that particular bottle in that particular lighting in that particular picture that causes some people to notice shadows and other people to write about other things.

More broadly, could we get the same information about people by just looking at their regular language? This might include their e-mails, transcriptions of conversations, blogs, or professional writing. The answer is yes. And this is the very essence of this book. People who are analytic or categorical thinkers tend to use articles, prepositions, and negations when describing a boring bottle, discussing a backyard party, or talking with their neighbor about Mrs. Gilliwitty's stomach problems. Of course, the ways we talk and think change depending on the situations we are in. In formal settings, we all talk more formally; when at wild parties, we are apt to talk, well, more wildly. Nevertheless, we take our personalities with us wherever we go, and no matter what the setting, we will leave behind a partial copy of our function-word fingerprint.

A THUMBNAIL SKETCH: OSAMA BIN LADEN THROUGH HIS WORDS

Consider the language of a public figure such as Osama bin Laden. Over much of his adult life, he left a record of his language in his interviews, speeches, letters, and written articles. Analysis of his words in Arabic or in English translation evidences his supreme self-confidence, even arrogance (very low rates of I-words, high use of we-words and you-words). Unlike most other leaders of extremist Arabic groups, including his sidekick, Ayman al-Zawahiri, bin Laden was a storyteller (high in narrative markers—past-tense verbs, social references) with a decidedly dour, hostile edge. Our overall analyses would peg him as high in need for power, moderate in need for achievement, and low in need for affiliation. Cindy Chung's meaning extraction technique reveals that his real obsession in life switched from rage at his homeland, Saudi Arabia, to America's incursion in Iraq and Afghanistan. Interestingly, he never showed much interest in Israel compared to his al-Qaeda colleagues. No data on whether he liked long walks on the beach at dusk.

USING WORDS TO UNDERSTAND OTHERS AND OURSELVES

Armed with the findings from this chapter, is it possible for you to "read" others better? Can the work on language help you to be a better or more effective person? Let's go with a qualified "yes" to both questions.

Recall from the second chapter the story about Senator John Kerry's aides urging him to use the word *we* more and *I* less in his speeches? His very bright group of advisers falsely assumed that a person who uses *we* in a speech makes listeners feel closer to the speaker. This should serve as an object lesson to anyone who wants to read others' personalities by analyzing their language. The primary rule of word counting: *Don't trust your instincts.*

If you want to get a sense of other people by examining their language, you will actually need to count their words. You can do this by hand—but it is a slow and painful process. Or you can use a computer program. (A brief overview of some programs can be found in the notes section at the end of the book.) Of course, simply counting their words is just the first step in decoding their personality.

What do you want to know about other people? As outlined in this chapter, it is fairly easy to detect different thinking styles—whether formal, analytic, or narrative. Later chapters provide clues to detecting deception, dominance, ability to socially connect, and other dimensions. Capturing what grabs their attention through techniques such as the Meaning Extraction Method can be more difficult. Fortunately, our brains are much better at hearing content words than function words and so actual word counting may be less needed.

If you want to find out what themes guide people's attention, listen to what they talk about. One friend of mine is insecure about his intelligence. He's undoubtedly smart but in virtually every conversation he drops information to prove how smart he really is. The last couple of times I saw him, he mentioned how he performed on an intelligence test in an airline magazine, a colleague's offhand comment about something smart he said, how smart people watched documentaries (oh, and he watches documentaries). This has been a guiding theme in this person's life and it is evident in virtually all his interactions.

A second way to capture the themes most important to people is to watch how they guide the conversation. Years ago, I had dinner with two old friends—one who is an insightful clinical psychologist and the other an architect. In the middle of the conversation, the clinician casually noted to the architect, "It sounds like you are having some financial problems." The architect was stunned by the clinician's out-of-the-blue comment. But then he painfully admitted that he had recently lost his life savings due to a risky investment. I was surprised myself by the clinician's comment because there was nothing I could discern in the conversation that hinted at the financial problems of my other friend.

Afterward, I asked the clinician what made him think that our friend had financial difficulties. He laughed because in his mind, it was obvious. Several times during the meal, the architect would change the conversational topic—and it always had something to do with money, some kind of financial loss, or investments. Neither the architect nor I saw the regularity of his switching topics. Indeed, I've since learned that when someone changes the conversational direction, it serves as a powerful marker of what is on his or her mind.

ANALYZING OUR WORDS TO KNOW OURSELVES BETTER

If you had access to all the words you used in a day, what could you learn about yourself? Through my language research, I've been able to answer the question for myself. And, at least for me, it has been quite helpful.

One way my laboratory team studies natural language is to record everyday speech in children, college students, married couples, and the elderly. One of my former graduate students, Matthias Mehl, was instrumental in developing a recording device called the Electronically Activated Recorder, or EAR. The EAR is a digital recorder that is programmed to come on for about thirty seconds once every twelve to fourteen minutes over the course of several days. Matthias, who is now an internationally respected researcher, spent thousands of hours perfecting the EAR so that it could withstand the punishment from its wearers.

Part of the testing phase was to ask all the members of my research team to wear the EAR for a few days and then transcribe everything that was recorded on it. I have now done this myself several times. The first weekend I wore the EAR, my son was about twelve years old. In my own mind, that weekend was uneventful—chores, a family outing somewhere, the usual. A couple of days later, I transcribed my EAR recording and was distressed to see the way I spoke to my son. My tone was often cool and detached—matching his own aloofness (or was he matching my own aloofness)? In our interactions, I used big words, high rates of articles, relatively few pronouns—especially I-words. With my wife and daughter, my language was more warm and approachable.

The experience of hearing my tone of voice and seeing my own words on paper had a profound effect on me. Thereafter, I made a conscious attempt to be warmer and more psychologically available to my son. Note that I did not make a conscious effort to change my pronouns and articles. Rather, I changed my behavior and attitudes with the assumption that my function words would follow.

Over the years, I have also analyzed my language in e-mails, classroom lectures, professional articles, and letters of recommendation. Sometimes my language behaves in predictable ways; sometimes it doesn't. And when it doesn't, I learn something about myself. Indeed, it is always most striking to see those instances when my own view of myself doesn't match the ways I'm objectively behaving. It also raises the question of what should I do—change the way I view myself, change my behaviors, or change my language.

And this brings us back to a recurring theme of this book: To what degree does language influence psychological state or merely reflect it? Is it possible to change our psychological state by changing the ways we use words? For example, would John Kerry have won the 2004 presidential election if his advisers had told him to use I-words more and we-words less? Would his change in language have changed his formal speaking style and rigid body posture? I seriously doubt it. People can be trained to change their language but there is no compelling evidence that the language affects their personality, behavior, or emotional state. Rather, had John Kerry attempted to loosen up, be more personal and genuine, his language would have followed. Language is a powerful reflection of a person but does not change the person on its own.

CHAPTER 5

Emotion Detection

*Who said there's no crying in football? [New York] Jets coach Rex Ryan . . .
in the wake of the previous day's devastating 24–22 loss to the Jaguars,
delivered an impassioned speech to his players that was so emotionally-
charged it brought* him *to tears. . . . "He didn't bash us at all; he was just
very emotional . . . he was crying," right tackle Damien Woody told The
Post. "Rex believes in our team so much I can't even put it into words and
it would be a shame if we didn't capitalize on our opportunity."*

*"I was a little upset to see him that way," cornerback Darrelle Revis
told The Post. "I'm upset for the same reasons he's upset."*

*Asked if he's ever been a part of a meeting with such high-powered
emotions, Revis said: "No, I haven't been a part of a meeting where a
coach cried like that. . . . In the future, I hope there are more tears of joy
than the one this morning."*

—MIKE CANNIZZARO, *New York Post*, November 17, 2009

*All signs point towards trouble for [the New York Jets] this week, as Coach
Rex Ryan cried as he addressed his team on Monday, feeling so over-
whelmed with emotions. Staged or not, Ryan's using tears to motivate
and bring his team together is the official signal that the wheels have
come off.*

—SAM HITCHCOCK, NewJerseyNewsroom.com,
November 20, 2009

WHEN PEOPLE BEHAVE emotionally, it gets our attention.
An adult football coach crying is important information for his

team, his opponents, and the football-watching public at large. The original *New York Post* article suggested that after Coach Ryan's emotional display, his team was ready to take the next bus to Boston to better prepare for their upcoming game with the New England Patriots. The article a few days later from the respected NewJerseyNewsroom website viewed the same emotional display as evidence that the team was headed for disaster. And, indeed, it was. The following Sunday the Jets were crushed by the Patriots 31–14. No tears were reported the following week.

Emotions change the ways people see and think about the world. They can motivate people to work harder or cause them to give up in despair. Emotions can broaden our perspectives or restrict them by causing us to ruminate about the same topics over and over. Emotions guide our thinking and affect the ways we talk and get along with others. Not only do we need to know our own emotions, we need to be able to read other people's emotions to understand what they are thinking and planning to do.

Reading other people's emotions is usually easy if they are crying, screaming, or laughing hysterically. At other times emotions are conveyed more subtly through facial expressions, tone of voice, or nonverbal behaviors. Much of the time, however, people may be feeling one thing but not conveying it. All of us have had the experience of not knowing if our date, parent, teacher, boss, or client likes us or not. In our close relationships, someone may have failed to pick up on important emotional cues that may have damaged the relationship. In reading others' e-mails, IMs, tweets, or letters, most of us have missed an emotional cue that the other person may have been intending to send.

The central question of this chapter is how can we detect people's emotions through their words. On the surface, this sounds like a simple task. If people are happy, they should use happy words. If sad, they should use sad words. If only it were this easy. Counting emotion words is a fine start to measuring feelings but these approaches miss the central point: *Emotions affect the ways people think*. If we could just come up with a way to measure the ways people think, we could come up with a richer way to study and understand emotions. There is just such a way. Function words do a fine job of tracking people's thinking styles. It should come as no surprise that these same words can provide insight into people's emotional states as well.

DIFFERENT EMOTIONS, DIFFERENT WAYS OF THINKING

A good starting point is to consider three distinct emotions: happiness, sadness, and anger. We all agree that these are common emotional states that have their own distinct physical and psychological feelings. These different emotions also cause us to look at the world differently. When thinking about emotions and words, it can be instructive to see how poets write. After all, poets spend much of their time writing about their emotional reactions. Do poets use function words differently when writing about happiness, sadness, and anger? Look at some of the work by Edna St. Vincent Millay, the first woman to win the Pulitzer Prize for poetry. Writing in the first half of the twentieth century, Millay was celebrated as a free spirit who wrote powerfully about love, loss, and relationships. Compare the ways she uses words in lines from the poems on the following page.

The examples from Millay illustrate what researchers have found. When writing about positive experiences people tend to use we-words at particularly high rates. People who are happy are also more specific, relying on concrete nouns and references to particular times and places. Other studies find that positive moods change people's perspectives so that they look at the world in a more open way—sometimes referred to as the broaden-and-build way of thinking. Sadness generally causes people to focus inwardly. Pronouns tend to track people's focus of attention, and when in great emotional or physical pain, they tend to use I-words at high rates. Sadness, unlike most other emotions, is associated with looking back in the past and into the future. In other words,

EXAMPLE OF HAPPINESS	EXAMPLE OF SADNESS	EXAMPLE OF ANGER
"Recuerdo"	"Interim"	"Witch-Wife"
We were very tired, we were very merry,	Ah, I am worn out—I am wearied out—	She is neither pink nor pale,
We had gone back and forth all night on the ferry.	It is too much—I am but flesh and blood,	And she never will be all mine;
We hailed, "Good morrow, mother!" to a shawl-covered head,	And I must sleep. Though you were dead again,	She learned her hands in a fairy-tale,
And bought a morning paper, which neither of us read;	I am but flesh and blood and I must sleep.	And her mouth on a valentine.
And she wept, "God bless you!" for the apples and pears,		She has more hair than she needs;
And we gave her all our money but our subway fares.		In the sun 'tis a woe to me!
		And her voice is a string of colored beads,
		Or steps leading into the sea.

people tend to use past- and future-tense verbs more when they are sad or depressed compared to other strong emotions.

Although classified as a negative emotion, anger has a completely different profile than sadness. When angry, people focus on others and rarely themselves. In addition to using high rates of second-person (e.g., *you*) and third-person (*he, she, they*) pronouns, angry people talk and think in the present tense.

When events happen to us that cause us to feel sad or angry, we tend to try to understand why they occurred. We use cognitive words that reflect causal thinking and self-reflection. Not true for positive emotions such as pride and love. When happy and content, most of us are satisfied to let the joy wash over us without introspection. In other words, negative feelings make us thoughtful; positive emotions make us blissfully stupid.

Most of the studies that have examined transient emotions in the laboratory have relied on asking college students to write about powerful events that had elicited feelings of happiness, sadness, or anger. The lab studies serve as a helpful road map by which to understand how we all feel and express emotions in the real world.

PRONOUNS AND MISERY:
THE LANGUAGE OF SUICIDAL POETS

In any given year, over 5 percent of all adults experience a major depression. Depressive episodes are associated with physical health problems, breakdowns in people's social and work lives, and greater risk of suicide. A number of factors are known to influence the likelihood of depression, including major life upheavals, genetic predispositions, and social isolation. One particularly prominent theory of depression argues that when people become depressed, they tend to focus on their own emotions at a pathological level. They ruminate on their feelings of anxiety, sadness, and worthlessness while paying less and less attention to the world around them.

Recall that pronouns reflect people's focus of attention. Given that depression causes people to look inward, it follows that a depressive episode would be associated with higher rates of self-referencing pronouns, especially first-person singular pronouns such as *I*, *me*, and *my*. Several studies have found this. The more depressed a person is, the more likely he or she will use I-words in writing or speaking. Most striking is that use of I-words is a better predictor of depression among college students than is the use of negative emotion words.

Depression rates are particularly high among writers, most notably for successful poets. Recent studies indicate that published poets die younger than other writers and artists and as many as 20 percent commit suicide. Although the job of writing poetry may be stressful, a more compelling explanation is that depression-prone individuals are drawn to writing poetry, in part, to try to understand their mood swings. This is especially true for a form of depression called bipolar depression, sometimes referred to as manic depression. Bipolar disorder is especially toxic because it has a clear genetic basis and often catapults people through extreme mood swings without any apparent cause. Unlike other forms of depression, people diagnosed with bipolar disorder are much more likely to commit suicide.

Kay Redfield Jamison, a respected scientist at the Johns Hopkins School of Medicine, has written extensively on the close link between the artistic temperament and bipolar disorder. In her research, she finds that a disproportionate number of poets have symptoms consistent with bipolar disorder, which she discovered through their memoirs; reports from family members, friends, biographers; or the authors' poetry. Would it be possible to identify bipolar disorder and suicide proneness through the computer analysis of the poets' published works? Working with Shannon Stirman, who is now a clinical psychologist, we examined the published poetry of eighteen poets, nine of whom committed suicide. We discovered that suicidal poets used far more I-words in their poetry than non-suicidal poets. Particularly striking was that the two groups of poets did not differ in their use of negative emotion words. Although this was a small sample of poets, the effects were statistically impressive.

As we started looking more closely at the language of the suicidal and nonsuicidal poets, something caught our eyes. The suicidal poets, in using I-related pronouns, seemed to be psychologically close to their sadness and misery in ways that the nonsuicidal poets were not.

For example, consider the first line of Sylvia Plath's well-known poem "Mad Girl's Lovesong" where she is mourning the loss of love: "I shut my eyes and all the world drops dead; I lift my lids and all is born again. (I think I made you up inside my head.)"

Compare her sadness with the words of the well-respected poet

Denise Levertov in the first line of her poem, "The Ache of Marriage": "The ache of marriage: thigh and tongue, beloved, are heavy with it, it throbs in the teeth."

Although both poems deal with a similar topic, Plath's use of *I* suggests that she is embracing her loss. Levertov, on the other hand, seems to be holding her pain away at arm's length—almost as if she is looking at it from a more distant (and safer) third-person perspective. Indeed, as one reads the collected works of these two authors, it is apparent how the two differ in owning or embracing their feelings of loss, alienation, and depression. Plath may be the more popular poet for this reason. With the tool of first-person singular pronouns, she takes us closer to the edge so that we can get a feeling of her personal despair.

ARROGANCE, LOSS, AND DEPRESSION:
THE CASE OF MAYOR GIULIANI AND KING LEAR

Closely linked to sadness and depression are the feelings of loss that come from failure or rejection. In the year 2000, a front-page article in the *New York Times* reported on some apparent personality changes that members of the press were witnessing in Rudolph Giuliani, the mayor of New York City at the time. In my experience, people's personalities don't change very often and the *Times* piece intrigued me enough to start digging a little deeper.

During his eight years as mayor, Rudolph Giuliani was variously referred to in the media as an insensitive bully, a man seething with anger and self-righteousness as well as someone with a reservoir of warmth, charm, and compassion. Such contradictory assessments were often made by the same people as Giuliani changed over his term. One thing that the majority of New Yorkers agreed on was that he was an effective mayor. He helped rescue the city financially, reduced crime, and restored tourism. Because of his mayoral success, he had begun a campaign for the 2000 U.S. Senate seat against Hillary Clinton.

In late spring of 2000, Giuliani's life turned upside down within a two-week period: He was diagnosed with prostate cancer, withdrew from the senate race against Hillary Clinton, separated from his wife on national television (before telling his wife), and, a few days later, acknowledged his "special friendship" with Judith Nathan, whom he later married. By mid-May, he was living in a friend's apartment while undergoing treatment for his cancer. By early June, friends, acquaintances, old enemies, and members of the press all noticed that Giuliani seemed more genuine, humble, and warm.

One of the most reliable predictors of depression is experiencing traumatic life events. In fact, the more traumatic upheavals people experience at any given time, the higher the probability of depression and illness. Could we see changes in Giuliani's personality by looking at his language? Fortunately, the New York City mayor had frequent press conferences that we were able to analyze. Specifically, we wanted to know if his function words had changed over the course of his emotional upheavals compared to earlier in his term.

Compared to his first years as mayor, Giuliani demonstrated a dramatic increase in his use of I-words, a drop in big words, and an increase in his use of both positive and negative emotion words. He also shifted away from first-person plural pronouns, or we-words. Recall from earlier chapters, we-words are used frequently when people are arrogant, emotionally distant, and high in status. Males especially use *we* in a distancing or royal form: "We need to analyze that data" or "We aren't going to put up with higher taxes." In Giuliani's case, his language suggested an interesting personality switch from cold and distanced to someone who was more warm and immediate.

When the first phase of the Giuliani project was complete, there was something about the results that seemed eerily familiar. And then it hit me: Shakespeare's *King Lear.* In the play, King Lear starts off as an arrogant ruler who demands that his daughters publicly declare their love and admiration for him. His favorite daughter, Cordelia, refuses and ultimately leaves England and marries the king of France.

Wars, fights, recriminations, and misery follow. (Note: this is the Cliffs-Notes version of the play.) In the final act, the mortally wounded King Lear confronts the corpse of his beloved daughter. He is transformed. After facing the trauma of his losses, his personality exudes warmth and humanity. See the connection with Giuliani? Read Shakespeare's first and last speeches by Lear:

Act 1, Scene 1. King Lear speaks:
Know we have divided in three our kingdom; and it is our fast intent to shake all cares and business from our age, conferring them on younger strengths while we unburdened crawl toward death. Our son of Cornwall, and you, our no less loving son of Albany, we have this hour a constant will to publish our daughters' several dowers, that future strife may be prevented now . . . Tell me, my daughters (since now we will divest us both of rule, interest of territory, cares of state), which of you shall we say does love us most? That we our largest bounty may extend where nature does with merit challenge.

Act 5, Scene 3. King Lear's final lines:
Oh, you are men of stone. Had I your tongues and eyes, I'd use them so that heaven's vault should crack. She's gone forever! I know when one is dead, and when one lives. She is dead as earth . . . A plague upon you, murderers, traitors all! I might have saved her; now she's gone for ever! Cordelia! Stay a little. What is it that you say? Her voice was ever soft, gentle, and low . . . I have seen the day, with my good biting falchion. I would have made them skip. I am old now, and these same crosses spoil me. Who are you? My eyes are not of the best. I'll tell you straight . . . Pray you undo this button. Thank you, sir. Do you see this? Look on her!

The analyses of these two speeches make for a fascinating parallel with the changes seen with Mayor Giuliani. In fact, the relative usage of pronouns and big words by Giuliani and Lear in their early arrogant periods compared with their post-trauma warm-and-honest periods is almost disconcerting. During the arrogant periods, both Lear and Giuliani used low rates of I-words and emotion words and, at the same time, high rates of we-words and big words. These patterns were reversed for both when faced with life-changing (and, in Lear's case, life-ending) personal upheavals. Life imitates art and science is here to record it.

The Giuliani story unfolded in another interesting and important way after his personal crisis in 2000. A little over a year after his personal crises, Giuliani was serving his last months as mayor when the September 11 attacks brought down the Twin Towers at the World Trade Center, killing almost three thousand people. By all accounts, Giuliani emerged as a powerful and compassionate leader of New York and the United States.

Giuliani's news conferences in the first weeks after the attacks were marked by genuine warmth and grace. Analysis of his language

THE LANGUAGE OF KING LEAR AND MAYOR GIULIANI:
PERCENTAGES OF TOTAL WORDS

	LEAR ACT 1	GIULIANI FIRST YEARS	LEAR LAST ACT	GIULIANI CRISIS
I, me, my	2.0	2.1	7.4	7.0
We, us, our	12.0	2.5	0	1.0
Big words	18.9	17.0	7.4	12.5

Note: The Shakespeare analyses are of the first and last speeches by King Lear; the Giuliani data are based on press conferences during the first four years of Giuliani's administration and during the two months immediately following his announcement of his prostate cancer. Numbers are percentage of total words within speeches (for Lear) and within press conferences (for Giuliani).

revealed a new pattern of word use. His use of I-words was moderately high (3 percent) as was his use of we-words (3.2 percent). His use of we-words, however, stood out in another way. Early in his administration, his we-word usage was often vague, referring to society at large. After the attacks, his we-words were much more targeted and personal, referring to the residents of New York City or particular groups in government.

The Giuliani project complements the suicidal poet results in demonstrating the links between emotional states and function words, particularly pronouns. Emotions both reflect and affect our social connections with others. Pronouns, by their very nature, track the relationships between speakers and those they are communicating with. Pronouns and other stealth function words serve as subtle emotion detectors that most of us never consciously appreciate.

HOW TRAUMAS UNFOLD: USING WORDS AS WINDOWS

There are at least two ways people deal with emotional pain— acknowledging it and avoiding it. The suicidal poets, the imaginary king, and the real mayor all acknowledged their pain and loss. Socially, their elevated I-word usage made them appear more introspective and vulnerable. Looking inwardly can intensify the pain, motivate the person to understand and come to terms with it, and alert others about his or her emotional distress.

Another common strategy people adopt in dealing with pain is to avoid it or, in some way, distance themselves from it. Recall Denise Levertov's poem "The Ache of Marriage," where she analyzed the experience in a less personal, more distant way. Other avoidance strategies include trying to put the unwanted emotional experience out of mind altogether. In fact, distancing oneself from pain can be a very effective way to regulate emotions, especially in the short run. If I receive bad news about the death of my dog just prior to a business meeting, it behooves me to ignore my feelings and to continue the meeting as though nothing has happened even though part of me wants to collapse onto the floor and wail.

There appears to be an art form to avoiding emotional pain in the short run. In a series of brilliant laboratory studies, Dan Wegner and his colleagues have shown that people can't just stop thinking about an emotional event. Rather, they need to start paying attention to something else. If something terrible happens before that meeting, Wegner would advise you to think about the meeting itself and not say to yourself "Don't think about the dog, don't think about the dog."

When do people naturally use avoidance versus acknowledgment strategies in dealing with traumatic experiences? Only recently have scientists been able to track the ways people react to traumas as they unfold. Through a mix of technological innovations, it is becoming clear that most people tend to adopt both avoidance and acknowledgment strategies in the short run when dealing with upheavals.

THE SHOCK OF A TRAUMA IN THE FIRST HOURS

A few years ago my family and I were staying at the house of my friend Hector over the holidays. He asked me to listen to his voice messages and to contact him if there was an emergency. Several days into our stay, he received a message from a male who spoke in a quiet and flat tone:

> Hector, it's Nolan. Just calling to say that Marguerite died last night. She took a turn for the worse a couple of days ago. Thanks for calling last week. Really appreciate it. There will be a memorial service on Monday. Will try to call you later. Stay in touch. Take care. Bye.

I didn't know Nolan or Marguerite nor did I know their relationship. But it was obvious that Nolan was completely crushed. As I listened to the message again, I tried to figure out why I knew that he was so devastated. He never said he was sad or in pain. He didn't cry and his voice didn't waver. The starkness of his language, however, was something I was not used to.

As a connoisseur of pronouns, I was struck that Nolan never used *I, me, or my* in his message. In fact, in the years since hearing Nolan's voice message, I have heard at least three others where friends called to tell me about the death of someone close. And, like Nolan, they rarely used the word *I*.

More recently, I cataloged the first lines of blog posts from people who wrote about the death of a parent, spouse, or sibling that had occurred within the same day of their posting. Comparing their language with another post they made just prior to the death, the same pattern emerged. In the peak hours of suffering, most people used relatively few I-words and a low rate of negative emotion words. Their language was relatively simple, using smaller words, shorter sentences, and fewer cognitive words.

Immediately after a traumatic loss, people are often disoriented, numb, and in excruciating pain. As a way to reduce the pain, they regulate their attention away from their bodies. Intense grief causes people to pay less attention to themselves and their emotions. Instead, they focus more on the person who has died, their family, and the details of the death.

TRACKING THE EMOTIONS OF A COUNTRY: BLOGS OF SEPTEMBER 11, 2001

It makes sense that people psychologically distance themselves from a personal trauma in the minutes or hours after hearing emotionally overwhelming news. Does this happen on a broader scale when large groups of people face a traumatic experience? In the United States, when people heard the news of the assassination of Abraham Lincoln or John F. Kennedy, the attack on Pearl Harbor in 1941, or the September 11 attacks, they recalled where they were and what they were doing for the rest of their lives. Do people emotionally distance them-selves when learning of a culturally shared trauma in the same ways we have seen with intensely personal events?

Unlike earlier cultural upheavals, the 9/11 attacks occurred when a sizable group of people were starting to blog regularly. An under-graduate on my research team with considerable computer expertise, Michael Cohn, dropped by my office a couple of weeks after the attacks and proposed analyzing the text of thousands of blogs to track how people changed in their writing and thinking from before the attack to the weeks and months afterward.

Working with a popular blog site at the time, LiveJournal.com, Michael, Matthias Mehl, and I saved the postings of over a thousand people who blogged at least three or four times per week in the two months before and after 9/11. We selected blogs from people who lived in the United States and who represented a wide range of ages. By all accounts, the bloggers were regular people who simply liked to blog about a broad array of topics. Analyses of over seventy thousand blog entries revealed startling changes in pronoun and emotion word use from before to during to after the attacks.

Consistent with the telephone messages and blog entries soon af-ter a death, online bloggers immediately dropped in their use of I-words as soon as they learned of the September 11 attacks. In the top graph on the next page, you can see that use of I-words dropped substantially from the baseline level of 6.2 percent. From a statistical perspective, this was a jaw-dropping, breathtaking change.

Hold on to your seats; there's more. Just as I-words dropped, use of first-person plural we-words jumped at an even higher rate. As you can see on the bottom graph, use of we-words almost doubled from before to after the attacks. Recall from earlier chapters that there are different types of we-words. The types of we-words people used were a mix of *we* meaning Americans and *we* referring to family.

Here are two examples.

A twenty-five-year-old female, whose previous blog entries

USE OF I-WORDS AND WE-WORDS IN
BLOGS SURROUNDING SEPTEMBER 11, 2001

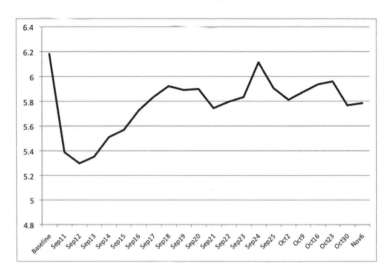

I-words

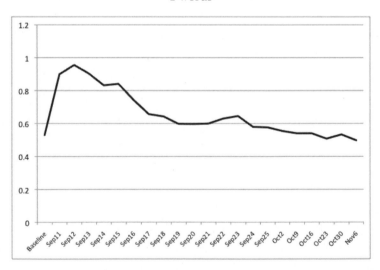

We-words

Note: Graphs reflect percentage of I-words (top) and we-words (bottom) within daily blog entries of 1,084 bloggers in the two months surrounding September 11, 2001.

described her attraction to another man and the awkwardness of running into an old boyfriend, was deeply shaken by 9/11:

> I watched the buildings collapse, I cried as the WTC [World Trade Center] came tumbling down . . . My sadness was replaced with anger . . . and fear. The idea that our home is no longer safe. I think we are as angry for loss of safety . . . as we are for the lives that were lost.

This man's earlier blogs were generally devoted to philosophical and cultural topics. The day before the attacks, he wrote at length about Ayn Rand and libertarianism. The next day he became the epitome of social responsibility:

> What can we do to help? Blood banks are probably VERY crowded right now, and may be for several days. Don't let that stop you. YOU are needed. YOU can help.

Approximately 92 percent of the blog entries mentioned the attacks in the first twenty-four hours after the collapse of the buildings. In a powerful way, it forced people to embrace others in their family, community, and nation.

Analysis of people's use of emotion words in the blogs bolstered the pronoun findings. After relatively brief drops in positive emotions and increases in negative emotions, people's use of emotions returned to normal. And, in fact, they tended to express more positive emotions than they did before the attacks occurred. To capture these effects, our computer counted the percentage of words that reflected positive emotion (e.g., *love, happy, gift*) as well as negative emotion words (*hate, cry, worry*). As you can see in the next figure, during the two months prior to the attacks, people generally used far more positive than negative emotion words. People are basically quite positive in the ways they communicate with each other.

Across the seventy thousand blog entries, the terrorist attacks

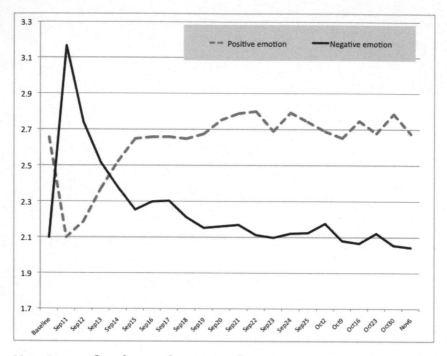

Note: Lines reflect the use of positive and negative emotion word usage of 1,084 bloggers. Baseline is the average of two months of blog posts prior to September 11. Data points through September 25 are by day, and thereafter by week through November 6.

resulted in an immediate surge in the expression of negative emotions that lasted about two days; then negative emotions returned to pre-attack levels in about eleven days. At the same time, the drop in positive emotion word use showed an even more striking pattern. After a precipitous drop on 9/11, the use of positive emotion words returned to pre-attack levels within four days. By ten days after the attacks, people's positive emotions were *higher* than they were before the attacks.

One final important finding emerged from the 9/11 project. In the five or six days after the attacks, the bloggers used cognitive words at much higher rates than before 9/11. Recall that cognitive words include words that reflect causal thinking (e.g., *because, cause, effect*) and self-reflection (e.g., *understand, realize, meaning*). The cognitive words typically indicate people's trying to understand what is happening in their lives.

An increase in the use of cognitive words immediately after an unexpected event makes sense—we all want to know what happened and why. However, starting about a week after the 9/11 attacks, the bloggers' use of cognitive words dropped to unprecedented lows for the next two months. In fact, markers of thinking were far below the levels that existed before the 9/11 attacks.

Consider the implications of all these effects. The analysis of the thousand bloggers paints a picture of how normal, everyday people think following a large emotional upheaval. Note that within a few days of the 9/11 attacks most of the bloggers returned to writing about their usual topics—shopping plans, boyfriends, pornography, pets, the usual. Across all topics, however, the same patterns were emerging. A summary of the bloggers' language suggests:

- **Shared traumas bring people together.** They pay more attention to others and refer to themselves as part of a shared identity—as can be seen in increased use of the warm you-and-I form of *we*.

- **Shared traumas deflect attention away from the self**. Even though people may feel sad, they are not depressed. Recall that people who are truly depressed show higher I-word usage, not lower I-word usage.

- **Shared traumas, in many ways, are positive experiences.** For at least two months after the 9/11 attacks, people expressed more positive emotions and were more socially connected than they had been in the months before the attacks.

- **Shared traumas make people stupider.** OK, maybe not stupider but certainly less analytic. Within a week of the attack, people wrote in simpler ways, suggesting that they weren't thinking deeply about their writing topics. In fact, they seemed more passive and accepting of new information.

- **People's reactions to traumatic experiences change over time.** The ways people think, feel, and pay attention to their worlds change drastically in the hours, days, and weeks after an emotional upheaval.

BEYOND 9/11: MAN-MADE AND NATURAL DISASTERS

Evolutionary psychologists look at the 9/11 findings and note how they make evolutionary sense. If we are in a small group on the savannah and are attacked by another group, it is critical that we band together, focus outwardly, and prepare for possible future attacks. These are adaptive reactions that can help to increase the survival of the individuals and the group itself.

Do the same language patterns exist for shared emotional upheavals that do not directly threaten the group? The answer appears to be yes. Over the course of my career, I have studied the social and psychological effects of a number of large-scale upheavals, including the Mount St. Helens volcano eruption in Washington state in 1980, the Loma Prieta earthquake in the San Francisco bay area in 1989, the first Persian Gulf War in 1991, the death of Princess Diana in 1997, and the tragic death of twelve students at Texas A&M university during the building of their traditional bonfire in 1999.

Across all of the studies, similar themes emerge that bolster the 9/11 findings. The most striking phenomenon is that all kinds of upheavals bring people together. People become more selfless, more concerned with others, and actively seek out relationships with others. Interviewing people in Yakima, Washington, several weeks after Mount St. Helens had dumped almost four inches of sandlike ash on their community, most of the residents reported that it had been a frightening experience but that, despite their losses, they were glad it happened in their lifetimes. Most reported meeting and talking with neighbors they never knew.

The university community of Texas A&M was shaken by the deaths of twelve students caused by the collapse of their symbolic bonfire. Again, in interviews, online blogs, and newspaper accounts, the language of the community was selfless and warm. In fact, the social bonds of the university ended up being tighter than anyone had seen before. In tracking the physical health of the student body over the following year, we found that the students went to the student health center for illness 40 percent less compared to the year before the bonfire disaster. No such effects occurred at A&M's neighbor, the University of Texas at Austin.

It's almost heretical to admit but terrible experiences can bring out the best in us. By their very nature, traumas can destroy some lives and enrich others.

USING LANGUAGE ANALYSES TO GUIDE MENTAL HEALTH TREATMENT IN THE IMMEDIATE AFTERMATH OF AN EMOTIONAL UPHEAVAL

One of the best-kept secrets in the mental health world is that most people actually cope quite well when faced with truly horrible life events. Most of us think just the opposite. When researchers ask us how we might react if something horrible happened to us, they find that we tend to believe that personal traumas would psychologically cripple us. In fact, the majority of people who have experienced torture or rape or who have survived terrible car or plane crashes or other unimaginable events don't evidence symptoms of post-traumatic stress disorder (PTSD) or major depression.

Humans, it seems, are remarkably adaptable. They also naturally know what to do when a trauma strikes. Keep in mind that the overwhelming number of bloggers that have been studied are in good psychological health—meaning that whatever they do is probably not a bad idea. One finding is clear and a little counterintuitive: It can be healthy to distract yourself from your pain. Paying bills, helping others, playing video games, or cleaning your house are all time-honored methods of coping with profoundly disturbing news. If you want to talk with people about the event, talk to them. If you want to be by yourself, be by yourself. There is no convincing evidence that any single coping method works well for all people.

If you are a mental health professional, this advice is very unsatisfying. If a disaster hits and you see people in great distress on television, your natural inclination is to run out and help. Again, all the evidence indicates that the best way you can help is to make sure people have their basic needs fulfilled, that someone can answer their questions, and that someone will listen to them. People do not need indepth psychotherapy right after a disaster hits. Far from it.

In the 1990s, a well-meaning psychological intervention became popular that encouraged traumatized people to disclose their deepest emotions about their trauma within the first seventy-two hours after it occurred. The movement, then called Critical Incident Stress Debriefing (CISD), sounded quite reasonable and was adopted by emergency workers, large corporations, and wings of government around the globe. Despite the good intentions behind the program, there were some serious problems with it. After a large number of studies, it is now generally agreed that CISD probably causes more harm than good. In looking at the ways people use language online in the first hours after a trauma, deep emotional processing immediately after an emotional event is not what healthy people do.

Most people need social support after an upheaval. One of the most striking phenomena my students and I have seen in studying blogs is the degree to which people seek and receive support from others. When people are distressed after an upheaval, they merely mention their emotional state and a flood of well-wishing comments from friends and strangers follows.

As part of her doctoral dissertation dealing with the language of diet blogs, Cindy Chung tracked what factors led to successful weight loss across several hundred dieters in a diet blog community over several months. Many of the bloggers focused on the details of losing weight but the majority also wrote about their relationships, life experiences, and emotional issues. Many dieting experts would recommend that the best way to lose weight is to obsessively list the foods you eat, the number of calories you have taken in, and the amount of exercise you have done on a daily basis. Not true according to Chung's research. Instead, she found the very best predictor of successful weight loss was being involved in the online social network. That is, the more comments or posts a person sent out and received, the more successful they were at losing weight. In addition, bloggers writing about personal and emotional issues were far more successful in losing weight than those who wrote only about their foods and diets.

THE LONG-TERM EFFECTS OF TRAUMAS: HOW WORDS CAN HEAL

As the blog data suggest, most people initially cope with a traumatic experience by seeking out friends and family. The ways people talk or write about the upheavals vary considerably and may not involve any deep emotional discussions.

If people could always respond to emotional events the ways they wanted or needed, there would probably be less of a demand for therapists and physicians. Traumas, even highly personal traumas, are deeply social. If I have been raped or mugged, I may be hesitant to tell others because of the humiliation or the fear that others will treat me differently. Consequently, my natural reactions to talk openly about the experience will be stifled. Similarly, I may need to appear strong and happy to my family to avoid their becoming anxious or depressed.

THE DANGER OF SECRETS

Events that are shameful, embarrassing, or could damage one's reputation are often kept secret for years. I discovered this early in my career when I included a questionnaire item that asked people if they had experienced a traumatic sexual experience prior to the age of seventeen. In surveys of thousands of adults, approximately 22 percent of women and 11 percent of men said they had. Particularly striking was that this same group had terrible health compared to people who had not had traumatic experiences. Later studies showed that the problem was that the sexual traumas were almost always secret traumas. Any type of major upheaval that people kept secret from others tended to compromise their physical and mental health.

Big emotional secrets are toxic for several reasons. One of the first interviews I conducted that illustrated this was with a thirty-five-year old woman I'll call Laura, who had been about twelve when her mother remarried. Starting a few months after the marriage, her new step-father, Jock, would occasionally sneak into Laura's bedroom in the middle of the night and fondle her. Terrified, she tried to get him to leave even though he would make light of the situation. This continued off and on until Laura was fifteen, when she left home to live with an aunt. As she described it:

> I had always been close to my mother. The divorce had nearly killed her and she was so happy with Jock. If she had known what Jock was doing to me, it would have broken her heart. I wanted to tell her so much. Do you know what it is like to be in a family like that? I'd get up in the morning and Jock and my mother would come down together. He would smile and be friendly, like nothing had happened. I hated his guts but could never tell anyone why. Every morning, every evening, every time I saw that bastard, I felt sick to my stomach.
>
> Looking back on it all, the very worst thing was that I couldn't talk to my mother anymore. I had to keep a wall between us. If I

wasn't careful, the wall might crumble and I'd tell her everything. The same was true of my friends. I'd go out with my girlfriends and we would all giggle about boys and dating. Their giggles were real, mine weren't. If they had known what was happening in my bedroom they would have died.

I have heard or read variations on this theme hundreds of times over the last twenty-five years. In Laura's case, the fondling was horrible but the collateral effects were worse. All of her close relationships with family and friends were damaged, her physical health deteriorated, and she was not able to talk about the experience to anyone until several years later.

Not talking about a major emotional upheaval violates our natural ways of behaving. As we have seen, emotional events provoke conversations. If we witness a terrible accident, discover that our favorite sports team has won an important game, learn that our closest friend has just left her husband, we feel the need to talk about it. This urge to talk about unexpected and upsetting events is fundamentally human. It is found in all cultures that have been studied. People talk about emotional experiences to learn more about them. Talking, it seems, is one of the primary ways that we are able to understand complex experiences. Conversely, when people are not able to talk about emotional events, they tend to think—even obsess or ruminate—about them.

TRANSLATING SECRETS INTO WORDS: EXPRESSIVE WRITING

As described in the first chapter, the links between secrets and illness motivated me to turn this idea on its head. If we encouraged people to talk or write about upsetting experiences, would their health improve? The answer turned out to be yes. In our first experiment, college students took part in a writing study where they were initially told that they would be writing about assigned topics for fifteen minutes a day for four consecutive days. After agreeing to participate, half of the people were told that they would write about deeply traumatic or stressful experiences for the four days. The other half of the students were instructed to write about superficial topics, such as describing objects or events.

Overall, people who were asked to write about emotional topics exhibited better physical health than those who wrote about superficial topics. Those in the experimental condition who wrote about traumas went to the doctor at half the rate of people in the control condition in the six months after the experiment. Later studies found similar patterns. Writing about traumatic experiences improved people's physical and mental health.

Other researchers soon found that expressive writing affected immune function and other biological processes associated with health and illness. Josh Smyth from Syracuse University and his colleagues published a powerful study with arthritis and asthma patients showing that writing influenced the course of the diseases. Other projects with people dealing with AIDS, cancer, heart disease, depression, cystic fibrosis, and a range of other physical and mental health problems benefited from expressive writing. Now, almost twenty-five years later, over two hundred scientific articles have been published pointing to the power of writing.

The early writing studies were the impetus to develop a text analysis method that could help us figure out why writing worked. Awakening people's emotions about earlier upheavals forces them to think differently about them. Exploring emotional topics demands that people look inward (as we see by their increasing use of first-person singular I-words). It helps them to organize their thoughts and construct more meaningful explanations or stories of their lives (as seen in the increasing use of cognitive words). By tracking the ways people write about their traumas, we are witnessing how they are changing in their thinking.

Writing is not a panacea and its effects are limited. For example, there is no evidence that writing about an emotional upheaval immediately after it occurs is helpful. Although writing for a relatively brief time over a few days has generally worked, it is unclear that long-term diary writing is necessarily helpful. In fact, writing too much about a particular problem may be a form of rumination. My recommendation is if you are interested in expressive writing, try it out for a few days. If it is beneficial, great. If not, try something else.

TYING IT TOGETHER: EMOTIONS AND THINKING STYLES AS TWO SIDES OF THE SAME COIN

Remember Rex Ryan, the coach of the New York Jets football team who cried in front of his players after losing an important game? His emotional display reflected a change in the ways he was thinking about his team and its potential. Equally important, his tears were a powerful social signal to the players. You will recall that one of his players was quoted as being impressed by the coach's commitment to the team and how his crying brought the team together. In a separate article, the same crying scenario signaled to a sportswriter that the New York Jets were falling apart.

Emotions are not just reactions to events. Different emotions can change the ways we think and influence how we respond to others. Emotions are intensely social in that they can draw us closer or push us farther apart. Emotions are also meaningful signals about other people's motivations, goals, and intentions. The intimate connection between function words and emotional state naturally follows. Emotions make us think about the world differently and function words reflect this change in thinking.

The relationship between thoughts and feelings has been the subject of heated debate in philosophy and psychology for centuries. Both Aristotle and Plato argued that logic and emotions were fundamentally different processes. Descartes, writing in the seventeenth century, went farther by claiming that emotions undermined people's abilities to think rationally. The early American psychologist William James also emphasized how emotions and passions frequently blinded people's judgments. Sigmund Freud argued that fundamental emotional issues were the driving force of personality and behavior.

We are now beginning to think very differently about emotions and reason due, in part, to discoveries in the brain sciences. One of the most eloquent spokesmen for this new perspective is Antonio R. Damasio, a neuroscientist who has studied and written about the behaviors of people who suffer damage to the frontal lobe of the brain. The frontal lobe integrates information from primal emotional centers as well as regions associated with abstract reasoning and language. Many of the connections are so extensive that it makes no sense to make a sharp distinction between emotions and thoughts.

In his book *Descartes' Error*, Damasio describes a procedure whereby people play a competitive card game. Healthy people with no brain damage are highly sensitive to rewards and punishments in making their decisions. Those with damage to their frontal lobes, however, seem to ignore the feelings they get from failure. He concludes that the emotions associated with losing help people to behave more rationally. Emotions inform thoughts.

That our feelings affect the ways we think about the world is the take-home message of this chapter. Our emotions influence our thinking, which is reflected in the ways we use function words. By extension, function words can give us a sense of how other people are thinking and feeling. They also serve as subtle public announcements alerting others to our own emotional states, our thinking patterns, and where we are paying attention.

CHAPTER 6

Lying Words

L IE DETECTION EXPERTS have always known that lying is associated with specific biological changes. What is the biology of
true confessions? Early in my expressive writing career, volunteers
came to the lab and were asked to describe a powerful emotional
event while they were hooked up to sensors that measured their blood
pressure, heart rate, breathing, muscle tension, and skin conductance
(sometimes called galvanic skin response, or GSR). They were then left
alone during the time they talked about a traumatic experience into a
tape recorder. One student stands out in my mind. An edited version of
what he said:

> On December 20, at 10:35 P.M., my father would have been driving
> north on State Highway 27. He was going approximately sixty-five
> miles per hour in a 1990 Buick LeSabre when a deer jumped in
> front of his car. He could not stop. His car swerved and lost control
> which caused it to roll over three times before it would have hit a
> tree. According to the coroner's report, he would have died in-
> stantly. My mother would have received a phone call at approxi-
> mately 12:15 A.M., who then reported the incident to me. Although
> fourteen years old at the time, the death was manageable for me
> and its effects have been minimal . . .

The student's voice on the recording was matter-of-fact and eerily distant, much like his language. Biologically, however, he evidenced signs
of tremendous conflict and stress. While talking about the event, his
heart rate and blood pressure levels were elevated and his facial muscles

were tense. Nevertheless, on a questionnaire he completed immediately after the study, he reported that talking about the traumatic event was not at all upsetting or stressful.

THE LANGUAGE OF SELF-DECEPTION

Rarely had I seen such a clear case of self-deception. The student was fully aware of the facts of the experience but he failed to acknowledge the emotional impact of it while describing it and, I suspect, in the months and years after his father's death occurred. His case reminded me of other studies involving expressive writing where the occasional participant would write about terrible traumas but not mention negative feelings or emotions. In fact, people who were unable to acknowledge their emotional reactions to disturbing experiences rarely benefited from expressive writing. The people who are honest with themselves when exploring their past are the ones who find the greatest value in writing.

The costs of self-deception are somewhat controversial. Much of modern religion and psychotherapy is based on the premise "To thine own self be true." There is a bit of irony in that Shakespeare's famous quotation was spoken by the deceptive Polonius to his deceptive son Laertes, who eventually killed the deceptive Hamlet in a deceptive way. Nevertheless, there has been a long tradition of thinking that self-awareness is associated with greater mental and physical health. It makes sense. People who know themselves should be better able to gauge their strengths and limitations in making decisions.

The alternative view is that harboring positive illusions about ourselves makes for a happier life. If Maya Angelou had truly understood the infinitesimal odds of becoming a world-famous author and poet, would she have done it? If Phil Hellmuth knew that the odds of winning the World Series of Poker were less than one in ten thousand, would he have entered? (Hellmuth has won eleven times.) And if Uncle Jake really appreciated that the odds of winning the lottery were one in several million, would he continue buying lottery tickets? (Yes. And he has never won.) From the beginning of time, humans have been compelled to try things that are unlikely to pay off. They are motivated by a self-deceptive belief in their abilities. Statistically, virtually no one becomes a world-famous poet, champion poker player, or lottery winner. Nevertheless, a small group of people succeed in these domains and their successes often fuel our illusions.

Holding positive illusions about our abilities, relationships, and the world around us can be reassuring and stress reducing. One downside is if the overconfidence we have in our abilities leads to a gross distortion of reality that produces disastrous consequences. Examples, of course, abound. In his intriguing book *Deceit and Self-Deception*, the evolutionary biologist Robert Trivers details catastrophic results of self-deception, from airplane crashes to ill-advised wars to worldwide depressions.

Self-deception comes in many forms. As evidenced by the student who spoke about his father's death, people can deny or fail to appreciate the emotional impact of an event. Another form is a brash overconfidence in one's own abilities or situations. Yet another is a firmly held belief that is either demonstrably false or not proven. Examples include the man who is convinced of his ex-girlfriend's love even after she has married someone else and has issued a restraining order against him. At the extreme, delusions by people suffering from serious mental disorders such as schizophrenia could also be an example of this form of self-deception.

Can self-deception be captured by language? To some degree, yes it can. Look back to the student's story about the death of his father. Three language features jump out:

- **Impersonal language.** Most people, when writing about a personal upheaval, take the experience, well, *personally*. They use phrases like "I saw" or "I felt." Notice how the student never uses the word *I*.

- **Lack of emotions.** Despite his writing about the death of his father when he was fourteen years old, the student uses virtually no emotion words, especially negative emotion words. His only emotion-related words, in fact, are implied—the experience was *manageable* and *minimal*.

- **Concrete, stiff, and oddly distant language.** You can see he tends to use a high rate of concrete nouns (as measured by his use of articles—*a*, *an*, and *the*). He also uses a large number of verbs, especially words like *would*. Words such as *would*, *could*, and *should* introduce a type of distance between the actual event and the person's perception of it.

SELF-DECEPTION IN LITERARY CHARACTERS

Self-deception of all forms is frequently portrayed in literature. Consider Ebenezer Scrooge in Charles Dickens's *A Christmas Carol*. At the beginning of the story, Scrooge is an emotionally cold older man who is contemptuous of the Christmas season, family, and close human connections. We first see Scrooge in his business office on Christmas Eve excoriating his clerk Bob Cratchit about his plans to not work on Christmas. When Scrooge's nephew drops by to invite Scrooge to Christmas dinner, Scrooge replies:

> What else can I be . . . when I live in such a world of fools as this? . . . What's Christmas time to you but a time for paying bills without money; a time for finding yourself a year older, but not an hour richer; a time for balancing your books and having every item in them through a round dozen of months presented dead against you? If I could work my will . . . every idiot who goes about with "Merry Christmas" on his lips, should be boiled with his own pudding, and buried with a stake of holly through his heart.

Self-deception at work? Indeed. Dickens later lets us see a younger Scrooge whose childhood was difficult but who was close to his sister and had warm ties to his first mentor in the business and especially an old girlfriend whom he lost. We see that he was actually a decent human being who now hides his emotions in his greed. During the night of Christmas Eve, a series of ghosts appear at Scrooge's bedside. Horror and havoc ensue. And by Christmas morning, the real Scrooge emerges. As soon as he awakens, he opens his window and exclaims:

> I don't know what to do! . . . I am as light as a feather, I am as happy as an angel, I am as merry as a schoolboy. I am as giddy as a drunken man. A merry Christmas to everybody! A happy New Year to all the world!

He eventually runs to his nephew's house, where dinner with Bob Cratchit's family is about to begin:

> Now, I'll tell you what, my friend . . . I am not going to stand this sort of thing any longer. And therefore . . . I am about to raise your salary . . . A merry Christmas, Bob . . . A merrier Christmas, Bob, my good fellow, than I have given you for many a year. I'll raise your salary, and endeavour to assist your struggling family, and we will discuss your affairs this very afternoon, over a Christmas bowl of smoking bishop, Bob. Make up the fires, and buy another coal-scuttle before you dot another *i*, Bob Cratchit!

Dickens nicely captures the language of self-deception and self-awareness. Scrooge uses I-words half as often in his first speeches as in his last. He is also slightly less emotional at the beginning. You can discern more distancing in the first dialogue as well. In addition to greater use of discrepancy verbs such as *would* and *could*, he deflects attention away from himself by using much higher rates of words like *you* at the beginning. The only anomaly is Dickens's overuse of concrete nouns and articles in the second speech. If only he had had LIWC when this was written in 1832, he would have known that Scrooge needed to say more *a*'s and *the*'s at the beginning of the book.

SELF-DECEPTION IN EVERYDAY STATEMENTS
ON THE INTERNET

The language of the student whose father died and of Scrooge points to the type of self-deception associated with the denial or avoidance of emotion. How about the self-deception of overconfidence? There are a number of simple yet fun ways to answer the question. One is to think of common phrases that we all use when we are almost too certain of something versus when we are reasonably certain. For example, the phrase "There is absolutely no doubt that . . ." would only be used by someone with a tremendous amount of confidence—some might say overconfidence. But the phrase, "There is a possibility that . . ." would likely be embraced by speakers who are more tentative.

When people start sentences with these two differents phrases, what do they actually say? With search engine queries (using something like Google, Yahoo, or Bing), it is easy to answer the question. Here are some of the statements that resulted from each of the searches.

There is absolutely no doubt that:

superficial breathing ensures a superficial experience of ourselves.

high definition television is the way to go.

all who entered the Summer Holidays Picture Framing Competition produced pieces of an exceptional standard.

blackjack is a beatable game [and] you can have an edge over the casino.

God will forgive sex before marriage. God's love for a person is not diminished because of the mistakes that person has made.

boxer shorts rule the planet for the ultimate comfort and style. Now crushing the hat industry will be HEAD BOXER HEAD-WEAR!

taking a few minutes to locate the rabbit breeder hobbyists near you is well worth the time.

anyone who does hear or read this amazing story will join in the fight to save our Country and our Nation's Youth.

It is interesting to look at each of these statements for which there is absolutely positively no doubt. Maybe it's just me but I harbor some serious doubts about a few of them. Did *everyone* who entered the framing competition really produce pieces of exceptional standards? And will boxer-short headwear really destroy the hat industry?

The language of these certainty statements is also striking. Phrases starting with "There is absolutely no doubt that" included few I-words, high rates of positive emotion words, and sentences that are simple and less specific. Now compare the certainty statements with those that start with a more humble, "there is a possibility that."

There is a possibility that:

you could be pregnant. Arrive twenty minutes prior to your appointment time to complete registration.

I will be grounded if my parents find out about their car.

your former spouse may be entitled to financial information about your spouse from your second marriage in certain circumstances.

you may receive this survey from more than one source; if so, I apologize in advance for the duplication.

Who could disagree with any of these statements? The tone for most of the statements is measured and reasonable. You will also notice that the language is less formal and more personal. For example, phrases starting with "there is a possibility that" use more personal pronouns, especially I-words. The sentences are more complex and specific. A good way to evaluate specificity is to see if there are references to time, space, and motion. Finally, the tentative phrases are actually less emotional— especially in the use of positive emotions. It is almost as if the overconfident writers make up for truth with optimism.

SELF-DECEPTION IN LETTERS
OF RECOMMENDATION

Most university faculty members write a large number of letters of recommendation every year. These letters are for undergraduates trying to get into a graduate or professional school and for graduate students trying to land jobs. In addition to writing letters, we also read letters of recommendation—for people applying for graduate school and jobs. Over the years, my colleagues and I have noticed that it is very difficult to distinguish among letters. They all seem to be quite positive. Is there a way to sort out the genuinely positive letters from the pro-forma positive letters?

I like to think of myself as an honest, straightforward person. When I sit down to write a letter of recommendation, it is important that what I say is truthful but also portrays the student in a positive yet fair light. One thing I've noticed is that as I start writing a letter I gradually start to see more and more positive things about the student. By the time I have finished, I come away with the belief that *there is absolutely no doubt that* the student I'm writing about is perfect. Ouch. That sounds a little like self-deception. In talking with colleagues, many report the same feelings.

Is it possible to use language analyses to tell which of my letters are real and which ones are self-deceptive? To find out, I analyzed about two hundred letters of recommendation that I had written. To begin, I went back and rated how I truly felt about the student's potential. This rating was made often several years after writing the letters and was not tainted by the post-writing self-deceptive glow. I then simply correlated the word use in my letters with my ratings. Four reliable patterns emerged.

In my letters for the students I truly felt would do the best, I tended to:

- **Say more, use longer sentences and bigger words.** The better I felt they would ultimately perform, the more words I wrote. Longer letters reflect the fact that I had more to say about the student. My sentences were also more complex.

- **Use *fewer* positive emotion words.** This shocked me. The more potential I believed the student had, the *less* likely I was to use words like *excellent, nice, good,* and *happy.* As I went back to the original letters, the reason became clear. For people best suited for graduate school or a particular job, I tended to give specific examples of their accomplishments. For people not as suited, I tended to wave my hands a bit more and simply say they were great at what they did.

- **Provide more detailed information.** I noticed that in the stronger letters, I paid more attention to what the students had done rather than just talk about the students themselves. For the promising students, I spent a disproportionate amount of time describing their work and their contribution to whatever projects they worked on. To do this, I used more words that referenced time, space, and motion. Relatively few of my sentences used pronouns like *he* or *she* because I was focusing on the projects as opposed to the people.

- **Pay little attention to the potential reader of the letter.** Recall that the ways people use pronouns reveals where they are paying attention. Apparently, when writing letters for somewhat weaker students, my mind would float to the reader and away from the student. I included phrases like "as you can see from the candidate's résumé . . ." or "I'm sure you will agree that . . ."

The language analyses indicated that my letters of recommendation said more than I thought they did. I suspect that I'm similar to most earnest letter writers who are not intentionally lying to try to place a student. There is little doubt, however, that some self-deception is at work. The findings point to how I subtly and unconsciously engineer a letter to make a student appear stronger than he or she might be. Do other letter writers employ the same techniques as part of their own self-deceptions? No studies have been conducted on the topic yet. My sense is that there are wide variations in the ways self-deception is expressed. Nevertheless, there appear to be common language markers across the different types of self-deception.

It is easy to imagine creating a system to automatically analyze letters of recommendation. Many companies might be interested in this product. This is both an intriguing and an unsettling idea. For a computerized system to work efficiently, multiple letters of recommendation would need to be collected from each letter writer. It is likely that the computer would do as well or perhaps slightly better than human readers. The real problem is that letters of recommendation are currently not very diagnostic in predicting students' future performance. A computer program may help in the selection process but the danger is that company executives may start taking the program's results too seriously. Remember that language analyses are all probabilistic and recommendation letters are often a small part of the decision to hire someone.

THE LANGUAGE OF LYING, LIARS, AND SCOUNDRELS: IN SEARCH OF THE LINGUISTIC LIE DETECTOR

The line between self-deception and all-out deception is not entirely clear. Is the self-deceptive student who claims that the death of his father was not a problem actually trying to deceive his family or friends into thinking he was stronger than he really was? Is the self-deceptive writer of letters of recommendation being deceptive by attempting to influence the people who receive the letters? If there is a linguistic fingerprint for self-deception, is it similar to one that might emerge when people are actively lying to others?

The prospect of a linguistic lie detector has intrigued parents, spouses, teachers, car buyers, people in law enforcement, and just about everyone else for generations. In theory, developing such a system should be possible. Sigmund Freud, for example, suggested that people's true feelings sometimes leak out and can be seen through subtle speech errors, such as slips of the tongue. Slips of the tongue are most likely to occur when a person is thinking of one thing but having to talk about something else.

Once you start paying attention, slips of the tongue are surprisingly common—in natural conversation, e-mails, online chats, and even formal lectures and speeches. Just last week a friend who works in an office with a domineering boss sent me a message from work: "Are you free for coffee after work? I'd like to have a quit talk with you." What she meant to say was a "quick talk" rather than a "quit talk." When we met, I opened our conversation with "So tell me why you want to quit your job." My friend was amazed at my brilliant psychological insight.

There are many other ways that the words we use can reveal our deceptions. In 1994, Union, South Carolina, residents were horrified to learn that the car of one of their neighbors, Susan Smith, had apparently been hijacked on a nearby country road with her young children still in it. Smith claimed that an African-American male had forced her from the car and had sped away. For over a week, Smith made powerful appeals to the hijacker on national television to return her children. Before she was an official suspect, Smith told the reporters, "My children wanted me. They needed me. And now I can't help them."

The FBI agents on the case paid particular attention to that statement. Why had she used past tense when talking about her children? Only someone with knowledge of her own children's death would talk of them in the past. Several days later Smith confessed to the drowning of her children by driving her car into a lake. Her motive was to get rid of the children so that she could marry a local businessman who didn't want to be burdened with an instant family.

ON THE SURFACE, building a linguistic lie detector should be simple. Find a large number of instances where people tell the truth and compare their word use with instances where people lie. The problem is that there are dozens of ways that people can deceive. Some are intentional, others are not. Some are large lies with life-changing consequences if the liar is caught, others are no more than parlor games. Some lies involve creating elaborate stories whereas others may simply involve omitting or adding some crucial information to an otherwise true story. Lies also differ in their ultimate goals, which may include gaining status, money, or sex; avoiding shame or punishment; or just having fun. Perhaps most important is the context in which lies are told. A person who is being interrogated by the police is likely to use words differently than the same person who is trying to get an elderly couple to buy some nonexistent ocean-side property. Although the work on linguistic lie detection is in its early stages, some exciting language patterns are beginning to emerge.

CATCHING FALSE STORIES

One reason for Susan Smith's downfall was that her stories about her missing children didn't match her language use. Telling a false story is harder than you might think. A convincing lie requires describing events and feelings that you have not directly experienced. In a sense, you don't "own" a fictional story in the same way you do a true one. Similarly, when constructing a false story you have to make an educated guess about what realistically could have occurred.

Real and Imaginary Traumas   In the 1990s, Melanie Greenberg, Arthur Stone, and Camille Wortman at the State University of New York at Stony Brook ran a wonderfully creative expressive writing study to see if there were health benefits to writing about imaginary traumas. The authors first enlisted approximately seventy people who reported having had a major traumatic experience in their lives. Half of the people who came to the lab wrote about their own traumas. The essence of each trauma was then summarized in a few lines. Soon, the other half of the participants visited the lab, but this group did not write about their own traumas. Instead, each was given a brief trauma summary from someone who had already written about a trauma. The new group was told to imagine that they had experienced that particular trauma and to write about it as if it had happened to them.

Half of the essays, then, were people's real traumas and the other half were imagined traumas. Both sets of essays were surprisingly powerful. In fact, the researchers discovered that writing about an imaginary trauma was almost as therapeutic as writing about a real one. In reading the essays it is often impossible to know which ones were real and which ones were made up.

However, computer analyses of the two sets of essays revealed a large number of striking differences. First, people writing about their own real traumas simply wrote more words than people writing about imaginary traumas. They were able to supply more details about what they did and didn't do. They also used first-person singular pronouns more—words such as *I*, *me*, and *my*. Real stories also included *fewer* emotional words—both positive and negative emotions—than imaginary stories. Finally, the real stories used fewer verbs and cognitive (or thinking) words than the imaginary ones.

This jumble of effects is not that surprising. Consider the meaning of each of the language differences. Writing about real experiences is associated with:

- **More words, bigger words, more numbers, more details.** If you have experienced a real trauma in your life it is easy for you to describe what happened. You can describe the details of the experience without having to do much thinking. Some of the details include information about time, space, and movement.

- **Fewer emotion and cognitive words.** If you have lived through a trauma, your emotional state is obvious. For example, if your father died, most people don't then say "and I was really sad." It is implicit in the experience. However, people who haven't experienced the death think to themselves, "Well, if my father died I would feel very sad so I should mention that in my essay." The person who has had a trauma in the past already has a reasonable story to explain it. The person who is inventing the story must do more thinking—and use more cognitive words to explain it.

- **Fewer verbs.** There are a number of different types of verbs that can serve different functions in language. When a person uses more verbs it generally tells us that they are referring to more active and dynamic events. For a person who has had a trauma in the past, much of it is over. If you are writing about an imaginary trauma, you are living it as you tell about it. In addition, imaginary traumas cause people to ask themselves, "What would have happened? How would I have felt?" Discrepancy verbs such as *would, should, could,* and *ought* were used at particularly high rates in the imaginary traumas.

- **More self-references: I-words.** Recall that I-words signal that people are paying attention to themselves—their feelings, their pain, themselves as social objects. By the same token, the use of first-person singular pronouns implies a sense of ownership. Not surprisingly, people writing about their own traumatic experiences were more acutely aware of their feelings and, at the same time, embraced their traumas as their own.

These language dimensions do a very nice job in distinguishing the real from the imaginary essays the participants wrote. Using some elegant statistics (a cross-validation strategy), we can estimate that our word categories would accurately classify 74 percent of essays as either real or imaginary. This is an interesting case because no deception was involved.

Real Versus Fabricated Stories: The Case of Stephen Glass   In 1995, the magazine the *New Republic* hired a young and promising writer, Stephen Glass, who had just graduated from the University of Pennsylvania. Within a few months, he began publishing comments and then full-blown articles on a wide range of topics. Between December 1995 and May 1998, Glass published forty-one high-profile and often beautifully written articles. His colleagues and readers often marveled at his ability to find such interesting people to interview and to draw such colorful quotes from them.

Glass, it seems, was able to get such great stories and quotes by just making them up. When he was finally caught by the magazine's editors, he was fired. An investigation revealed that at least six of his articles were completely invented, another twenty-one were partially fraudulent, and the remaining fourteen were likely trustworthy. An excellent movie on the Glass scandal was eventually made, *Shattered Glass*. And, in an ironic twist of fate, Glass ended up going to law school, presumably in search of truth and justice.

Is it possible that Glass left a linguistic fingerprint on his fabricated stories? Using our computerized text analysis program, I checked them out. By and large, the language analyses found that the completely fabricated and the likely true stories were quite different from each other and the partially fraudulent fell somewhere between the two. Glass's real or likely true stories were characterized by the use of the following word categories:

- More words, more details, more numbers
- Fewer emotion (especially positive emotion) and cognitive words
- Fewer verbs
- Fewer self-references: I-words

Sound familiar? With the exception of self-references, Glass's honest stories used language that was similar to people writing about their own traumas. His fabricated stories had virtually identical language fingerprints to the study where students wrote about imaginary traumas.

The one interesting and very important exception was the use of I-words. Recall that people writing about their own traumas used I-words at higher rates than people writing about imagined traumas. The explanation was that writing about your own traumas provokes more genuine emotion and is associated with a greater sense of ownership. Relying on these processes, it is easy to see why Stephen

Glass used more I-words when fabricating his stories. Look at the lead for his last known likely true story:

> "Test 1, 2, 3, 4," Alec Baldwin says, clearing his throat. "Test 1, 2, 3, 4." The star of such films as *The Hunt for Red October* and *Glengarry Glen Ross* holds the microphone a few inches away from his mouth and stares at it with a sense of pride. "This bus has a microphone," he says to the few of us who have gathered to watch his debut into grassroots politics.
>
> —*New Republic*, December 8, 1997

Compare this with the beginning of his final and completely fabricated story:

> Ian Restil, a 15-year-old computer hacker who looks like an even more adolescent version of Bill Gates, is throwing a tantrum. "I want more money. I want a Miata. I want a trip to Disney World. I want X-Man comic book number one. I want a lifetime subscription to 'Playboy,' and throw in 'Penthouse.' Show me the money! Show me the money!" Over and over again, the boy, who is wearing a frayed Cal Ripken Jr. t-shirt, is shouting his demands.
>
> —*New Republic*, May 18, 1998

In his fake stories, Glass is far more flamboyant in his writing style than when writing about true events. You can sense his excitement in confabulating experiences that can't possibly be true. You feel his pride and his ownership of the story—even his excitement from creating such daring and deceptive stories. In his completely fabricated stories, Glass uses I-words both in his fake quotations and as the "impartial" author at dizzying rates. When lying, Glass exudes earnest pride and self-focus, the way most people do when they are telling the truth.

CATCHING FALSE ATTITUDES AND BELIEFS

People in sales, candidates for political office, administrators, and many others in positions of authority sometimes proclaim beliefs that we later discover were not entirely true. The art of espousing deceptive beliefs is practiced by more than just politicians and crime bosses. How many of us have proclaimed attitudes that we didn't believe in order to curry favor with an attractive, powerful, or potentially helpful friend? We should be ashamed of ourselves. Fortunately, our abilities at self-deception are sufficiently intact that we know that the *real problem* is when other people are deceiving us by their deceptive statements.

Attitudes About a Hot Topic: Abortion and Choice   How well can a computer program detect if people are expressing their true beliefs about an emotional topic? Several years ago, Matt Newman, Diane Berry, Jane Richards, and I ran a series of experiments to answer the question. We recruited about two hundred students and asked them to provide us with two opinions on the highly emotional topic of abortion—one that they believed and another that they did not believe. Some of the students were asked to write the two essays at home and to mail them in to us at a later time. Another group simply typed out two essays in a laboratory cubicle in the psychology department. And yet another group was asked to state their true and false beliefs out loud while they were videotaped.

If you are like most people, you have a fairly well-articulated view of the abortion issue. Some readers believe it is a woman's choice and others are against its ever being performed. Imagine now that you are asked to write a persuasive essay supporting your belief as well as an essay that argued against your true belief. It might be a distasteful task but most people can do it.

Can human judges tell which is your true belief? We recruited several students to read each of the four hundred essays and guess if each one was the writer's true belief or not. The student judges were accurate 52 percent of the time—where 50 percent is chance. In other words, it can be difficult for a reader to discern people's true beliefs on the abortion issue.

The computer did a far better job, accurately predicting people's real beliefs about 67 percent of the time. The word markers of honesty overlapped considerably with some of our other studies. When expressing their true beliefs, students said more words, used bigger words, and relied on longer and more complex sentences. Their arguments were more nuanced and less emotional. Particularly interesting was their relatively heavy use of exclusive words (e.g., *except*, *but*, *without*). Exclusive words are used when people are making a distinction between what is in a category and what is not; "I did this but not that." When people were describing their own beliefs using exclusive words, they tried to circumscribe them in a way that clarified what they believed and what they didn't.

When telling the truth about their beliefs, people relied on more self-references, using the word *I* at much higher rates. When being deceptive about their beliefs, the students expressed more positive emotion.

Turning Up the Heat: Attitudes With Consequences   Writing or talking about your own view of an emotional topic versus the opposite view is not exactly a high-stakes test of deception. Some might argue that this isn't an example of deception at all. A more compelling approach was developed several years ago by Paul Ekman, Maureen O'Sullivan, and Mark Frank. Ekman has been considered the premier expert on nonverbal communication for the last generation. In addition to mapping cross-cultural displays of emotion, he has studied changes in facial expressions when people are induced to lie. Several years ago, I heard Ekman deliver a spellbinding lecture on his recent research with lie detection. He had conducted an experiment with about twenty people that was a delicious mix of science and theater.

Imagine you read about an experiment that will take an hour or so that will pay you money. You call to sign up, and in the mail, you receive a questionnaire that asks your beliefs about a number of current topics—things like capital punishment, smoking, the environmental movement. A few days later, someone calls to make an appointment for you to participate in the study. You are told that you will meet Professor Ekman for a brief interview about one of the topics on which you reported holding a strong belief. Some people are asked to tell their true beliefs and the others told to falsely claim the opposite of what they had reported on the questionnaire. You are told that Ekman will talk with you for a few minutes and try to determine if you are expressing your true belief.

Here's the interesting part of the deal: If you tell him the truth and he believes you are telling the truth, you will receive a $10 bonus. If you lie and he thinks you are telling the truth, you will receive a $50 bonus. However, if he thinks you are lying you will receive no bonus and, in fact, you may be punished by a trip to the Noise Room. The Noise Room is a small dark room where you must sit alone for an hour or so while you listen to occasional bursts of loud noise. In other words, it is to your advantage to try to convince Ekman that you are telling the truth.

Ekman's group made videotapes of the interviews and ultimately showed the tapes to a wide array of people, including psychologists, local and state law enforcement personnel, and high-level federal officers with training in interrogation, and asked them to distinguish those who were lying from those being truthful. Overall, the accuracy rates ranged from 51 to 73 percent accurate, where 50 percent was chance.

After hearing Ekman's presentation, I asked if he would be willing to share the transcripts of the interviews so that I could subject them to our computer program. Our arrangement was that he would send the transcripts but not tell us who was truthful. I would then send back a list of my conclusions about who were the liars and who were the truth tellers. A few weeks later I had analyzed his data and made my determinations. His co-author Maureen O'Sullivan responded almost immediately saying that I had done an amazing job. With this small sample, the computer accurately predicted between 65 and 75 percent.

The Ekman project revealed that pretty much the same group of words were related to deception as the other studies found. That is, those who were honest in their discussions with Ekman used more and bigger words, had longer and more complex sentences, and expressed less positive emotion than did the liars. And, as before, the truth-tellers relied on more I-words.

Sweating It Out After Committing a "Crime"   The Ekman project required people to try to deceive someone else in a face-to-face inter-action. In a sense, it was a test of wills concerning the students' beliefs about a particular topic. The students hadn't done anything wrong nor had they behaved in a way that called into question their basic honesty. A slightly edgier method to study deception in the laboratory is to ac-tually induce people to engage in a questionable behavior and then, with their permission, lie to an interrogator about what they have done. One standard technique to accomplish this is called the "mock crime." The idea is that participants agree to "steal" something—usually money—and then when "caught," they agree to lie to a researcher who doesn't know if they stole the money or not.

Working with Matt Newman a few years ago, we did such a study. Students who had signed up for an experiment were first met by Matt, who explained that they would be sent to a room for several minutes. Once seated in the room, they were to look in a book by their chair and go to page 160. If there was any money on that page, they should steal it and then put the book back. Later, they were informed, someone would enter the room and ask if they took the money. They were to deny tak-ing the money. Everyone agreed to the rules.

Once in the room, half of the students found the money (a single dollar bill) and for the other half, no money existed. Another experi-menter then came in, looked at page 160, and said, "There's no money here, did you take it?" All said no. The experimenter then announced that they would be taken to another room and interrogated to determine if they were telling the truth. The interrogation was fairly minor and simply asked students to say in detail what they did when they entered the room. The transcripts of the students' statements were later computer analyzed, and as with our other projects, we did much better than chance at catching the liars.

The mock-crime study and the various attitude studies all found similar effects: There are reliable "tells" in language that provide clues to deception. Soon afterward, several labs began testing the language-deception link. Judee Burgoon, one of the most respected researchers in the field of communication, conducted a striking number of experiments demonstrating that different types of deception—especially deception in natural interactions—have their own language fingerprints. She has repeatedly shown that lab-based deception studies generalize to groups other than college students. Gary Bond and his colleagues have found similar language effects with deception tasks among men and women prisoners across different prisons in the United States.

Although these studies are impressive, a recurring criticism of the various deception projects has been that virtually all are based on highly contrived laboratory studies. In fact, most of the studies are remarkably similar to parlor games. At the very worst, if any of the participants had been "caught" in these studies, they would have lost a few dollars—probably the equivalent of a single hand in a moderate-stakes poker game. What about language markers of deception when the stakes are real and potentially life changing?

CATCHING DECEPTION WHEN IT MATTERS: AVOIDING PRISON, HEARTBREAK, AND WAR

The advantage of running controlled experiments is that the researchers can get a nice clean picture of what causes what. Conducting real-world projects with life-and-death consequences is far messier. Researchers generally have no control over the situation and it is often hard to find situations where you know with certainty that people are lying and others where they are telling the truth.

LYING ON THE WITNESS STAND:
PERJURY AND EXONERATION

After publishing some of our deception studies, I received one of the most interesting graduate school applications I've ever seen. The applicant, Denise Huddle, had run her own successful private investigation firm for the previous twenty-one years. She was ready to retire and felt she needed to go to graduate school to get the knowledge to build a foolproof lie-detection system based on language analysis. Everything in her application pointed to the fact that she was brilliantly smart and fiercely tenacious. We soon met and agreed that graduate school was not the way to go. Instead, I would work with her in developing a more real-world-tested language lie detector.

Denise's idea was to find a real-world analog of the mock-crime study Matt Newman and I had conducted. Having spent thousands of hours in courthouses, Denise had watched hundreds of people testify in trials—many of whom were lying. Over several weeks, she and I hatched an imaginative study. We (meaning Denise) would track down the court transcripts of a large number of people who had been convicted of a major crime and who had clearly lied on the witness stand. In certain cases in the United States justice system, defendants who have been convicted of a major crime can also be subsequently convicted of perjury. The perjury conviction is usually the result of overwhelming evidence that the defendant lied on the stand. (Note to future criminals: If you are on trial for a crime you have committed and there is very strong evidence against you, *do not lie*. Just say, "I refuse to answer that question." You'll thank me for this advice.)

We also needed a separate group of people who clearly did not lie on the witness stand but who were found guilty anyway. Fortunately, Denise was able to track down eleven people who were convicted of a crime but were later exonerated because of DNA or other overwhelming evidence. This was an important comparison group because the exonerated sample was made up of people who were clearly poor truth-tellers.

This certainly sounded like a simple project from my perspective. Just get the public records, run them through the computer, and bam! Fame and glory was right around the bend. As often happens, it wasn't as simple as I had imagined.

Denise spent almost a year tracking down the eleven exonerated cases as well as the thirty-five people convicted of felonies. To qualify for the study, people had to have testified on the witness stand and the full records had to be intact. Denise had a small trailer that she would drive to federal court archive facilities. Every day, she would use the court's copy machines to make copies of the courtroom records—which were sometimes hundreds of pages in length. At night, she would return to her trailer and then scan the copies into her computer. She would usually spend two weeks at a time in the trailer before taking a few days off. On returning to her home, she spent additional time poring over the court transcripts, pulling out sections that were pivotal to the juries' decisions and those sections that were uncontested.

Denise's work eventually paid off. Although the number of cases was somewhat small, the effects were meaningful. Most striking were the differences in pronoun use. As with most of the other studies, the exonerated defendants used first-person singular pronouns at much higher rates than those found guilty of a felony and perjury. I-words (primarily just the single word *I*) signaled innocence. Interestingly, the truly guilty defendants used third-person pronouns at elevated rates. They were trying to shift the blame away from themselves onto others. Also, as with many of the earlier projects, the truth-tellers used bigger words, described events in greater detail, and evidenced more complex thinking.

The pattern and strength of the effects were remarkable. I was thrilled but Denise was disappointed. The computer correctly classified

76 percent of the cases, where 50 percent is chance. This is better than the juries did but was far below the 95 percent that Denise was hoping for. As of this writing, Denise remains optimistic that a language-based deception system is a realistic possibility. She might be right but if she could get a system that reliably identified deception 80 percent of the time, it would be a cosmic breakthrough.

DETECTING DECEPTION: A LESSON IN REALITY

Having been connected to parts of law enforcement for much of my career, I've been impressed by the number of ridiculous claims people have made about detecting deception. Researchers with sterling reputations who have spent years studying the biological correlates of deception (such as those measured by the polygraph), nonverbal indicators of deception, the language of deception, and now the brain activity of deception have always come away with the same conclusions: We have a system that works much better than chance. No system has ever been shown to reliably catch liars at rates much higher than 65 percent. And even those with hit rates in that neighborhood (including me) have done so in highly controlled and artificial circumstances.

Nevertheless, I have heard over and over again about specific individuals or companies that claim to have a system that can catch deception 95 percent of the time. *This is not possible.* This will never happen in any of our lifetimes.

It is interesting that polygraph evidence is not allowed in the courtroom. The polygraph is actually impressive because it can accurately identify guilty people at rates close to 60–65 percent. Eyewitness identification, which is allowed in the courtroom, is probably accurate at comparable rates to the polygraph.

It is time that we begin to think about scientific evidence in the courtroom. Specifically, it is all probabilistic. If polygraph, nonverbal, eyewitness, brain scan, and any other type of evidence can help classify the guilt or innocence of a witness it should be introduced in court. However, it should be introduced in a way that calibrates its accuracy to the jury. Each type of evidence is simply something else for the jury to weigh, knowing that there are problems with each type. Life is probabilistic—courtroom evidence is no different.

LYING FOR LOVE: EVALUATING HONESTY IN POTENTIAL DATING PARTNERS

Deciding on whether to go on a date with someone doesn't have the same gravitas as deciding if someone should go to prison for the rest of their lives. Leaving the prison metaphor aside, online dating sites can determine who you may live with the rest of your life. Deception in selecting a date and possibly a mate for life is serious business. And word on the street is that people are sometimes deceptive in terms of what they say about themselves online.

Just ask Jeff Hancock. Hancock and his colleagues at Cornell University conducted a riveting study with eighty online daters in the New York City area. The people—half male and half female—were selected based on their profiles on one of four commercial dating sites. All included a picture; information about their weight, height, and age; and a written description of who they were along with their interests. After agreeing to participate, each visited the research lab, where they completed several questionnaires. Their pictures were taken, their driver's licenses scanned, and their height and weight measured.

As you can see, Hancock was able to determine how deceptive the daters' online information was now that he had independently validated age (from the driver's license), height, and weight. He was also able to get a group of raters to compare the photo he took in the lab with the one displayed on the online posting. Men tended to lie about their height and women their weight. Both sexes posted pictures that were flattering compared to their lab pictures—although some people's online pictures were much more flattering than others. From all the objective information he collected, Hancock calculated a deception index for each person.

The heart of the research was to determine if the word use in the online ads differed between the daters who were most deceptive and those most honest. Yes, there were differences and they were comparable to the other deception studies. Those who were most honest tended to say more, use bigger words and longer sentences, including fewer emotion words (especially positive emotions). The best general predictor of honesty was, not surprisingly, use of I-words.

Although the function words distinguished honest from deceptive online ads, there were also differences in content words. That is, people who were dishonest about their profiles tended to shift the focus of their self-description away from their sensitive topic. For example, women and men who lied about their weight were the least likely to mention anything about food, restaurants, or eating. Similarly, those whose pictures were the most deceptive tended to focus on topics of work and achievement in a way that built up their status and downplayed their physical appearance.

Do you really need a computer to assess how trustworthy a potential online match might be? Can't we intuitively pick out the honest from the deceptive people by taking in all of the information that is available to us? Hancock's research team paints a rather bleak picture. He solicited the help of about fifty students to rate each online profile for trustworthiness. The students' estimates of honesty were no better than if you chose a trustworthy date by flipping a coin. One reason is that we tend to look at precisely the wrong language cues in guessing who is trustworthy. As raters of online ads, most of us assume that an upbeat, positive, simple, selfless, down-to-earth person is the most honest. And that, my friends, is why our "love detectors" are flawed instruments.

DECEIVING FOR WAR: THE LANGUAGE OF
LEADERS PRIOR TO THE IRAQ WAR

Any student of history will undoubtedly look back on the relationship between the United States and Iraq after about 1950 and ask, "What were they thinking?" The "they" will refer to both countries. Perhaps the most puzzling turn of events in this relationship was the decision by the United States to invade Iraq in March 2003.

Immediately after the attacks on the World Trade Center and Pentagon on September 11, 2001, the administration of George W. Bush was convinced that Iraq may have played some role in the attacks. Without detailing the intricate history between the United States and Iraq, it should be noted that there was already some bad blood between the countries. Over the next year and a half, the Bush administration began raising more and more concerns about Iraq—including claims that it was harboring terrorists, building weapons of mass destruction, and planning for attacks on the West. With the benefit of hindsight, most of these concerns were unfounded. There were no terrorist training sites, no weapons of mass destruction, and no plans to attack anyone. Nevertheless, the increasing rhetoric about the danger of Iraq helped to propel the invasion and occupation of Iraq in March 2003.

The social dynamics of a democratic government starting a war are tremendously complex. During periods of high anxiety, rumors spread quickly and people are vulnerable to distorted information. Rumors and speculation, with enough repeating, slowly transform themselves into firmly held beliefs. The distinctions between deception and self-deception can quickly erode.

The Center for Public Integrity (CPI), an independent watchdog agency, is a nonprofit and nonpartisan organization that supports investigative journalism on a wide range of issues (www.publicintegrity .org). In the months and years after the Iraq invasion, CPI began to comb through all of the public statements by key administration officials about Iraq in the time between 9/11 and the war. Indeed, anyone can access the hundreds of statements from speeches, press conferences, op-ed pieces, and television and radio interviews. For the researcher, the task is made even easier in that those portions of text that have been verified to be false are highlighted. It makes you think . . . A word count researcher could simply compare the words in the non-highlighted sections with the highlighted sections.

In fact, the very same Jeff Hancock who studied deception in online dating analyzed the CPI data bank. The Cornell group compiled 532 statements that contained at least one objectively false claim along with an equal number of true claims from the same sources. The statements, which were made between September 11, 2001, and September 11, 2003, were from eight senior Bush administration insiders: Bush himself, Vice President Dick Cheney, Secretary of State Colin Powell, Secretary of Defense Donald Rumsfeld, National Security Adviser Condoleezza Rice, Deputy Secretary of Defense Paul Wolfowitz, and White House Press Secretaries Ari Fleischer and Scott McClellan.

An example of information from the CPI database is an interview of Vice President Cheney on CNN's *Late Edition* on March 24, 2002. The interviewer, Wolf Blitzer, asked Cheney if he supported the United Nations sending weapons inspectors into Iraq to try to find any evidence of weapons of mass destruction. Cheney responded (note that the highlighted sections were identified by CPI as deceptive; those not highlighted are presumed to be truthful):

> **What we said, Wolf, if you go back and look at the record is, the issue's not inspectors. The issue is that he has chemical weapons and he's used them. The issue is that he's developing and has biological weapons. The issue is that he's pursuing nuclear weapons.** It's the weapons of mass destruction and what he's already done with them. There's a devastating story in this week's *New Yorker* magazine on his use of chemical weapons against the Kurds of northern Iraq back in 1988; may have hit as many as 200 separate towns and villages. Killed upwards of 100,000 people, according to the article, if it's to be believed.

This is a man of great evil, as the president said. And he is actively pursuing nuclear weapons at this time, and we think that's cause for concern for us and for everybody in the region. And I found during the course of my travels that it is indeed a problem of great concern for our friends out there as well too.

Computer text analyses comparing the truthful with the deceptive statements resulted in findings comparable to the others reported. Truthful statements were associated with higher rates of I-words. In addition, they were more nuanced, focused on more detail, and tended to be associated with fewer emotions. The above quotation is a good example of these differences. In the truthful section, Cheney is more detailed in his information, uses more complex sentences, and uses I-words.

As with the other deception projects, it is possible to estimate how well the computer could have picked out truthful versus deceptive statements. Hancock's group reports that the computer could accurately distinguish between the true and false statements at a rate of 76 percent, where 50 percent is chance.

Be careful in interpreting these numbers, however. The ability to distinguish the truth from a lie is much easier after the fact when we know that deception was going on. If we are trying to guess the trustworthiness of statements of people for whom we have no evidence of deception, our guesses will likely be uninterpretable. There are two overlapping problems in determining deception—the first is that we don't know what "ground truth" is. That is, what parts are, in fact, truthful. Second, we don't know the base rate of truth. If we know that 50 percent of Cheney's clauses are deceptive, we will interpret our computer output differently than if only 2 percent are deceptive. In the months leading up to the Iraq War, there was no reliable ground truth and certainly no sense of the degree of deception. And, to make issues even more troublesome, many of the deceptive statements made by the administration were likely believed by the people telling them.

WATCHWORDS: WHICH WORDS BEST PREDICT
HONESTY AND DECEPTION

This chapter has described several types of deception—from the self-deception associated with the denial of emotions and overconfidence to the intentional deception people employ to avoid prison. Even though the motives, strategies, and people associated with these various types of lies are all quite different, the language patterns are surprisingly similar.

Every project, of course, is unique. However, as the studies have mounted, we can stand back and take the Squint Test. The Squint Test is a nonscientific way of trying to assess if there are reliable patterns to deception across the various studies. As you can see in the chart on page 162, there are five general word categories. Each word is associated with a bar on the right. The closer the bar is to the right of the page, the more that word category is associated with honesty and telling the truth. Bars on the far left indicate words that typically occur with people who are lying or being deceptive. Words linked to bars in the middle tend to be either unrelated to deception or are too unreliable to classify.

SELF-REFERENCES: THE I-WORDS

In virtually every chapter of this book, first-person singular pronouns are important. In deception research, the word *I* (including *I'm, I'll, I'd, I've,* and related contractions) is the best single marker of a person's being honest.

The use of I-words has tremendous social and psychological significance. By definition, it is an identity statement. Using *I* in conversation is announcing to your speaking companion that you are aware of yourself, that you are paying attention to yourself. There is a certain degree of vulnerability in doing this—especially if there is a chance that your companion is judging you or seeking to harm you in some way. I've often thought of the use of *I* as a subtle submissive gesture—much like the lower-status dog rolling over and baring his belly to the bigger, more dangerous dog. "Hey, I'm not a problem. I'm at your service. I'm not a threat."

There have been several studies that suggest that when people are forced to pay attention to themselves, they become more humble and honest. Robert Wicklund, who is now at the University of Bergen in Norway, pioneered a theory of self-awareness in the 1970s. He and his colleagues devised dozens of imaginative studies where people would have to do some kind of task in one of two conditions—in front of a mirror or away from a mirror. If they completed a questionnaire in front of a mirror, they reported having lower self-esteem and generally less positive moods. More intriguing, their answers to questions tended to be more honest—their reports of their weight, grades, and behaviors tended to match objective measures of their true weight, grades, and behaviors. Also, completing questionnaires in front of a mirror caused people to use the word *I* more.

Why does self-attention make people more honest? Wicklund posited that paying attention to the self made people briefly ponder who they ideally wanted to be. Perhaps their lifelong dreams were to be strong, honest, beautiful, brave, and compassionate. Looking in the mirror made them realize that they had not attained these ideals. Ultimately, then, people would see the gulf between their ideal and real selves, which made them feel bad about themselves but, at the same time, motivated them to try to be better people. Self-awareness, in Wicklund's view, drives us all to be the people we always wanted to be.

Indeed, most of us usually want to be honest with others and with ourselves. Self-attention provokes honesty. I-words simply reflect self-attention. Across the multiple studies, when we see the use of I-words increase, it is likely that self-attention is higher. And, with self-attention, people tend to be more honest.

COGNITIVE COMPLEXITY

The stories that people generate when telling the truth are generally more complex than false stories. Not only do people say more when

WORDS ASSOCIATED WITH HONESTY AND DECEPTION

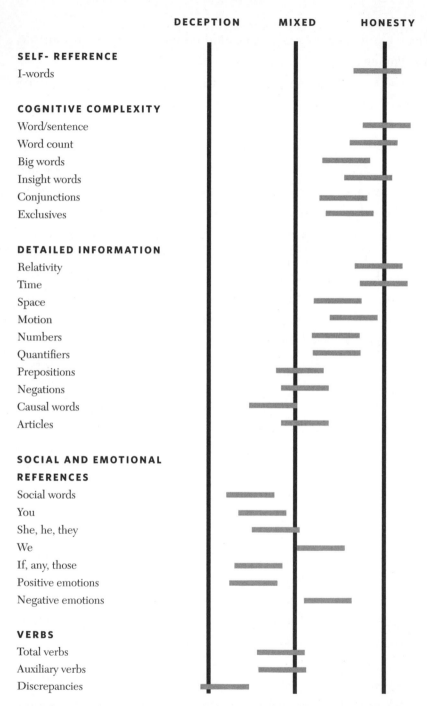

Note that words with bars on the left side of the table are reliably associated with deception. The farther to the left, the less trustworthy. Those on the right side are markers of honesty. Those words with bars close to the center line are not reliably associated with either truth or deception.

telling the truth but each sentence they put together is longer and more complex. Their words are bigger, suggesting that their statements are more precise and nuanced. The statements of truth-tellers also come across as more thoughtful, using insight words such as *realize, understand, think*, and the like.

One reason truth-tellers have longer sentences is that they are linking multiple phrases with conjunctions. Conjunctions include words such as *and, or, but, because*, etc. Many of these conjunctions are exclusive words such as *but, or, except, without, excluding*. As described in previous chapters, exclusive words are used when people are making distinctions. They are distinguishing what did happen versus what did not, what they were thinking and what they were not thinking about, what was in the category and what was not in the category.

The ability to talk about what you did not do, did not see, or did not think about is a remarkably difficult task when you are lying. If you are telling a completely fabricated story, everything you are saying is something you didn't experience. In making up a false story, you can quickly get a headache trying to add what you didn't not do. Most lies, then, are made up of simple and straightforward statements about what the person presumably did or saw. Relatively few specific comments are about what they did not do.

DETAILED INFORMATION

When conveying a true incident, we have access to a rich group of memories about the event and exactly where we were as it unfolded. More specifically, we have knowledge of precisely where our bodies were at the time. Our bodies and the relevant events existed in three-dimensional space that unfolded in real time. It is not surprising, then, that when we describe an event that really happened, we naturally include information about time, space, and motion. Together, these dimensions are captured by relativity words. As can be seen in the table, truth-tellers are far more likely to include words that invoke time (e.g., *before, ten o'clock, morning*), space (e.g., *above, next, around*), and movements (e.g., *went, put, leap*). Along the same dimensions, truth-tellers are more specific in using numbers and quantifiers, which include words like *more, less, few, larger.*

The use of words signifying greater cognitive complexity and detailed information fits nicely with recent research on statements found in the questioning of witnesses. Aldert Vrij, one of the world's experts on the analysis of interviews of people suspected of crimes, points out that the detection of lying depends on the ways people are asked questions. A policeman, parent, or friend who is accusatory in their interview will likely just get brief statements full of denials—which can be extremely difficult to evaluate. Instead, Vrij and his colleagues recommend that interrogations or interviews should be more open-ended, less judgmental, and aimed at information gathering. The more that a suspect is allowed to say, the more likely that their stories will exonerate or convict them.

Although Vrij and other law enforcement researchers have only recently started to use computer-based methods, they have independently discovered that truth-tellers make statements that are more complex and more detailed.

SOCIAL AND EMOTIONAL DIMENSIONS

Many forms of deception are associated with optimism and overconfidence. The person trying to sell you a new rug, a new religion, or a new war often brims with the certainty of truth. Part of the effective salesperson's approach is convincing you that once you buy the product *there is absolutely no doubt that* you too will be as happy and confident as the salesperson.

Counter to common sense, people who are deceptive make more references to other people and rely on more positive emotion words. The stereotype of the liar is the lonely, furtive, shifty, self-loathing, treacherous, and nervous person who is desperately avoiding capture. There may be a few such liars around but I would urge you to hang on to your wallet more tightly when you happen upon the bubbly, enthusiastic, outgoing, warm, and self-assured person who has a great deal just for you.

Social words, by the way, are a mix of words that indicate a social relationship—including nouns like *friend, pal,* and *mother* as well as actions such as talking, calling, and listening. In reading over many of the deception transcripts, it is impressive how frequently people bring up other individuals to try to validate their own statements or to shift the blame to someone else.

VERBS AND ACTIONS

Verbs are complicated. Hang around a language expert such as Steven Pinker for a few hours and your head will soon be swimming with an ocean of verb types. Regular verbs generally express a particular action and can distinguish between past tense and present (but not future). Auxiliary verbs, sometimes called helping verbs, are really only a handful of verbs such as *to be, to have,* and *to do.* Auxiliary verbs are associated with a passive voice and are frowned on in American English classes but celebrated in British English classes. Another type, called discrepancy verbs (or modal verbs), includes words like *should, could, ought, must,* and *would.* Discrepancy verbs are used when people suggest some kind of subtle discrepancy between how the world is and how it could, should, or ought to be.

As you can see in the chart, people who use verbs at high rates tend to be more deceptive than people who use fewer verbs. This pattern is particularly strong for auxiliary verbs and discrepancies. Let's say that you are a grade school teacher and three of your students give practically the same excuse:

1. I finished my homework but the dog ate it.
2. I had finished the homework but the dog must have eaten it.
3. The homework was finished but must have been eaten by the dog.

The first excuse is far more likely to be true. It includes two past-tense verbs that indicate that the actions were specific and were completely finished. The second excuse relies on five verbs that hint that the actions were not completed and, with the word *must*, may not have even happened. And the third person's excuse is the most scurrilous lie of the three—six verbs, past tense, and not a single I-word.

In English, verbs provide a remarkable amount of information about actions. They hint at whether an action is ongoing, partly completed, or completely finished. Some verbs, such as discrepancies, subtly assert that an action may have occurred—but possibly didn't. Saying that dog *could* or *must* have eaten the homework strongly implies something about the dog's behavior but, at the same time, distances the speaker from asserting that the behavior actually occurred.

OTHER COMMON DECEPTION MARKERS

The use of discrepancy verbs points to one of several ways we all try to mislead others while, at the same time, not technically lying. Some of my favorites:

> **Passive constructions: "Mistakes were made."** In a delightful book on misinformation, *Mistakes Were Made (But Not By Me)*, Carol Tavris and Elliot Aronson examine how people frequently avoid responsibility through ingenious linguistic maneuvers. For example, historians are in general agreement that Secretary of State Henry Kissinger frequently deceived the American people about the direction and scope of the Vietnam War during the 1970s. Years later, in an interview, Tavris and Aronson quote Kissinger as saying, "Mistakes were quite possibly made by the administrations in which I served." Note his wording. Obviously, Kissinger didn't make any mistakes. Rather, someone probably did.

> **Avoiding answering a question.** In the mock-crime experiment where students were asked to "steal" a dollar, we asked each person point-blank: "Did you steal the dollar that was in the book?" People who actually did take the money said things such as:

I don't believe in stealing. I have a problem with it. I did it once a long time ago; I was . . . younger. I really didn't like the feeling of knowing they're going to catch me. I just, you know, especially you said for a dollar? I wouldn't have taken it.

Why would I? I would never even think to look in the book to look for a dollar. I was just writing in my journal for my freshman seminar.

It really offends me that you would accuse me of something like that. I would never do something like that.

The most common response of people who were telling the truth was "No, I didn't take your dollar." Unlike the liars, the truth-tellers answered the question directly without any embellishment. As these examples attest, when someone doesn't directly answer your question, there is a good chance they are hiding something no matter how earnest they may sound.

Let me be clear about that: performatives. Linguists and philosophers have long been intrigued by a language device called a performative. Performatives are statements about statements. In the statement "I promise you that I did not steal the money," the phrase "I promise you" is a performative. It is simply claiming "I say to you" or "I am uttering the following words to you." What is interesting about performative statements is that they cannot be assessed on their truthfulness. In the sentence starting with "I promise you," the claim "I did not steal the money" is not directly asserted. The truth of the phrase is that the speaker is merely saying that he or she promises that they didn't steal the money. It's a fine distinction but one used surprisingly frequently.

Toward the end of his term, President Bill Clinton was being hounded by the press concerning rumors of sexual misconduct with

a White House aide, Monica Lewinsky. In a January 26, 1998, press
conference, Clinton announced:

> I'm going to say this again: I did not have sexual relations
> with that woman, Miss Lewinsky.

A naïve human being would think that the president did not have sex
with Lewinsky. Actually, the statement he said is true: "I'm going to say
this again . . ." In fact, it is technically correct. He was saying it again.
OK, so he later admitted that he had had sexual relations with "that
woman" but in the press conference, he was not officially lying.

One of the great baseball pitchers of all time, Roger Clemens, was
accused by former teammates of taking performance-enhancing drugs
during his baseball career. In a press conference several months before
later admitting that he had, in fact, taken drugs, Clemens said:

> I want to state clearly and without qualification: I did not
> take steroids, human growth hormone or any other banned
> substances at any time in my baseball career or, in fact, my
> entire life . . .

There again, you can see that Mr. Clemens was technically honest. He
did, in fact, state clearly and without qualification. What he stated was
a lie but it was truthfully a statement.

WE ALL TELL lies to ourselves, to our friends, and to the world at
large. Most of these are innocent lies intended to avoid hurting others'
feelings or to try to make ourselves look a bit better than we should. In
the same way, we are constant victims of deception from friends, politicians, advertisers, and just about everyone else. Lies, of course, are
not entirely bad. They make our lives more interesting. As the writer,
director, and star of the movie *The Invention of Lying*, Ricky Gervais,

claims, without lies we would have no fiction, no good stories. In other words, without lies and deception, there would be very little need for art, literature, philosophy, and psychology.

One of the primary vehicles for the art of deceiving others is language. Not surprisingly, the language of lies is generally seen in the function words we use. As noted in other chapters, function words are essentially social. They tell us about our relationships with objects, events, and most importantly other people. As we've seen, lies ultimately reflect a subtle shift in the relationship between the speaker and the listener. At the moment of deception, the human relationship changes, which is reflected in the function words being used.

CHAPTER 7

The Language of Status, Power, and Leadership

T HE MOVIE IS *The Godfather.* The scene is a boardroom in New York City. Around the table are the Mafia dons from the Five Families, including the Godfather, Vito Corleone. The meeting is to discuss whether the families should get into the illegal drug business. The two dons with the most to gain from the meeting are Philip Tattaglia and Emilio Barzini. Corleone, who called the meeting, suspects that Tattaglia was behind his son Santino's murder. After some discussion, a solution is reached:

> DON BARZINI: Then we are agreed. The traffic in drugs will be permitted, but controlled—and Don Corleone will give up protection in the east—and there will be the peace.

> DON TATTAGLIA: But I must have strict assurance from Corleone—as time goes by and his position becomes stronger, will he attempt any individual vendetta?

> DON BARZINI: Look—we are all reasonable men here; we don't have to give assurances as if we were lawyers . . .

In the next scene, Corleone is leaving the meeting in his limousine with his lawyer Tom Hagen. Hagen assumes that he will next meet with Tattaglia to discuss the details of the arrangement. Corleone interrupts him, indicating that the real decision maker is actually Barzini rather than Tattaglia: "Tattaglia's a pimp . . . But I didn't know until this day that it was Barzini all along."

Whoa. How did the Godfather know that Barzini was the strongman? In the boardroom scene, Barzini appeared more at ease whereas Tattaglia was more rigid and nervous. The language of the two men also differed. Barzini's dominant pronoun was *we*, whereas Tattaglia used the word *I*. The use of we-words is, in fact, a consistent indicator of high status and I-words of lower status. Although Mario Puzo, the author of *The Godfather*, didn't know about pronoun research linking we-words to power and status, he intuitively knew how to shape the language of his characters.

If you hang around with a bunch of murderers, the ability to detect the real boss can save your life. In fact, knowing who is in charge of any group is adaptive. At work, those above us can promote or fire us. The journal editor can accept or reject our papers. With a warm smile or raised eyebrow, the high school cheerleader or football quarterback can make us popular or pariahs. As social animals, we are enmeshed in social hierarchies. We see them in ant colonies, dog packs, chimpanzee troops, elementary school playgrounds, boardrooms, and nursing homes. No matter what group we happen to be in, most of us are trying to fit in and, at the same time, seeking to have as much influence as possible.

There is something inherently unpleasant about the topic of social status. Being consciously aware of it seems, well, inappropriate. After all, most of us have been brought up to believe that we are all equal. Unfortunately, to paraphrase George Orwell, some people are more equal than others. The grim truth is that to be a healthy human being you must be attentive to social status. Indeed, those individuals who are most successful and happy in life are particularly good at decoding and working within social hierarchies.

FIGURING OUT WHO'S THE BOSS: DECODING SOCIAL HIERARCHIES

We have all found ourselves among a group of strangers who all know each other. Part of the puzzle of being the new guy is in trying to determine who is who and how everyone fits together. Some of the mental calculations involved in understanding the social hierarchy include figuring out who is the person in charge, who else may be new or uncomfortable in the situation. Two types of information are available—nonverbal and language cues.

NONVERBAL INDICATORS OF STATUS

A generation of researchers has tried to identify how people behave if they are high versus low in the social hierarchy. It isn't as easy as it appears. In a thoughtful analysis of dozens of good scientific studies, Judith Hall of Northeastern University was able to identify only a small group of behaviors linked to status:

Loudness High-status people tend to talk more loudly than lower-status people.

Interruptions High-status people are more likely to interrupt others than are lower-status speakers.

Physical closeness Higher-status people tend to stand or sit more closely to others than do those lower in status.

Openness Higher-status people have a more open body orientation, meaning that their arms and legs extend out more. Lower-status individuals are more likely to have their arms and legs in a more closed position.

Before you memorize these four nonverbal factors associated with status, you should note that even these dimensions are not too reliable. Hall concluded that some nonverbal cues are trustworthy in some situations but not others. Loudness, for example, is a modest predictor of dominance when people are talking to others who share the same social class. However, when people of different social classes are talking with each other, the person from the lower social class tends to speak more loudly.

What made Hall's analysis so important was that many of the behaviors that most people believed were related to status weren't. For example, most people are convinced that higher-status people fidget less, smile less, talk more quickly, have a more relaxed and deeper voice, touch others more, and stand farther away from others. Not true. In other words, what you think is signaling status and power in a group probably isn't.

One reason people are so bad at detecting the powerful people in the room is that the less powerful often do things to make themselves appear more important than they really are. A few years ago I attended a museum exhibit that tested people's abilities to identify status. A video displayed a series of brief office encounters between pairs of adult men. The viewer guessed which of the two people was the boss and who was the underling. Generally, one of the two people sat upright, didn't smile much, and leaned forward in his chair. The other sat back in his chair and seemed more informal. Because there was no sound, the viewer had to guess status based solely on nonverbal behaviors.

Most of the viewers wrongly thought that the serious and more rigid person was the one in command. In fact, the videos were job interviews and the person sitting upright was the person looking for the job. The job seekers were trying to look in control, serious, and not nervous. The interviewers were simply being themselves. They had interviewed dozens of people before and were much more relaxed in their roles. The museum visitors were fooled because they thought that people who acted dominant were really dominant.

LANGUAGE INDICATORS OF STATUS

The words people use in their conversations, e-mails, and letters predict where they rank in the social hierarchy surprisingly well. As you might guess, status is revealed by function words rather than the content of what is being said. Of all the types of function words, the single dimension that separates the high- from the low-status speakers is pronouns. And even among the pronouns, only a small group of words is important:

Low use of I-words People higher in the social hierarchy use first-person singular pronouns such as *I*, *me*, and *my* at much lower rates than people lower in status. In any interaction between two people, the person with the *higher status* uses *fewer I-words*. This is not a typo. High-status people, when talking to lower-status people, use the words *I*, *me*, and *my* at low rates. Conversely, the lower-status people tend to use I-words at high rates.

High use of we-words Those higher in status use first-person plural pronouns (*we, us, our*) at much higher rates than those lower in status.

High use of you-words In written and spoken conversation, the person who uses more second-person pronouns like *you* and *your* is likely to be the person higher in status.

Depending on the situation, other classes of words can be related to status as well. But in reality, the pronouns *I*, *we*, and *you* are by far the words that consistently reveal status. In many ways, it isn't too surprising that pronouns are so tightly linked with status. Pronouns are the most social of all word categories and we use them at particularly high rates in conversations. Recall from chapter 2 that pronouns reflect where people are paying attention. People who use the word *I* at high rates are focusing on themselves. Those using *you* are looking at or thinking about their audience.

In fact, there is some interesting experimental research that tracks people's attention as they are involved in a conversation. Those who are more dominant tend to look at their audience while they speak but look away while listening. Low-status people tend to do just the opposite. They focus on the speaker when listening but look away when talking. Where are they looking? Probably inwardly at themselves.

It is quite reasonable that I-words reflect attention to the self and, at the same time, go along with being lower on the social ladder. The you-word findings are also logical. You can think of using you-words as the equivalent of pointing your finger at the other person while talking.

You hear what I'm saying?

I mean you there.

You better be paying attention.

If you pop that gum one more time . . .

The link between I-words and you-words with attention and status make sense. What about we-words? Remember from earlier chapters that words such as *we*, *us*, and *our* are tricky. On the surface, we-words sound warm and fuzzy and should, in theory, be related to feelings of group solidarity. The problem is that, in conversations with others, the word *we* is really at least five different words:

The you-and-I *we*. This is the *we* that everyone wants to be part of. Let's you and I get a cup of coffee. The two of us enjoy coffee. The you-and-I *we* is a public acknowledgment that a specified person or group of people and I are all part of the same group. We do, in fact, share an identity. Note, however, that there is a subtle problem with the you-and-I *we*: It can be a little presumptuous. I may think that you and I are in the same group, but you might not. In fact, in both Japanese and Korean, speakers are extremely careful in their uses of the word *we* in normal conversations for that very reason. It can be insulting to say *we* to others who may not share the same group identity.

The my-friends-and-not-you *we*. You have just returned from a camping trip with high school friends and are explaining this to your office mate. As the tale unfolds, you will likely say something like "and then we ate breakfast." Very often when talking to people, it is necessary to tell them some action or experience that you shared with others but not with the listeners of your story. Use of *we* in this case is exclusionary in the sense that the message is being broadcast that this tightly knit *we* does not include you.

The we-as-you *we*. My personal favorite. This is where the speaker makes a *we* statement but is politely asking or telling someone else to do something. At the beginning of class when the students are all talking with one another, I have been known to say, "Could we please stop talking with one another?" Or last night at a restaurant, the server asked, "Have we decided what we are going to order for dinner tonight?"

The we-as-I *we*. Sometimes referred to as the royal *we*, the we-as-I *we* is invoked to diffuse responsibility and imply support from others that may not exist. I've overheard an administrator say to an employee, "We don't feel as though you have completed the forms accurately enough." The only person who knew about the forms was that particular administrator.

The every-like-minded-person-on-earth *we*. The politician's favorite, the every-like-minded-person-on-earth *we* is the vaguest of all. "We need a better government." What distinguishes this form of *we* is that it is virtually impossible to specify who the *we* refers to.

As you look back at the five types of *we*, only the you-and-I *we* is truly personal and helps to cement or acknowledge a bond between the speaker and listener. The other four forms of *we* erect a barrier between the participants in the conversation. It is not surprising that as people move up the social hierarchy, they use the more distancing forms of *we* more often.

Taken together, both nonverbal cues and language can signal relative status in both formal and informal groups. To outsiders watching a group of people interact, the various types of cues typically reveal themselves periodically in an interaction. The problem is that the cues may appear briefly and then disappear. One person who is the leader may speak more loudly, have a more open body language, and use the words *we* and *you* for just a few moments—perhaps just long enough for others at the meeting to notice. If previous research is any guide, most observers will be able to identify the status hierarchy of a group at rates somewhat better than chance. With computer analyses of the group's language, however, you will be far more successful.

DISCOVERING YOUR OWN STATUS THROUGH YOUR CORRESPONDENCE

Let's get personal for a minute. What is your status compared to your friends? Are you intimidated by some friends more than others? Do you really want to know? The best way to appreciate status in human relationships is to see it in your own dealings with others.

It's surprisingly simple. Look at the last ten e-mails that you sent to someone and compare them with the last ten they sent you. Calculate the percentage of I-words each of you used. If you have a great deal of time, you can do the same with the you- and we-words that you both used as well. Statistically, I-words are the most trustworthy. Here's the rule: The person who uses fewer I-words is the person who is higher in the social hierarchy. If the two of you are about the same in I-word usage, you probably have an equal relationship.

We know this because of an e-mail study that Matt Davis and I conducted a few years ago. We recruited ten volunteers—some graduate students, undergraduates, and even a couple of faculty who let us analyze their incoming and outgoing e-mail to and from about fifteen people. Matt wrote a computer program that scrambled all of the e-mails so that they were unreadable and preserved the anonymity of the e-mailers and what they actually said.

In addition to the e-mails themselves, we asked each of our volunteers to rate each of their fifteen correspondents along several dimensions: sex, age, how well they knew them, how well they liked them, and similar questions. The pivotal question was about relative status. That is, for each of the fifteen correspondents, the volunteers made judgments in response to the question:

Evaluate this correspondent in terms of relative status:

1	2	3	4	5	6	7
OTHER PERSON HAS			**OTHER PERSON HAS**		**OTHER PERSON HAS**	
MUCH LOWER			**ABOUT THE SAME**		**MUCH HIGHER**	
STATUS			**STATUS**		**STATUS**	

All correspondents were rated for their relative status on the seven-point questionnaire. So if the volunteer was a graduate student, they might rate a senior professor as a 6 or a 7 and a high school student as a 1 or a 2.

The results were clear-cut. The person with the higher status used fewer I-words, more you-words, and more we-words. This was not a subtle finding. For most of the people, the effects were quite large.

As I pondered the findings, I kept asking myself if I did the same thing. You should know that I have always harbored the illusion that I am a very egalitarian guy. I have tried to treat undergraduates, graduate students, staff, people in the community, and my superiors in the academic world with respect. Certainly these analyses would not show large status effects in my e-mail. I'm the egalitarian guy, remember? I analyzed my data and that was the day I abandoned my I-treat-everyone-the-same self-view. The analysis of my words revealed the same status differences as others in our study. Some edited examples:

Dear Dr. Pennebaker:

I was part of your Introductory Psychology class last semester. **I** have enjoyed your lectures and **I've** learned so much. **I** received an email from you about doing some research with you. Would there be a time for **me** to come by to talk about this?

—Pam

Dear Pam—

This would be great. This week isn't good because of a trip. How about next Tuesday between 9 and 10:30. It will be good to see you.

Jamie Pennebaker

Pam, as you may guess, had been a first-year college student in my Introductory Psychology class. Notice how she uses I-words in every sentence. Pennebaker manages to avoid the use of a single I-word in his return e-mail. Not coincidentally, Pam uses the honorific "Dr. Pennebaker" and Pennebaker refers to her by her first name. But now watch the same Pennebaker when writing to a world-famous faculty member trying to get him to attend a conference:

Dear (Famous Professor):

The reason **I'm** writing is that **I'm** helping to put together a conference on [a particular topic] . . . **I** have been contacting a large group of people and many have specifically asked if you were attending. **I** would absolutely love it if you could come . . . The only downside is that we can't pay for any expenses . . . **I** think the better way to think about this gathering is as a reunion rather than a conference . . . **I** really hope you can make it.

Jamie Pennebaker

Dear Jamie—

Good to hear from you. Congratulations on the [conference]. The idea of a reunion is a nice one . . . and the conference idea will provide us with a semi-formal way of catching up with one another's current research . . . Isn't there any way to get the university to dig up a few thousand dollars to defray travel expenses for the conference?

With all best regards,
Famous Professor

All of a sudden, the formerly distant, high-status Pennebaker is writing like the lower-status, slightly groveling student. If you look a little more closely at the e-mails you will also see that all the e-mails are friendly and enthusiastic. Not using I-words does not make the writer appear cold or arrogant, just slightly less accessible and more distant.

Many people ponder these findings and think the differences in I-word usage simply go along with making a request of some kind. If you want something, maybe you use *I*. When you are in the position to grant the request, perhaps you don't. Some other studies indicate this isn't the case. A good example are some e-mails I sent a few years ago in my capacity as an administrator in my department. We were running low on office space and I had to ask a few people to move to different offices. Here are some edited versions of an e-mail I sent to a Very Important Professor and another one to a Humble Graduate Student. The results were painfully predictable:

Dear (Very Important Professor):
I've been trying to avoid this but **I** think **I** may need to ask you if you would be willing to give up your office . . . **I** can find you something significantly less grand should worse come to worse.

Dear (Humble Graduate Student):
As you probably know, office space in the department is at a premium. We are doing our best to accommodate all the students. However, would you be willing to move your office . . . ? Thanks so much for your help with this.

As with the earlier examples, the tones of the e-mails are honest, warm, and constructive. Even though the content is essentially the same, they convey slightly different messages. The request to the Very Important Professor is written as though I have my hat in my hand. You can see me stooping over a little and speaking in a quiet voice. In the second e-mail, I'm not speaking at all. I'm merely conveying information from "us"—the department. "We really don't want to bother you but we want you to move. Nothing personal, mind you."

Did I consciously adjust the language of these e-mails? No. I have no memory of specifically writing them. My brain must have kicked in on its own and adjusted the writing style knowing who would read the e-mail later. Don't blame me. It was my brain that was so sensitive to status differences.

I love the e-mail study because it demonstrated an important effect that held up across several people and, more important, revealed my own hypocrisy. Status hierarchies are everywhere yet they go on right below our noses. We are generally oblivious to them, especially when corresponding with friends whom we may have known for years.

THE SPEEDY UNFOLDING OF SOCIAL HIERARCHY
IN CONVERSATIONS WITH STRANGERS

Think back to the scene from *The Godfather* at the beginning of the chapter. Do we have the ability to detect pronoun use in natural conversations so, like Vito Corleone, we can determine who is the powerful person in any given situation? In a word, no. People talk too quickly and we simply can't detect small differences in pronoun use with our ears. Once the conversations are transcribed, however, computer programs have little problem.

Unlike e-mails or letters, when talking with others, the words fly out of our mouths with very little forethought. Despite these very different forms of social interaction, the same general word categories can identify social status in conversations as in written communications. Several studies have now been conducted with college students and, in a manner of speaking, in the White House with top administration officials.

In one of the first studies linking pronoun use to status in natural conversations, my graduate student Ewa Kacewicz invited students to participate in a get-to-know-you task. Pairs of strangers entered a room and talked about anything that interested them for ten minutes while they were videotaped. The conversations were fairly standard—where are you from? What's your major? How do you like the university? At the end of the conversation, the two people went to separate rooms where they each evaluated the interaction. Both tended to agree on which person had more status and who tended to control the interaction more.

The findings from Ewa's project and others like it have been clean and consistent. High-status people use we-words and you-words at high rates and use I-words at low rates. In fact, this same pattern emerges when people are chatting with each other on the Internet. What is most striking, however, is how fast the social hierarchy emerges in the conversation. In Ewa's first study, the two people who were going to have an interaction met just as they were going into the laboratory. They were asked not to talk until both were seated and the video cameras were turned on.

Within the first minute of the conversation, the social hierarchy was established. I suspect that the two people had a rough sense of the hierarchy within seconds of seeing one another. Perhaps they noticed each other's height, weight, attractiveness, clothing, or general bearing. Whatever it was, their relative use of pronouns was fixed almost immediately.

When two strangers meet and chat on the Internet, you would think that it would take a little longer for the hierarchy to emerge. Surprisingly, it doesn't take much longer. The Internet project was part of a large classroom exercise that I conducted with my colleague Sam

Gosling and graduate student Yla Tausczik. Hundreds of students were asked to go online at particular times where they were randomly connected with another person. They were simply asked to chat about anything they wanted for fifteen minutes. At the end of the fifteen minutes, they completed a questionnaire about the conversation.

Just like the face-to-face natural conversation project, the status differences were apparent in the first three minutes of the interaction. This amazed us because there were no physical appearance cues, voice tone, or anything else that could prejudge status for the two participants. How was it possible for the two people to tacitly agree who was more dominant so quickly?

Reading some of the online transcripts helped to understand the process. Early in the conversation, both participants tossed out cues about themselves and, at the same time, fished for cues about the other person. Some participants would also make subtle moves that diminished the other person's stature. Here is an example of two females at the beginning of their conversation. Person B (Brittany), whose comments are in bold, is the one who both agree was more dominant when they completed questionnaires at the end of the conversation:

A: hello, is anyone here?

B: I am. Hi.

A: oh hey

B: I'm Brittany

A: what are we supposed to talk about? I'm Chris, nice to meet you.

B: dont take this the wrong way, are you a boy or a girl?

A: haha girl

B: Chris is kind of ambiguous, lol, nice to meet you. what year are you

A: freshman. What about you?

B: cool. im a junior. Major?

A: studio art but i am going to be transferring to communications to do photo journalism. You?

B: history

A: are you involved in any organizations or anything like that here

B: um, im getting certified to teach high school but other than that, no. you?

A: i am thinking about being a photographer. I don't want to draw for a living

B: photography is great

A: i'm not a serious art student . . . i did art in high school so i could get into the art school here

Notice at the beginning the two people appear to be approaching the interaction in the same way. By the third time she writes, however, Brittany makes an underhanded power play, "don't take this the wrong way, are you a boy or a girl?" I ask you, dear reader, can you imagine any sentence that starts with "Don't take this the wrong way . . ." that can end well for the listener? Brittany has already put Chris on notice that she has the potential to be a bully.

Afterward, both look for information about the other that can help peg them on some kind of social hierarchy. However, once Brittany discovers that Chris is younger and in a less prestigious major, she psychologically takes control. Once Brittany has established her dominance, Chris begins to focus on herself in a more nervous, submissive way. Much later in the conversation (not included here), the higher-status Brittany works to give Chris advice about how she can (and should) get teacher certification.

Interestingly, both Chris and Brittany reported that they enjoyed the conversation and liked one another. At the end of the time period, the two exchanged e-mail addresses and promised to get in touch with one another in the future. And it is safe to say should they meet for coffee, Brittany will still be the person with the higher status in both of their eyes.

In reading over hundreds of interactions such as this, it is fascinating to watch the unfolding of the status hierarchy. "Innocent" status-related questions include asking the other person about their parents' occupation, last vacation, exercise habits, ethnicity, living location on campus, grade in the psychology class, and others. Not surprisingly, the person with high status in a particular domain usually is the one who asks a question about it. Notice how the higher-status Brittany is the one who asks about the other person's year in school and major.

Assessing each other's status is not unique to English-speaking college students. It is something that happens around the world. In fact, some societies have much simpler rules in assessing status. In South Korea, for example, relative age is one of the most strict determinants of who is higher in the social hierarchy. If the age is the same, wealth or income is assessed next. In these societies, it is common for people to directly ask one another about their lives, which, in the West, might be viewed as impolite. On a recent trip to South Korea, for example, I sat next to a Korean man roughly my age. Within the first ten minutes of the flight, he started a conversation asking me about my age. When it was clear that we were exactly the same age, he asked what my yearly income was. When I answered, he smiled warmly and simply said, "We make about the same." I got the impression that his income was far higher, which made him somewhat more comfortable in talking with me afterward.

PEGGING STATUS HIERARCHIES IN THE NIXON WHITE HOUSE

Laboratory experiments to study status are pale imitations of the natural social processes that often take months or years to develop. In real-world organizations, the person who has emerged as the boss is likely to be someone who has been groomed for years and has the respect of others within the group. On occasion, an opportunity arises to capture natural conversation among well-known individuals with known levels of status. When this happens, we can begin to see the overall social hierarchy of the group. One of the best natural experiments of relative status emerged through tape recordings made a generation ago. The recordings were released as part of the famous Watergate scandal that shook the United States and resulted in the resignation of a president.

Two years after his 1968 election as president, Richard M. Nixon had a secret recording system installed in his office in the White House. Only a couple of his staff knew about it, and based on the recordings, he himself was rarely inhibited by the presence of the hidden microphones. After serving for four years, Nixon ran for reelection against a Democratic candidate who hopelessly trailed in the polls from the very beginning. Partly because of the paranoia that ran rampant in the Nixon administration, some of his high-level aides approved a number of illegal activities to help ensure Nixon's reelection. One scheme was a late-night break-in of the Democratic National Headquarters in the Watergate office building in Washington, D.C. The burglars, some of whom worked in the White House, installed listening devices on the phones of the election strategists. Because of the vigilance of a single night watchman, the burglars were caught by the local police as they left the building.

Because the burglary was so peculiar, very few people could imagine that it had been initiated by responsible people in the White House. In the first months after the break-in, few took it seriously and its occurrence had no discernible impact on the election four months later. However, two young reporters from the *Washington Post* newspaper, Bob Woodward and Carl Bernstein, doggedly pursued the story until Nixon's closest aides began to be implicated. The Watergate scandal made headlines from early 1973 until Nixon's resignation in August 1974.

The turning point in the investigation occurred when it was revealed by a midlevel White House staffer, Alexander Butterfield, that the White House taping system always recorded conversations when Nixon was present. In the subsequent months as their legal problems mounted, the White House released several of the transcribed recordings to the public. When the final one (also known as the "smoking gun" tape) was made public in the summer of 1974, Nixon was forced to resign.

The most pertinent tapes involved Nixon's conversations with his lawyer John Dean, his chief domestic adviser John Ehrlichman, and his chief of staff H. R. Haldeman. The recordings, which were published in the spring of 1974, have been a treasure trove for historians and for language analysis researchers like me. Of the initial transcripts, we were able to analyze fifteen conversations where Nixon had one-on-one conversations with Dean, Ehrlichman, or Haldeman. For each conversation, we compared Nixon's words with those of his aides.

Consistent with the lab studies, the high-status Nixon used far fewer I-words than his aides. Overall, 3.9 percent of Nixon's words were first-person singular pronouns, compared to his aides' 5.4 percent. Nixon also used more we-words (1.4 percent versus 0.8 percent) and you-words (3.4 percent versus 1.8 percent) than his aides.

Closer inspection of the transcripts suggested that Nixon had very different relationships with the three men. In their conversations, Nixon's use of the first-person singular was significantly lower when talking

PERCENTAGE OF I-WORDS USED BY NIXON AND HIS VARIOUS AIDES

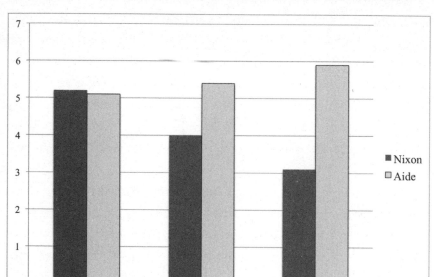

to Dean and Ehrlichman than in his interactions with Haldeman. These pronoun patterns suggested that Nixon distanced himself much more from Dean and Ehrlichman, but that Nixon and Haldeman spoke to each other as equals. This is a great hypothesis, but is it true?

Of the four men, only John Dean was still alive when we began analyzing the Watergate transcripts in the early 2000s. He consented to an e-mail interview with me about Nixon's relationships with the three aides. Haldeman and Nixon had known each other since the early 1950s and, in Dean's words, were peers in running the White House. "They were not friends however. [Haldeman] once said that [Nixon] had no idea how many children he had, and they only shook hands once— the day [Nixon] fired him." But ultimately "it was a partnership."

Dean's own relationship with Nixon was formal and respectful. Interestingly, Dean characterized Ehrlichman, who was often in "over his head" with respect to Washington politics, as arrogant yet insecure. In listening to the Watergate tapes himself, Dean was impressed with the degree to which Ehrlichman was making a power play in the hopes of getting Haldeman's job. In his interactions with Nixon, Ehrlichman was overly solicitous, almost groveling. Nixon's reaction was that of even greater psychological distance than with Dean, with whom he had a more formal relationship.

One final analysis with the I-words is noteworthy. The Watergate tapes that were released in 1974 were recorded from June 1972 (soon after the break-in) through July 1973, when the scandal was front-page news most every day. Remember that people who enjoy very high status and high self-esteem and who tend to be overconfident generally use I-words at very low levels. And in his interaction with his aides in June through about November 1972, Nixon's rate of I-word usage ranged between 2 and 4 percent. However, as the scandal continued to develop and Nixon's status began to erode, his use of I-words increased month by month. By the last recordings in July 1973, his average I-word usage with his aides hovered around 7 to 8 percent of all his words. In other words, as Nixon's political world began to crumble, he became less dominant and powerful in all his dealings with others.

The Watergate transcripts point to our ability to distinguish the social hierarchy of Nixon's aides through Nixon's own eyes (or, perhaps, mouth). We can infer that he was most responsive and open to what Haldeman may have said compared to others such as Ehrlichman. Interestingly, the pronoun analyses can't tell us about the relative hierarchy among the aides themselves. Nixon may have conferred more status on Dean than Ehrlichman inside the Oval Office. However, when Dean and Ehrlichman were together in other settings, it is possible that Ehrlichman could have had more status than Dean. Only through analyses of different groups of people can we begin to uncover the complexities of a group's status hierarchy.

Finally, there is a large difference between status and liking. As Dean pointed out, there is no evidence that Nixon and Haldeman particularly liked one another. Respecting another person and liking them is not the same.

THE LANGUAGE OF LEADERSHIP

Can the research on status be extended to our understanding of leadership? Is it possible to identify good leaders by the ways they use words? Can leaders become more effective if they change the ways they use words? Surprisingly few studies have examined the language of leaders. Even fewer have studied the words of people in everyday life in order to predict what kinds of leaders they might be in the future.

ASSUMING A LEADERSHIP ROLE AFFECTS THE LEADER'S LANGUAGE

Within small groups, leaders do, in fact, talk differently than followers. Ethan Burris from the Red McCombs School of Business at the University of Texas and his colleagues conducted a project where about forty groups of business students worked together on a group task. Each of the four-person work groups were told that they represented a small consulting firm that was to offer advice to a fictitious company to improve its customer service division. The task was complex and required each small group to work together to achieve a solution.

The Burris project stands out because he dictated who the leader would be. He told each group that he had chosen the best possible leader based on an analysis of each student's personality test scores. In truth, he made the leadership assignment randomly, akin to drawing one of the people's name out of a hat. What is important, however, is that the groups truly believed that their leader was skilled.

Each group's interactions were tape-recorded and transcribed. The results were consistent with everything we have found before. Those who were assigned leadership roles ended up using I-words the least and you-words and we-words the most. In other words, *people's language changes once they adopt a role*. I can't emphasize enough how important this finding is. Almost every other study that has been conducted with leadership and language was based on people who were already the leaders or who already had high status. This study indicates that the words reflect the leadership role. In other words, most people if thrust into a high-status leadership position will likely start to talk like a leader.

DOES A PERSON'S LANGUAGE PREDICT THEIR FUTURE LEADERSHIP ABILITY?

Hundreds of millions of dollars are spent annually in predicting and selecting the future leaders in industry, government, the military, and other large organizations. Most consulting firms that specialize in leadership selection and the companies they consult with make many of their decisions on intuition and/or questionable research methods. Even the very best scientifically grounded methods in selecting leaders are far from perfect in their hit rates.

Reliably selecting leaders is very difficult. The biggest problem is that a person could be a brilliant leader in one setting but terrible in another. In the past, I consulted with a company where the corporate head was unable to lead his management team in a direction that satisfied anyone. This same person had been a brilliant leader in a very different company just two years earlier. He hadn't changed in his approach, intelligence, or abilities. The only thing that had changed was the setting.

A second problem that consulting firms face is in building assessment tools. For example, some firms give prospective leaders a raft of questionnaires. Others have people undergo grueling interviews or problem-solving tasks. Yet others just send their prospective leaders into a company and have them give a talk, shake a few hands, and undergo a series of meetings with the relevant people in the organization. By themselves, each of these methods is only slightly better than a flip of the coin in selecting between two candidates with similar backgrounds.

If we know that there is a particular language profile for effective leaders, can we use natural language to select future leaders? In reality, it is too early to tell. Word analyses can help us determine how people think, relate to others, and view themselves. They will be far less helpful in predicting how people will react in completely novel settings with an unpredictable group of people with different motivations and backgrounds.

DOES A DOMINANT LANGUAGE STYLE
MAKE A PERSON A BETTER LEADER?

After almost a hundred years of group research, scientists in psychology, sociology, and business now appreciate that different groups work effectively depending on the task, the group structure, and the people in the group. In the Burris project, for example, the more the leader used high-status language, the more likely it was that the group would come up with objectively better results. The effects were not large, however. In another project with a looser group structure, just the opposite was found: Dominant language by the leader resulted in the groups' performing worse.

We return to the same problem of the tension between a leader's characteristics and the job that needs to be accomplished. Dozens of studies have shown that if a company, a sports team, or an entire country is generally productive, with very little infighting and not facing any major threats, leaders who are warm and friendly are particularly effective. Such leaders would probably not exhibit extremely dominant language. However, if the organization is facing a series of hardships from outside as well as conflicts from within, most people want a stronger, no-nonsense leader who will get the job done. A no-nonsense style often includes a leadership style marked by clear chains of command and an agreed-upon social hierarchy.

CAN LEADERS BECOME MORE EFFECTIVE
BY CHANGING THEIR LANGUAGE?

Yes, I think so. But not for the reasons most people think. Simply using words differently won't automatically change speakers' psychological states. As noted throughout the book, words reflect our personality and social situations but rarely directly affect them.

In speeches, commercials, and brief interactions, it is possible that the words individuals use can influence how their audience perceives them. Our brains do, in fact, register if a speaker is using *I* or *we* and react accordingly. And, in fact, if the goal is merely to make a person sound leader-like, then the careful crafting of their words can be effective in the short run.

But, speechwriters, beware. Do you want your presidential candidate to sound presidential or folksy? To sound high status or low status? In both his election campaigns for president, George W. Bush sounded more personal, folksy, and low status than either of his opponents Al Gore or John Kerry. In the 2008 election, Barack Obama's language was far more presidential and high status than his opponent John McCain's. The words that the candidates used clearly influenced our perceptions and ultimately our votes.

Note that attaining a leadership position is different from being an effective leader. In most cases, an effective leader is someone who works and interacts with others, who makes decisions that others will agree with. Leadership is not just making speeches. It demands a wide array of thinking and social skills.

Leaders can become more effective by first listening to and analyzing their own language. Think back to the case of John Kerry's use of we-words in his presidential campaign against George Bush in 2004 described in chapter 2. Recall that his advisers mistakenly believed that if Kerry increased in his use of we-words, he would come across to audiences as more warm and approachable.

Had I been Kerry's language adviser, I would have first analyzed his speeches and interviews. His high use of we- and you-words and low use of I-words would immediately have signaled that he was trying to sound too presidential, which came across as arrogant. My language therapy would have been to try to change his relationship with the audience and the way he was thinking about himself. He clearly needed to know that his use of we-words was coming across as cold and not authentic.

People can become better leaders by using their words as markers of how they are relating to others. Words are like a speedometer in a car that reflects how fast the car is going. You can't slow the car by directly affecting the speedometer. Rather, you use the speedometer to gauge your driving. Train a person to become a better driver and their speedometer will follow. Make a potential leader more attentive to their words and the meaning of their words and they can change their relationships with others and become better leaders.

FINAL THOUGHTS ON STATUS, POWER, ARROGANCE, AND LEADERSHIP

That status hierarchies are part of almost every relationship we have is, on a certain level, a bit depressing and threatening. Not only is a pecking order established within minutes of an interaction, but all the parties in the interaction then adopt their linguistic role. Sitting by a person on a plane, meeting a stranger at a party, or being introduced to a colleague in a business meeting triggers each person to see where they stand in the hierarchy compared to the others.

The almost-invisible status competition has been at play since we were young children and will continue to be through old age. Although the existence of social hierarchies may go against our beliefs in democracy and equality, the fast and efficient ways we create pecking orders helps to make all subsequent interactions run more smoothly.

Although the examples used in this chapter have come primarily from projects conducted in English, virtually identical patterns of word use are apparent in Ancient Greek, Arabic, Japanese, and all European languages that we have studied. For example, the characters in the plays of Euripides, writing in the fifth century B.C., use low rates of I-words and high rates of you- and we-words when they are powerful.

When the same characters fall from grace, their I-words skyrocket and their you- and we-words drop.

You will notice that the same pronouns—*I*, *we*, and *you*—are linked to status, power, self-confidence, arrogance, and leadership. This isn't to say that all of these constructs are the same. As recent research by organizational psychologists suggests, people can achieve high status without having direct power over others. Effective leadership sometimes does and sometimes doesn't involve arrogance or power. Whereas other word categories may be able to distinguish power from status, both can be thought of as markers of a social hierarchy.

What this means is that if you happen to be at a future cocktail party with Gandhi, Stalin, Einstein, and Emilio Barzini from *The Godfather* (but not that pimp Tattaglia), you can bet that you will likely use more I-words than any of them.

CHAPTER 8

The Language of Love

HOPEFULLY, YOU SHOULD now be convinced that function words reflect psychological states. Sadly, I've been keeping something from you: Word use rarely occurs in a vacuum. In most cases, when we use words we are talking or writing to another person, and at the same time, they are talking or writing to us. Most language use occurs among people in ongoing social relationships. What this means is that we can begin to use our word tools to investigate more than solitary individuals—we can begin to study human relationships.

Think what this means. The way that you and your lover, your parent, your boss, and your mortal enemy talk with each other provides important clues to the nature of your relationships. And not just the way you talk—the ways you and your friends e-mail, post updates on your respective Facebook pages or Twitter entries, inform us about your entire social network.

Social relationships have their own personality. One friend in my social network is someone I often talk to about personal and emotional topics, and when we meet, we always eat Mexican food; another friendship is characterized by our arguing and joking over beers. Even my e-mails to and from my two friends reflect the kinds of interactions we have during our periodic lunches. These different relationships have gone on for years and are both warm and fulfilling. If I were to analyze the language of these interactions, each would have its own fingerprint, its own conversational personality.

By inspecting the language of close relationships, a picture of the relationships themselves begins to emerge. Not only can we look at relationships over months or years but we can also track how two people are connecting with one another on a minute-by-minute level. For example, it is possible to tell how engaged two people are with one another by analyzing how similarly they talk with one another.

Consider this brief snippet of an IM interaction between two college students who are very much in love:

HER: I'm glad I can at least talk to you now, but I want to see you so badly. I hate being apart from you

HIM: ☺. I wish there was a heart-melting smiley . . . I love you

HER: Seriously though . . . I've always been the type of girl that I could go long periods of time and it wouldn't be that I wouldn't . . . think about you, it's just that the distance wouldn't get to me . . . but today, I felt like I was going crazy not seeing you! Like when I say I missed you like crazy . . . I mean CRAZY!!!!I love you too

HIM: I do love you . . . so much

Both members of the couple are closely attentive to each other and repeat many of the same words and phrases. Compare the words of intense love with words of intense, well, outrage. For several years, a daytime television talk show, *The View*, has commanded a large audience in the United States. The hosts are a group of smart and often opinionated well-known women with backgrounds in news, comedy, and politics. Over the years, occasional bitter disagreements have erupted that were both political and personal. On May 23, 2007, a long-simmering tension between the conservative co-host Elisabeth Hasselbeck and liberal Rosie O'Donnell erupted:

HASSELBECK: Because you are an adult and I'm certainly not going to be the person for you to explain your thoughts to. They're your thoughts. Defend your own insinuations.

O'DONNELL: I defend my thoughts.

HASSELBECK: Defend your own thoughts.

O'DONNELL: Right, but every time I defend them, Elisabeth, it's poor little Elisabeth that I'm picking on.

HASSELBECK: You know what? Poor little Elisabeth is not poor little Elisabeth.

O'DONNELL: That's right. That's why I'm not going to fight with you anymore because it's absurd. So for three weeks you can say all the Republican crap you want.

HASSELBECK: It's much easier to fight someone like Donald Trump, isn't it? Because he's obnoxious.

O'DONNELL: I've never fought him. He fought me. I told a fact about him—

. . .

HASSELBECK: I gave you an opportunity to clarify.

O'DONNELL: You didn't give me anything. You don't have to give me. I asked you a question.

HASSELBECK: I asked you a question.

O'DONNELL: And you wouldn't even answer it.

HASSELBECK: You wouldn't even answer your own question.

O'DONNELL: Oh, Elisabeth, I don't want—You know what? You really don't understand what I'm saying?

HASSELBECK: I understand what you're saying.

Obviously, the tone of the interactions between the two lovers and the two adult television hosts is different. Unlike the lovers' IMs, the women's sparring resembles a schoolyard fight between two bullies. Despite the striking differences in the two interactions, it is intriguing to see how in both exchanges, the two people converge in their use of words. In both interactions, the two people are completely focused on each other and practically mimic what the other person has just said— one in a loving way, the other in sputtering rage.

Conversations are like dances. Two people effortlessly move in step with one another, each usually anticipating the other person's next move. If one of the dancers moves in an unexpected direction, the other typically adapts and builds on the new approach. As with dancing, it is often difficult to tell who is leading and who is following in that the two people are constantly affecting each other. And once the dance begins, it is almost impossible for one person to singly dictate the couple's movement.

In his poem "Among School Children," William Butler Yeats asks, "How can we know the dancer from the dance?" In reading both transcripts, you get the feeling you can't. You can almost hear the players adjust their speaking rate, tone, and volume. As they both become more emotional, their uses of words converge. Less obvious, however, is their parallel use of function words. That is, both the happy lovers and the angry talk show hosts tend to use pronouns, prepositions, articles, and other function words with each other at almost identical rates. In both interactions, the two people are on the same psychological page and it is reflected in their language.

VERBAL MIMICKING

Social scientists have long known that people in a face-to-face conversation tend to display similar nonverbal behaviors. When one person crosses his or her legs, the other person follows. When one makes a grand hand gesture, the other will likely do the same a bit later. This nonverbal mimicking was first thought to reflect how much the two people liked one another. In fact, it is a marker of engagement, or the degree to which the two are paying attention to each other. If you are in love or you are outraged with your conversational partner, the two of you will match each other's nonverbal actions precisely.

The same is true for the words used in a conversation. If the two people are talking about the same topic then their words should be similar. After all, that's what a conversation is. More interesting is that people also converge in the ways they talk—they tend to adopt the same levels of formality, emotionality, and cognitive complexity. In other words, people tend to use the same groups of function words at similar rates. Further, the more the two people are engaged with one another, the more closely their function words match.

The matching of function words is called language style matching, or LSM. Analyses of conversations find that LSM occurs within the first fifteen to thirty seconds of any interaction and is generally beyond conscious awareness. Several studies suggest that LSM is apparent in some unlikely places.

Imagine, for example, that you were required to answer a series of open-ended essay questions as part of a class assignment. Imagine also that each of the open-ended questions was written in a very different style, ranging from very formal to extremely informal in style. Would you notice the differences in the writing styles of the questions? More important, would you change the ways you answered the questions by adjusting your answers to match each question's language style? Surprisingly, you would likely not notice the differences in writing styles but you would adjust the style of your answers.

Working with my colleague Sam Gosling and graduate student Molly Ireland, we set up an online class writing assignment for several five-hundred-person Introductory Psychology classes. Students were forewarned that they would need to answer four separate brief essay questions about aspects of a class writing assignment. We never told the students that the different questions would be written using different language styles. For example, one particular essay question was written either in a pompous, arrogant style or, in another version, the same question was written in a chatty "Valley girl" style. Here are two samples where students were asked to write about a particular theory that had been discussed in the textbook:

> **Pompous instructions:** Although your professors gave this topic rather minimal attention, cognitive dissonance is a common psychological phenomenon with which the vast majority of uninformed laymen will be familiar . . . generating an example should be simple enough once one has become reasonably familiar with this concept.
>
> **Valley girl instructions:** OK, we might not have talked about cognitive dissonance much. Which I think is totally crazy cause it's like, everybody should be able to see that cognitive dissonance is majorly relevant. Like, it's seriously happening ALL the time, you know?? . . . So OK, it's your turn. I mean, like really try to think of an example of cognitive dissonance and tell me everything about it.

At the end of both questions, everyone read the same instructions:

> In the space below, give a real-life example of cognitive dissonance, explaining what led to it and how it was resolved. Support your example with evidence from your book.

So, like, you get the idea of the differences between the writing styles of the two questions. Interestingly, the students provided equally knowledgeable answers no matter what the writing style. The only difference was that students who received the pompous question answered in pompous ways and those who read the Valley girl instructions wrote in the same freestyle informal lingo. Because everyone responded to four different essay questions, each written in a different style, many students later reported not even noticing the writing styles at all.

It's hard to look at those two essay questions and not notice the striking differences in the ways they are worded. Nevertheless, we all naturally adjust to the speaker (or exam writer) we are working with. In fact, Molly ran another experiment where she gave people two pages from previously published novels. She then asked her participants to pick up where the original author left off and to write another page of the novel. For half of her participants, she explicitly told them to try to match the author's writing style. Molly found that everyone, even those who were not explicitly told to do any language matching, naturally matched the writers' original styles. In fact, when people were directly told to match styles, they were slightly worse at style matching.

Language style matching is much more pervasive than you might think. You may have had the experience of watching a particularly riveting movie and then, afterward, talking like one of the characters you have just seen. Several people tell me that after reading a book with a distinctive writing style they find themselves writing and talking using that same style over the next few hours or even days. In fact, if I, like, started—you know—writing in a Valley girl style for like gobs of paragraphs, and, you know, if, uhhh, your phone rang and like you totally answered it? You would like majorly start talking like this.

I'll stop now to preserve our respective senses of dignity.

LANGUAGE STYLE MATCHING AND THE BRAIN

If style matching is so pervasive, why does it occur? One explanation is that it is hardwired in our brains. In the 1980s, a team of Italian neuroscientists measured the activity of a group of brain cells in a macaque monkey that fired whenever the monkey grasped a particular object. Later, they discovered that the same group of cells fired when the monkey watched a person's hand grasp the same object in the same way. Other studies suggested that there might be an entire group of brain cells that mirrors the actions of others. These groups of cells are collectively called mirror neurons or mirror neuron systems.

More recent studies have asked ballet dancers to watch videos of ballets while their brain activity was being scanned. The researchers found that mirror neuron systems became activated for ballet dancers while watching the ballet videos, whereas nondancers did not show the same activity. Most of us have had subjectively similar experiences. For example, if you have ever played tennis, you may have noticed that if you watch an intense match on television, you sometimes catch yourself subtly moving your arm in an attempt to hit the ball.

Particularly noteworthy is that most researchers report that mirror neurons are most dense in Broca's area in the brain. You will recall from chapter 2 that Broca's area is also the area implicated in the processing of function words. It's not coincidental that the ability to use function words is closely linked to mimicking nonverbal behaviors and, according to recent findings, voice intonation and inflection. Indeed, many scholars now claim that the ability to mimic social behavior and its close links to Broca's area explain the early development and evolution of language abilities.

The mirror neuron research is now relying on state-of-the-art brain imaging methods such as functional magnetic resonance imaging (fMRI), where it is possible to see which parts of the brain are active during highly specific tasks. For example, a research team from Princeton University recently found that people who are particularly empathic show more brain activity in Broca's area while watching short videos of people making emotional facial expressions than do people low in empathy. It should be emphasized that the mirror neuron research is still in its infancy with researchers often disagreeing about the best way to interpret the brain activity associated with empathy.

A question that emerges from the brain imaging research concerns the possible links between mirror neurons and language style matching. At this point, direct experiments have not been done. However, the studies we have conducted with style matching among students answering open-ended essay questions hint at some important parallels. Those students who evidenced the greatest style matching in response to the different question writing styles tended to be people who made the highest grades on the multiple choice exams. In other words, those students who were most committed to the class naturally paid closer attention to the essay questions. Paying closer attention resulted in greater correspondence between the function words in the questions and their responses.

We all have mirror neurons and have the basic ability to mimic and empathize with others. These abilities differ from person to person and also depend on whom we are talking with. We have all been in situations where we talked with someone who wasn't interested in what we had to say. Admit it, we have also been in conversations where we weren't interested in what the other person was saying. I might have a head full of mirror neurons but if I sit next to a stranger on a plane who spends the flight describing his joint pains, medication history, and phlegm observations, our respective function words will go in different directions.

HOW TO MEASURE LANGUAGE STYLE MATCHING

There are a number of ways that researchers have developed to tap the degree to which two people are using function words at comparable rates. Some of the techniques are mind-bogglingly complicated. Others are fairly simple. Here is a method that you can actually do with a calculator. The basic idea is that we want to find out the degree to which any two text samples are similar in their use of function words.

Although there are nine categories of function words (including personal pronouns, impersonal pronouns, prepositions, articles, conjunctions, negations, quantifiers, common adverbs, and auxiliary verbs), personal pronouns are the most common in everyday speech. Although our computer programs analyze all types of function words to calculate LSM, you can get a pretty good idea of people's engagement with each other by just looking at their personal pronoun use.

Look back at the nasty exchange between Rosie O'Donnell and Elisabeth Hasselbeck at the beginning of the chapter. To get a sense of how in synch the two women are, all we need to do is to calculate the rate of personal pronouns that each woman used, with the following formula:

$$1 - \frac{|\text{ \% Person 1's pronouns} - \text{\%Person 2's pronouns }|}{\text{\% Person 1's pronouns} + \text{\% Person 2's pronouns}}$$

In their brief exchange, Hasselbeck used 17 personal pronouns out of a total of 81 words and O'Donnell used 26 out of a total of 99 words. In other words, 21 percent of Hasselbeck's and 26.2 percent of O'Donnell's words were personal pronouns.

Recall that the vertical line, |, refers to absolute value. That is, when the personal pronouns from person 1 are subtracted from those of person 2, the result will always be positive. So in this case:

$$1 - \frac{|\ 21.0 - 26.2\ |}{(21.0 + 26.2)}$$

or

$$1 - \frac{|-5.2\ |}{47.2} = 1 - (5.2/47.2) = 1 - .110 = .890$$

Voilà! The LSM score based on personal pronouns alone is a high .89. Interestingly, when all nine dimensions of function words are averaged together, the two women's LSM score is even higher: an amazing 0.94—almost perfect synchrony. The LSM scale ranges from a perfect 1.00 if the two people are in perfect function word harmony and as low as 0 if they are completely out of synch. In reality, numbers below .60 reflect very low synchrony and those above .85 reflect high synchrony.

RIDING THE LSM ROLLER COASTER OF CONVERSATIONS

Mirror neurons help us to quickly synchronize our conversations with others. From a communication perspective, this makes good sense. Whether talking with an old friend, a business associate, a stranger on a plane, or a salesperson, we adapt our language style to set up a common social framework and to reduce friction. Style matching helps ensure that the people are similar in their emotional tone, formality, and openness, and understand their relative status with each other.

Further, our brains are highly attentive to changes in language style over the course of an interaction, constantly making corrections in the ways we use words. Style matching waxes and wanes over the course of a conversation. In most conversations, style matching usually starts out quite high and then gradually drops as the people continue to talk. The reason for this pattern is that at the beginning of the conversation it's important to connect with the other person. Both people need to know how the other person is thinking and feeling. As the conversation rolls on, the speakers begin to get more comfortable and their attention starts to wander. There are times, however, that style matching will immediately increase. The best examples can be seen when unexpected shifts in the conversational topic or tone occur.

Imagine you are planning a surprise birthday party for a close friend. The day before the party, your friend mentions that she is thinking of going to a movie the next evening at the time you have scheduled the party. You must quickly come up with a lie that makes sure she will be around for the party. From her perspective, this is an innocuous conversation; from yours, it has become highly charged. If we could track the words between the two of you, what would happen to your style matching? Surprisingly, it will go up but not in the way you might think.

TALKING TO LIARS

The tone and direction of a conversation changes drastically as soon as one of the people starts to lie. Jeff Hancock, the Cornell researcher who studies the language of deception, has conducted some experiments that demonstrate this. In one project, he brought pairs of students into his lab and told them that they would have four online conversations on four different topics. In other words, their chatting would be from computers in different rooms so that they couldn't actually see each other. So that both partners knew how the system worked, they were first asked to chat in a get-to-know-you kind of way for about five minutes. Once both were comfortable with the online chat systems, the experimenter gave both partners a list of the official conversational topics that they were to discuss for five minutes each. The sneaky part of the study was that one of the two partners received the topic list and, for two of the four topics, was instructed to blatantly lie about their views. Their partners never knew about this and so assumed that all of the conversations were, in fact, honest and straightforward.

We already know that when people lie, their language changes. You might have thought that style matching would drop during the deception topics. In fact, *partners'* style matching *increased* during the deception topics. Yes, the liars' language changed when they were deceptive but the innocent truth-tellers' language changed as much or more.

Think what is happening in this situation. Once the study starts, the innocent partner has already had at least one honest conversation with the person and then, out of nowhere, the other person starts speaking differently. Our brains are highly attentive to change. In this situation, the innocent person is detecting that something is "off" or not making sense. Consequently, he or she starts paying closer attention, resulting in higher style matching. This is clearly not a conscious process because most innocent partners later report that they thought the deceptive conversations seemed normal.

There is something about this study that has always puzzled me. Think back to the dilemma of the surprise birthday party. If I have to lie to my friend to convince her to stay home the next evening, I have to think fast and come up with a reasonable story. Lying is hard work and during my lie, I won't be paying much attention to my friend. Instead, she will be paying attention to me. Hancock's findings indicate that my friend's language use will accommodate to my deceptive way of speaking.

There is an interesting paradox about LSM. In the case of deceptiveness, one of the speakers—the person who is lying—is actually paying less attention to the other person. Intuitively, you would think that this would result in lower levels of style matching. Apparently when we talk with liars we start paying more attention in an attempt to decode their odd language change. In the case of deception, as one person becomes less attentive, the other becomes more attentive. Surprisingly, this occurs far more frequently than you might think.

TALKING WITH DISTRACTED MULTITASKERS

Recent studies indicate that multitasking is both quite common and surprisingly ineffective. When people multitask, they are attempting to do several things at once with the net effect that the quality of their work across all tasks is diminished. We have all had the experience of talking with someone who, at the same time, was reading a text message, watching something on television, or pondering a deep existential question. The deception research hints that conversations with multitaskers would result in high language style matching; common sense would argue just the opposite.

Common sense fails again. Yla Tausczik, a graduate student in my lab with extensive background in studying online social media, set up a simple experiment to test this idea. She had pairs of strangers initiate get-to-know-you conversations on separate lab computers as part of a psychology experiment. The computer displays were programmed to have random numbers continuously float across the top of the screens. For half of the conversations, the people were told to just ignore the floating numbers. In the other half of the conversations, one of the partners was told to count the number of times that the number 7 appeared. The people they were talking with, however, were told to ignore the numbers and didn't know that that their partner was multitasking by keeping track of the floating numbers. In other words, in half of the conversations, one of the two people was distracted during the entire conversation.

Much like the deception study, the distracted pairs actually showed slightly higher style matching than the non-distracted pair. Even odder, they tended to report liking each other more. In terms of actual word use, the distracted students were less negative, less complex, and more personal than non-distracted writers.

There have been very few times in my career that I didn't believe my own results. It just didn't make sense to me that style matching increases when talking to a multitasker. So I took things into my own hands and called two former students and asked if they would mind participating in a language project. The deal would be that we would have an informal talk on the phone that would be recorded, transcribed, and analyzed. The talk would actually be made up of three five-minute segments, and after each segment, they would complete a brief questionnaire. Both agreed to the rules. What they didn't know was that on one of the three segments, I would be sitting in my office madly doing arithmetic problems as fast as I could.

The phone calls started and we talked about work, our lives, our mutual friends, and other issues of the day. During the period I was working on the arithmetic problems, I recall thinking, "Wow, I'm really good at this. I'm as socially adept when I'm busy as when I'm not." Later, when I transcribed the conversations, I was startled to see how differently I spoke while engaged in the arithmetic problems. I stuttered and repeated myself. I deflected any complicated questions and tried to get the other person to talk more. Similar to the participants in Yla's experiment, I tended to laugh more and used more positive language in general.

Both of my students rated the distraction phases of the conversation as enjoyable as the other parts. In fact, the LSM measures indicated that we matched in our language use during the distraction period at rates as high or higher than during the nondistraction periods. What happened, however, is that both students started speaking to me in the ways I was speaking to them. As I psychologically distanced myself from the conversation, my conversational partners did the same. What intrigues me is that none of us were consciously aware of it. In fact, after the phone calls, I discussed the conversations with both students, asking their perceptions. One said that she was vaguely aware that I was slightly more distracted during the arithmetic problems but said, "You often are distracted in phone calls." Oooh.

Two people who respect and like one another learn how to dance with each other across conversational topics. They are both invested in paying attention to one another, even during periods of distraction or disagreement. What makes the conversational dance dynamic is that as one person's attention wanders, the other person attempts to adjust to it. An unspoken rule in this dance, however, is that both people are ultimately committed to it. If one or both members of the conversation simply doesn't care about the other person, the dance is at risk of falling apart.

CREATING A LANGUAGE LOVE DETECTOR

Wouldn't it be nice if there existed a device that could alert people if they were compatible? You could take it on dates with you, and at the end of the evening, the two of you would read the love detector's "date compatibility score" on the front of the meter and decide if you should meet again tomorrow or never see each other again.

Good news. We may have a prototype for your startup company. It's not a device, really. Instead, it just requires that you use a digital recorder to transcribe your interaction and then analyze the words to assess LSM. Oh, and for it to work, you should probably plan on having at least ten dates that are virtually identical in format. Hmmm. Perhaps a bit like speed-dating.

THE DATING DANCE

Indeed, Molly Ireland, several other colleagues, and I have found that the LSM between couples on a brief four-minute date predicts if they want to meet again. As you may know, in a typical speed-dating session, you meet and talk with eight to twelve different "dates" for a few minutes each. At the end of each date, each person rates the other person before moving to the next date. Usually the following day, the daters contact the speed-dating organizers and tell them which of the ten people they would be interested in meeting in a more relaxed setting. Most people report that the conversations range from superficial to passionate to exhausting. Sometimes people meet the loves of their lives; most times they don't.

Lonely hearts may not always like speed-dating but researchers love it. In a recent project, about eighty daters gave permission for us to record their four-minute conversations so that our research team could analyze their word use. Does LSM in the brief interaction predict whether the couple gets together in the future? Yes, to some degree. Those in speed dates characterized by above-average LSM were almost twice as likely to want future contact as those with below-average LSM.

More interesting, however, is that we could predict which couples would get together afterward better than the individuals themselves. Immediately after each brief date, participants completed a short questionnaire about the desirability of the person they just met. The individual ratings of desirability were, of course, related to their eventually meeting, but LSM was more strongly related. Why? Whether or not two people eventually meet up is dependent on both parties. A guy might find a woman attractive but she might find him repulsive. The two must tango together. And LSM is capturing the dance—whereas the questionnaire is just assessing the dancers separately.

PREDICTING YOUNG LOVE

Let's assume that a relationship advances beyond the four-minute speed-date and the young couple starts to date seriously. Would style matching between the two of them predict the long-term prospects of their relationship? Preliminary findings suggest yes.

Most people in passionate relationships are highly attentive to their partners. They detect subtle shifts in the other person's moods and behaviors. Linguistically, their levels of style matching are quite high. After a few weeks or months together, some couples begin to realize that their relationship may have a limited shelf life. As their attention to their partner wanes, their degree of language style matching drops as well.

By tracking the language style matching of young dating couples, it is often possible to predict which couples are most likely to survive. For example, my former graduate student Richard Slatcher and I worked on a project with young dating couples. Rich, who is now on the faculty at Wayne State University, wanted to see how the couples talked with each other using instant messaging, or IM. He recruited eighty-six couples who reported that they IMed with each other on a daily basis and who agreed to let us analyze several days of their messages. We then compared what happened to couples who had high LSM in their instant messages with each other and those who had low LSM.

Of the forty-three couples with the highest LSM scores, 77 percent were still dating three months later, compared with only 52 percent of the couples with low scores. In other words, those couples who naturally synchronized their function words with each other were more likely to maintain their relationship over time.

Reading the IMs of the various couples painted a clearer picture of how the relationships were succeeding or failing. The more successful high-LSM relationships revealed how both members of the couple were truly interested in each other. In addition, the overall tone of the IMs was positive and supportive. The relationships with lower LSM scores, which were more destined to fail, often revealed striking patterns of detachment between the two people. For example, the following couple had low LSM scores although they claimed that their relationship was passionate and satisfying. Nevertheless, their failure to connect with each other is obvious:

HIM: hey you! how ya doing?!

HER: fine you

HIM: great. me and jim are gonna go out on the town

HER: sweet

HIM: i have to find an oil painting of a cow for my mom's birthday and i'm gonna get my hair cut hopefully. what are you up to?

HER: not much

HIM: bout to jump in the shower too. we had a sweet christmas party last night. i got pics. pretty funny. listening to christmas music, its great

HER: good

HIM: ha ha, not very chatty today

HER: eh well . . . guess not

HIM: so. . . . you have a good week? what are you doing this weekend?

HER: yeah it was okay. working

HIM: ah . . . oh well at least youll have $$$$$$$! that's good. Im gonna jump in the shower. you think of somehting to talk about! be back in 10 min if you're still here. jim is waiting on me to get ready. bye bye

HER: then go!

HIM: miss ya! ha ha. fine bye

The male is chatty and, I would guess, falsely upbeat. His girlfriend is cool, detached, and unresponsive. His language is personal, with high rates of pronouns, and hers is noncommittal. By her relative silence, she is conveying her annoyance, which he avoids confronting.

Compare their interaction with another where the female is trying to emotionally engage her soon-to-be-ex-boyfriend. Over the previous two days of their occasional IMs, the female has tried to talk about their relationship and the male has constantly been busy with homework, exercising, even watching television. On the third day, she finally catches him when he might have some time to chat:

HER: are you there? are you gonna be able to talk for 5 minutes

HIM: yes. go

HER: what are you doing at the same time you're chatting with me?

HIM: cleaning

HER: i feel too mad to say anything to you

HIM: fine

HER: did you not even feel one bit of bad when you read the card?

HIM: of course i did

HER: are you sure

HIM: hang on for 1 min please . . . Yes.

HER: or are you just saying . . . please hurry . . . hello? . . . what is the problem

HIM: alright . . . sorry

HER: what were you doing

HIM: my friends got here. Go

HER: but tell me what made you feel bad about the card

HIM: that you were being so nice. but i still dont feel that im wrong

HER: so why did you feel bad . . .

HIM: it did, but the fact that you told me not to expect it

HER: i don't understand. the fact that i told you not to expect it made you feel bad?

HIM: look, i will call you @ nine. i cant speak like this

In this second case, the style matching numbers are also low. Although both use personal pronouns at similar levels, the computer analyses reveal that she is more concrete (using more articles) and more complex (e.g., conjunctions, prepositions) in her thinking than he is. She is also more personal and emotional, and focuses all of her attention on her boyfriend. He, on the other hand, is distracted and avoidant.

Whenever she tries to get closer or to connect with him, he slips out of reach. This pattern of interaction was consistent over several days of instant messaging. Nevertheless, when both members of the couple completed questionnaires about their relationship, both rated their levels of intimacy and relationship satisfaction as very high (!). As is typical, the language style matching numbers did a far better job at predicting the couple's later separation than their self-reports.

The LSM method allows us to make reasonable guesses about the success of relationships by tracking a few interactions between couples. Similar ideas have been tested with recently married couples. John Gottman and his colleagues at the University of Washington report that by listening to the ways a young couple fights during a laboratory exercise, he can predict the likely success of the marriage. Gottman brings the couples into his lab and has them discuss issues that they have conflicts about—usually topics dealing with money, sex, or household chores. If, during tense discussions, both members of the couple show respect, try to reduce tension, avoid accusations, and inject positive emotions, their marriage is more likely to last. On the other hand, if one or both spouses are dismissive of the other, actively avoid discussing an emotional topic, or use the task as a way to launch personal attacks on the other, the marriage is in trouble.

A happy marriage is more than the egalitarian sharing of pronouns and prepositions. When two people use function words in similar ways and at similar rates, they are seeing their worlds in parallel ways. Having a similar worldview, though, does not ensure marital bliss. Gottman's work reminds us that the strongest relationships are also characterized by shared positive emotions. Similar findings emerged in our dating couples—those with the highest style matching scores *and* the highest rates of shared positive emotions were the couples most likely to stay together. Interestingly, shared positive emotions on their own do not predict the long-term happiness or potential for survival of a relationship. The members of the couple must be both positive in their outlooks and engaged with each other.

BUILDING AN LSM DETECTOR

Imagine having a portable LSM detector that could track the quality of all your conversations. Perhaps you could point the LSM detector at your e-mails, text messages, or IMs and get a sense of the quality of your connection with your correspondents. Or, if you have been married for many years, you could keep tabs on your relationship and help point out to your partner when he or she isn't holding up their end of the conversation.

As discussed earlier, my research team and I have built a crude working version of an LSM detector. If you go to www.SecretLifeOf Pronouns.com/synch, you can enter text that you have sent and received from a friend, lover, or enemy. With the click of a button, you will receive feedback about the degree to which the two of you are in synch in your use of function words. You can then compare your LSM numbers with average LSM scores generated by others who have used the website. Even better, you can try out the LSM detector several times, comparing your interactions with different people. This should give you a sense of your general skill at matching your language with others.

The bad news is that a real-world LSM detector would be of only limited value. Yes, it could tell us when relationships were in synch and out of synch but not what the synchrony meant. Recall that LSM tends to be elevated when both people are passionate about each other and when they truly hate one another. Synchrony also increases when one of the two people is lying to the other. So, if your LSM detector registers a high number, you and your conversational partner are paying close attention to each other.

Think of the LSM detector as a device that can evaluate the synchrony of the conversational dance. Good dancing requires each of the two people to anticipate the other's next move and, in a sense, briefly inhabit their thoughts. The dancing may last only as long as the music is playing or could reflect the two people's interest in each other and ability to synchronize their thoughts and actions for years.

USING LSM TO UNDERSTAND PAST RELATIONSHIPS

One advantage of using computerized language analysis is that we can explore relationships over history wherever some kind of written record exists. For example, if we have access to old letters, poems, or lyrics that two people shared, we can get a glimpse of their emotional connection with each other. Computerized text analysis can illuminate our understanding of marriages, friendships, or alliances in history. Molly Ireland, who has been immersed in the language style matching research, has tracked down several enlightening cases, two of which include the poems of poets from one well-known happy marriage and from one equally famous unhappy one. By analyzing their works, we get better insight into each pair's relationship.

ELIZABETH BARRETT AND ROBERT BROWNING

The idea of measuring language style matching was initially developed to track word use in natural conversations. Conversations should be especially sensitive to the immediate back-and-forth of ideas and shared references implicated in the ways mirror neurons work. By standing back, it is possible to imagine that language style matching can occur on a much broader level. If I hear a rival politician make a speech on a given topic, I might write my own speech in reaction to it several days or weeks later that would linguistically match the original speech. If my spouse is an elegant writer of novels, her writing style could influence the way I write professional journal articles. It's not much of a stretch to imagine that two professional poets who read each other's work might begin to use function words in similar ways—especially if the two people were passionately attracted to one another. A wonderful example is the case of the mid-nineteenth-century British poets Elizabeth Barrett and Robert Browning.

The two poets already had sterling reputations by the time they first corresponded when she was thirty-eight and he was thirty-two. Elizabeth, whose health had been poor since the age of fourteen, had never left home and continued to live with her despotic father while she wrote about emotions, love, and loss. Robert was a vibrant man-about-town whose work was more psychological and analytic. After Elizabeth published a poem that referenced one of his poems, Robert wrote her and professed his love for her work and, more directly, for her—even though the two had never met.

Over the next several months, they corresponded and he proposed marriage—something that she initially resisted by trying to pull away from him. After Robert relentlessly pursued Elizabeth, the two eventually eloped, moving to Italy, where they spent most of their lives together. By all accounts, the marriage was supremely happy, with both continuing to publish their work. The only dark time in their fifteen-year marriage came during the last two to three years, when Elizabeth's health failed, resulting in her death at the age of fifty-five.

Over the course of their careers together, both Elizabeth and Robert were prolific, producing hundreds of poems. Even before they met, the two tended to use function words similarly. This may explain why the two were so attracted to one another long before they ever corresponded. As you can see in the graph, the LSM statistics indicate that their use of function words was quite similar before they met and for most of their marriage. During their one-and-a-half-year courtship, however, the poetry they wrote diverged. This was a period when Elizabeth struggled with the decision of breaking away from her father and, in her own mind, burdening Robert with her health problems.

As you ponder the figure, you might be curious to know who is responsible for the increasing and decreasing LSM over time. After all, LSM has been likened to a dance between two partners. Can we determine if one of the dancers is more responsible for the occasional faltering in the dance? In fact, we can. Closer inspection of both poets' use of function words suggests that Robert was impressively steady in his writing style over the course of his career, whereas Elizabeth tended to alter the ways she used function words from one period to the next. For example, during most of their time together, Elizabeth's use of

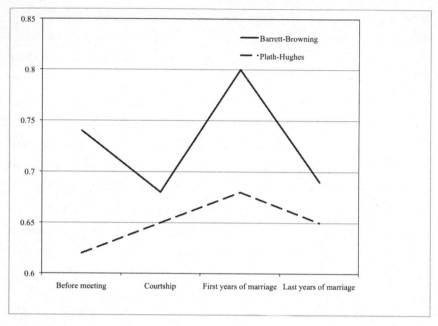

Language style matching (LSM) scores between the works of Elizabeth Barrett and Robert Browning and of Sylvia Plath and Ted Hughes. The higher the LSM score, the more similarly the two poets used function words.

function words tended to mirror Robert's. However, during her diffi-cult courtship year and as her health declined toward the end of her life, she tended to withdraw into her own world, writing less like Rob-ert and less similarly to her own writing at other times of her life.

SYLVIA PLATH AND TED HUGHES

Whereas the Brownings' marriage is often idealized by modern writers, the relationship between Sylvia Plath and Ted Hughes is not. Plath was born in Boston and met the British-born Hughes while she was on a Fulbright scholarship at Cambridge University. Both were con-sidered rising young stars in the poetry world. Her writing was often emotional, confessional, and occasionally whimsical. His was more cerebral, often dealing with nature and myth. Four months after meeting at a party, they married—she was twenty-four; he was twenty-six.

During the first four years of their marriage, both experienced personal and professional success. Relative to Plath, Hughes's writing came easily and he won several awards. About five years into the marriage, Plath's health started to fail, including several bouts with influenza, an appendectomy, and a miscarriage. She accurately suspected Hughes of being unfaithful—often causing her to fly into violent fits of rage. Within a year, Hughes left Plath for another woman. Plath, who had a history of depression before her marriage, sank into a period of despondency. Even though she continued with her writing, she became increasingly isolated from her friends. Less than a year after her separation from Hughes, at the age of thirty, she committed suicide.

It is interesting to compare the language styles of Plath and Hughes over the course of their relationship—especially in comparison with the Brownings. As is apparent in the figure, Plath and Hughes had very different linguistic styles before they met. Hers was far more personal and immediate compared to his more objective, distanced style. During their relatively happy years, their styles converged to some degree before veering apart during the last three years of her life.

It is also interesting to see how the two couples differed in their language style overall. The much happier marriage of the Brownings was associated with greater language style matching across all phases of their lives compared with the Plath-Hughes relationship. It would be a mistake to conclude that language style matching was the cause of the Brownings' success or the Plath-Hughes's marital failure. Instead, the matching of function words between two people merely reflects the fact that the two people tend to think alike. It is even riskier to make bold statements about LSM and relationships by looking at people's professional writing—especially when the two may be writing about very different topics aimed at different audiences.

BEYOND LOVE: ADMIRATION AND CONTEMPT
BETWEEN FREUD AND JUNG

LSM analyses can tell us something about close intimate relationships. The instant messages between dating couples helped reveal which couples were most likely to succeed and fail. The more esoteric poetry analyses allowed us to infer the similarity in thinking between married poets, and, by extension, pointed to the high and low spots in their relationships.

But there is much more to LSM than romantic love and heartbreak. The analysis of function words can be applied to any kind of relationship between two people. As long as we have ongoing communications between people—letters, e-mails, Twitter interactions—we can use the LSM technology to assess the degree to which the correspondents are in synchrony with each other. After studying the language and marital relationships of poets, Molly Ireland and I turned our attention to relationships where a complete set of correspondence existed between two people. Depending on your perspective, this could be a relationship of love, a relationship of identification, an unresolved Oedipal complex, or just two friends.

The relationship between Sigmund Freud and Carl Jung lies at the heart of the history of psychology and psychiatry. By the late 1800s, Freud's ideas about psychoanalysis were beginning to shake the foundations of Western thought. In a series of articles, he argued that people's personalities and daily behaviors were guided by unconscious processes, many of which were highly sexual. He also promoted the idea that early childhood experiences shaped people's mental health for the rest of their lives. Not only was Freud a creative thinker but he was also keenly aware of the mass appeal of his approach. One concern he harbored was that his work would be marginalized as reflecting a Jewish way of thinking.

Enter the young, ambitious, and Christian Swiss scholar Carl Jung. Fresh out of medical school, Jung became fascinated by the psychological underpinnings of thought disorders such as schizophrenia and the nature of the unconscious. In 1906, Jung mailed Freud a copy of

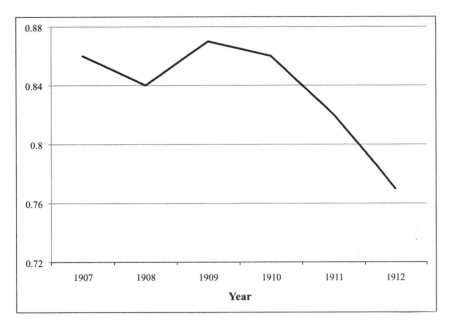

Language style matching scores in the correspondence between Sigmund Freud and Carl Jung. The higher the number, the more closely the two men matched in their use of function words in their letters to each other.

his first book and Freud reciprocated with a recent article. After a handful of letters back and forth, they became close friends. Most scholars agree that they both liked each other immensely but, at the same time, were not blind to the professional advantages of a close relationship. In fact, after their first face-to-face meeting, Freud proclaimed Jung to be his "dear friend and heir" in a letter. By 1908, Jung was able to write to Freud, "let me enjoy your friendship not as one between equals but as that of father and son. This distance appears to me fitting and natural."

Between 1906 and 1913, at least 337 letters were exchanged between the two men. During these years, Freud's reputation skyrocketed. Jung was becoming a force of his own, and by 1911, tension between the two men started to build. Jung felt that Freud was emphasizing sexuality too much; Freud felt Jung was disloyal in not adhering to Freud's own view. During the last months of their correspondence, Jung accused Freud of arrogance and being closed-minded. Freud responded that that they should "abandon . . . personal relations entirely."

Analyzing the function words of the letters between Freud and Jung revealed a predictable pattern in terms of their language style matching. As you can see in the graph on the previous page, their style matching was exceptionally high in their first four years but then dropped precipitously after that. Closer analyses indicated that both men were equally invested in the relationship during the first years. However, toward the end, Freud was the one who disengaged and whose language changed more. Indeed, in one of his last letters to Jung, where he recommended they cease being friends, he added, "I shall lose nothing by it, for my only emotional tie with you has long been a thin thread—the lingering effect of past disappointments."

UNDERSTANDING CLOSE RELATIONSHIPS WITH LSM

The conversational dance is played out in many ways. Who would have ever imagined that the ways people use pronouns, prepositions, and other function words could tell us so much about their relationships? With a little computer magic, we can use LSM as a barometer of the social links between two people. Or, more specifically, as a sign of the degree to which people are in synch with one another.

What does it actually mean to say that two people are in synch? At the most basic level, people who synchronize their use of function words are paying attention to each other. They may not like each other, they may not trust each other, but they are watching and listening to each other. Fortunately, people avoid spending much time with their enemies and opt to have their best talks with people they like. Most conversations with good friends or lovers are characterized by high LSM for the same reason—they are paying attention to each other.

It is difficult to fathom how two people can quickly adapt to each other's language styles. As we've seen, it generally happens in a matter of seconds when talking with strangers. The two people immediately adjust to each other's level of formality, concreteness, emotionality, and ways of thinking. Both people are constantly keeping track of which pronouns refer to which people and so keep a running tally in their heads of who the *she, he,* or *it* refers to. To keep the conversational ball rolling, both must adapt to shifting topics. In fact, if one of the two conversational partners is momentarily distracted or begins behaving oddly (as when lying), the other person must invest even more energy to maintain the interaction.

It is easy to understand why LSM is so high in both loving conversations and heated fights. Even in most boring discussions among people who do not care about each other, style matching is surprisingly high. Fortunately, the mirror neuron system constantly monitors what is being said and helps speakers convey what needs to be said with minimal effort. There are times, of course, when style matching fails terribly. Some individuals, for example, have great difficulty in language style matching. Certain disorders such as autism can interfere with people's ability to mimic in general and to socially connect with others. Some researchers believe that autism-spectrum disorders, which include diagnoses such as Asperger's syndrome, can impede interaction due to disruption in the function of the mirror neuron system.

In reality, we don't always click with our conversational partners. In most cases, one or both of the people are simply not interested in either the conversation or the person they are talking with. Sometimes, one of the conversational partners simply doesn't want to hear what the other person has to say. For example, I was recently at a gathering where I ended up sitting next to two people, let's call them David and Ahmed. Prior to the meeting, Ahmed had learned that David had made some disparaging remarks about Ahmed's wife. David, who was unaware of Ahmed's knowledge, started a friendly story about running into a mutual friend. During that time, Ahmed avoided eye contact with David and, as soon as David's story was finished, snatched the conversational ball and began talking with me about a recent book he'd read. Whenever David attempted to join the conversation, Ahmed either ignored him or changed topic yet again. Afterward, when I asked David about the conversation, he was unaware that Ahmed had ignored everything he said and felt that the interaction had been fine.

The Ahmed-David conversation is a reminder that people are not always aware of their failure to connect with others. Much like the study with the dating couples, people may completely fail to click with one another as measured by LSM numbers but think that their interactions are normal. Our research finds that both partners in these dysfunctional interactions often fail to appreciate the problems. Perhaps the thought that the other person is subtly rejecting them is too threatening to acknowledge. Perhaps the person who is dismissing the other can't see the process either. If only the two people had the LSM Detector with them.

CHAPTER 9

Seeing Groups, Companies, and Communities Through Their Words

Management consultants sometimes distinguish among I-companies, we-companies, and they-companies. To get a rough idea of an organization's climate, they ask employees to talk about their typical workday. If employees refer to "my office" or "my company," the atmosphere of the workplace is usually fine. People working in these I-companies are reasonably happy but not particularly wedded to the company itself. However, if they refer to "our office" or "our company," pay special attention. Those in we-companies have embraced their workplace as part of their own identities. This sense of we-ness may explain why they work harder, have lower employee turnover, and have a greater sense of fulfillment about their work lives. And be very concerned if an organization's employees start calling it "the company" or, worse, "that company" and referring to their co-workers as "they." They-companies can be nightmares because workers are proclaiming that their work identity has nothing to do with them. No wonder consultants report that they-companies have unhappy workers and high turnover.

How people talk about their company is only one way to tap the group dynamics of an organization. By listening to the words people use within any group, several features about the group's inner workings can be unmasked. Through e-mails, web pages, transcripts of meetings, and other word clues, we can measure how much group members think alike. It is also possible to profile groups in terms of their cohesiveness, productivity, formality, shared history, and, in some cases, their honesty and intentions to change.

This chapter may not be of relevance to some people. If you do not have any family, co-workers, or friends, or know anyone in any organization, neighborhood, or community, you can skip this chapter and jump to the next. Everyone else should keep reading.

WE-WORDS AS IDENTITY MARKERS

I learned about I-, we-, and they-companies from a consultant I sat next to on a flight several years ago. About the same time, couples researchers were discovering some similar patterns. In a typical study, married couples would be invited into the lab and encouraged to talk either about their marriage or about a problem in their relationship. Sparks would sometimes fly—sometimes in good ways, sometimes not.

In general, the more a couple used we-words when being interviewed about their marriage, the better. When couples used the warm-and-fuzzy *we* that said "my spouse and I," it signified a healthier relationship and, in some studies, predicted how long their marriage would last. Interestingly, the use of we-words only predicts a good relationship if the members of the couple are in the presence of an interviewer. Other studies where married couples were asked to wear a digital recorder for several days failed to find any patterns with we-words. The use of we-words around just one other person often means "you" or "everybody but you." A couple's use of we-words when talking to a *third party* predicts a satisfying relationship. However, *we* use for couples talking only to *each other* rarely predicts the quality of the relationship.

In the laboratory, when talking about marital disagreements, we-words indicated a good relationship whereas the use of you-words suggested problems. The use of you-words, such as *you, your,* and *yourself,* were most apparent in toxic conversations—usually where the two participants were accusing each other of various shortcomings.

We-words may even save your life. In one project, patients with heart failure were interviewed with their spouses. They were asked a series of questions, including "As you think back on how the two of you have coped with the heart condition, what do you think you have done best?" The more the spouses used we-words in their answers, the healthier the patients were six months later. The use of we-words by spouses indicated that they viewed their partner's health problem as a shared problem that both were committed to fixing. When both members of the relationship were working together to cope with the illness, it reduced the physical and emotional stress on the patient.

We-words may even save your life if you are perfectly healthy. Analyses of commercial airline cockpit recordings have found that poor communication among the flight crew has contributed to over half of all airline crashes in the last century. In some cases, pilots established a toxic atmosphere that discouraged dissent. In other cases, one or more crew members were distracted and failed to listen to critical information from others. A recurring theme has been that the most effective crews are ones that are close-knit and feel they are part of a team. For example, Bryan Sexton and Robert Helmreich analyzed the language of flight crews during extended flight simulations. The more the crew used we-words, the fewer errors it made. In analyses of cockpit recordings of airline crashes, the ones characterized by clear human error are associated with much lower use of we-words compared to those caused by unavoidable mechanical errors.

Words such as *we*, *us*, and *our* can be powerful markers of identity. When people tell complete strangers about "our marriage," "our business," or "our community," they are making a public statement about who they are and with whom they identify. "Our marriage," for example, is a shared and joint entity. Similarly, "our business" and "our community" are groups that are a part of who we are.

THE EXPANDING *WE*: THE PERSON AND THE GROUP

The ways people think about themselves are constantly shifting. The shift between the use of *I* and *we* can be remarkably subtle and can occur almost instantaneously. In conversations, both speakers and listeners may not even consciously hear which pronouns are uttered. Nevertheless, the speakers' use of *we* to refer to the listeners and themselves has psychological and social meaning.

You can get a sense of this shift in the following overheard conversation between two people talking about a real estate deal. Alex, about forty-five years old, is a lawyer who dabbles in real estate deals. Liz Ann, around forty years old, successfully got out of the stock market at its peak and has been involved in a number of investment projects.

ALEX: **I've** got a deal you might be interested in. It involves buying that property on Oak Street.

LIZ ANN: The last thing **I** need is another fight with the Darden Group.

ALEX: This isn't with Darden. The original owners have approached **me** about selling it for tax purposes.

LIZ ANN: What are they asking? What would be **my** risk?

ALEX: Probably 350, with the usual side deals. **We** could offer 300.

LIZ ANN: **I'm** not sure this is the right time. But if *we* sidetracked Darden, **I'd** be happy.

Clearly the two people know each other and have worked together in the past. At the beginning of the brief conversation, the two are separate beings with their own agendas. They both use I-words each time they speak. In the next-to-last line, Alex tosses out "We could offer 300." In Alex's head, the two people have subtly morphed from two individuals to one group with common goals. The final line by Liz Ann suggests a possible acceptance of their shared identity. Even though Alex might not have consciously picked up Liz Ann's use of *we*, his brain likely detected that she was leaning toward investing in the Oak Street property.

The use of we-words often signals that a person feels a part of the group. Experienced workers in sales jobs are often attentive to the ways people shift in their use of we-words. As suggested by the real estate conversation, when a customer starts tossing in we-words to refer to the salesperson-customer relationship, an important emotional bond has developed. If you are the one doing the selling, can you speed this relationship up by using we-words yourself? Probably not much. The premature use of we-words, much like the language of a politician, is often perceived as disingenuous and manipulative.

The sense of "groupness" is often illusory. Sometimes people feel that they are a solid part of the group they are in, and at other times, while around the exact same people, they feel detached, alienated, or alone. By tracking people's use of we-words and I-words, it is possible to detect their perceptions of group identity. The same language analyses can also tell us about the groups themselves.

THE GROWING SENSE OF GROUPNESS: FROM ME TO US

The longer people talk with others, the more they use we-words and the less they use I-words. As we get to know others, we let down our guard and start to accept them. The pattern of increasing we-words and decreasing I-words emerges across a wide array of groups.

Speed-dating is the perfect place to start. Think back to the speed-dating project in the last chapter where strangers met for ten consecutive four-minute "dates" back-to-back. Even in these ridiculously short meetings, people's use of we- and I-words changed quickly and predictably. Minute-by-minute in the brief speed-dating sessions, I-words for both people dropped and we-words increased.

The *I*-drop/*we*-jump effect can be seen far outside the dating context. In some studies, students visit a psychology laboratory and end up talking to a complete stranger for fifteen minutes in a get-to-know-you setting. In the first five minutes, both participants typically talk a little about their backgrounds, their majors, and where they live. Because both people are describing themselves, they tend to use I-words at relatively high rates. During the next five minutes, they talk less about themselves as they begin to establish common ground between them. By the final five minutes, their use of I-words drops between 10 and 50 percent compared to their starting levels. At the same time, their use of we-words increases anywhere from 20 to 200 percent. The patterns are even stronger in online get-to-know-you chats between two strangers.

The same shifts occur in larger groups. In a business school experiment with four-person groups, people worked on a complex group-decision task for thirty minutes. Same results: People in the groups decreased their I-word usage by 19 percent and increased their we-words by 39 percent from the first ten minutes to the last ten minutes.

More interesting are shifts in we- and I-words in real-world groups that last over hours, days, months, and even years. The airline cockpit project discussed earlier found similar patterns. The longer a crew is together, the more the group uses we-words.

And the *I*-drop/*we*-jump effect extends to bigger groups over much larger time frames. One project involved eighteen engineers, economists, and computer experts working on a complex online national defense project over almost two years. Another included around twenty professional therapists who met twice a year for three years as part of their professional training. Another project tracked the lyrics of the Beatles over their ten years of singing together. For all these groups, I-word usage dropped month by month, year by year, just as we-word use increased.

What does all this mean? The more time we spend with other people, the more our identity becomes fused with them. We may not necessarily like or trust them but as our history becomes intertwined, we see ourselves as part of the same group. An interesting corollary of this phenomenon happens as we age. By and large, the older we get, the more time we have spent with virtually everyone around us. One might even predict that older people would use fewer I-words and more we-words than when they were younger. And it's true. In a study of language use among almost three thousand people, those over the age of seventy used 54 percent more we-words and 79 percent fewer I-words than adolescents.

BRINGING "US" TOGETHER: WHEN EVENTS CREATE GROUP IDENTITY

Gradually adopting the identity of a group is a natural process that we rarely notice. One minute in a conversation our opinions are sprinkled with *I* and the next with *we*. It just happens. There are other times, however, when the ways we identify with a group change quickly and dramatically.

The simplest examples can be seen with our allegiances to sports teams. One of the most clever social psychology experiments to demonstrate this was run in the mid-1970s by Robert Cialdini and his colleagues. Students who were attending universities with top-ranked football teams were called in the middle of football season as part of a survey purportedly dealing with campus issues. In the previous weeks, their home football teams had won a major game but also had lost another. After a few preliminary questions, the interviewer asked about one of the two pivotal games in the season, "Can you tell me the outcome of that game?"

If their team had won, they usually answered, "We won." But if their team had failed to win the game, their answer was more likely "They lost." Taking partial credit for your team's winning is a form of basking in reflected glory. Basically, we want to be close to groups that are successful and distance ourselves from losers.

The sense of wanting to belong to a powerful group may have its roots in evolution. Most social animals seek the protection of a group when they are threatened. Even the appearance of an outsider can make people more aware of their own social network. In the same football project, Cialdini's interviewers sometimes claimed that they lived in the same town as the respondents. Other times, the interviewers reported that they were from out of state. In other words, half the time the participants thought they were talking to someone like them whereas the other half they believed that they were being interviewed by a football foreigner. The us-them effect was much stronger when talking with the outsider. When reminded of competing groups, our own membership in a successful group becomes more important.

The need to be part of a group is most likely to occur when an outside group threatens the very existence of our own group. Nothing galvanizes people more quickly than a physical attack against them. In the United States, the September 11, 2001, attacks provided a powerful example. In the first days of September, George W. Bush had been president for less than eight months and had an approval rating of about 54 percent. Within a week of the 9/11 attacks, his ratings skyrocketed to almost 90 percent. In every city in the country, people flew American flags and all the news stations discussed the outpouring of patriotism and national pride.

You may recall the large-scale project that we conducted on thousands of blog entries that spanned a four-month period starting two months before 9/11. Within minutes of the attacks, LiveJournal.com bloggers started switching from the use of I-words to we-words. In fact, this pattern continued for several weeks afterward. Coinciding with the elevation in we-words was the brief drop but then long-term increase in positive emotion words. A horrible trauma such as 9/11 has the unintended effect of bringing people together, making them less self-focused, and within a few days, making them more happy.

That natural and man-made disasters can bring people together is not a new idea. When residents of London were enduring an extended period of nightly bombings by the Germans in World War II, several indicators pointed to the much tighter social bonds among the people. One frequently cited statistic is that suicide rates dropped dramatically during this period. More recent data found large drops in suicide rates in the weeks after September 11, 2001, and, in the United Kingdom, after the 2006 subway bombings. You will recall similar findings discussed earlier surrounding the eruption of the Mount St. Helens volcano in 1980. Those from cities that had suffered the most damage later reported they were glad that it had happened in their lifetime and that the eruption had brought the community together.

Study after study has found the same pattern of effects, many of which have been mentioned elsewhere in the book. The *we*-jump and *I*-drop phenomenon is as reliable as, well, taxes and death. Examples include:

- Newspaper articles, letters to the editors of newspapers, and online tributes following the A&M bonfire tragedy that killed twelve students in 1999. The disaster galvanized the student body, resulting in tighter social connections than ever before. Illness rates over the next six months dropped 40 percent from the year before, unlike all other large universities in the region.

- Online chat groups talking about the death of Princess Diana in a car accident in 1997. The effect lasted about a week.

- Online bulletin boards discussing the Oklahoma City bombing that killed 168 people in 1995. Even in the earliest days of shared online communication, people rushed to talk about their feelings.

- Hundreds of essays of college students in New Orleans four months after Hurricane Katrina destroyed the city.

- Hundreds of interviews and surveys of people across Spain in the weeks after the March 11, 2004, Madrid subway bombings.

- Google Internet searches in England following the London underground bombings in 2005, Pakistan after the assassination of Benazir Bhutto in 2007, India after the attacks in Mumbai in 2008, and

Poland after the airline crash that killed the country's president and other leaders in 2010, which all showed comparable trends.

THE USE OF we-words and the sense of group solidarity is not something that just occurs when people are threatened. Much like the football example, people embrace their group identity when it succeeds or behaves admirably. Google Labs has developed a marvelous application called Google Trends (www.google.com/trends) that allows users to track the words people use when searching the Internet. With it, anyone can see how particular cities, states, or countries use words over time. Using Google Trends, it is easy to come up with examples of increased we-word use during times of cultural pride. Nationwide, use of we-words increased in the United States following the election of Barack Obama in 2008 and in Britain after the success of the Conservatives in their 2010 national election. In Canada, use of we-words spiked in February 2010, during the Winter Olympics, which it hosted.

THE IMPORTANCE AND LIMITS OF GROUP IDENTITY

We-words tell us about group identity. By analyzing them closely, it is possible to get a sense of the speakers' connections with others. Knowing if someone feels that they are an integral part of a marriage, a family, their company, their community, or their country is valuable information. In fact, many psychologists and sociologists have devoted their careers to understanding group identity. People who identify with a group are simply more loyal to it. They tend to rely on people in their group and distrust people outside it. Group identity has frequently been associated with stereotyping, prejudice, and discrimination. Many family feuds, regional battles, instances of genocide, and world wars have been fought where group identities served as the rallying cries.

If you are interested in groups and how they work, knowing about the people's identities is a good first step. But it's only part of the story.

Just because I am a member of various types of groups doesn't mean that I necessarily like all the people in each group, would work well with them, or would even like to eat lunch with them. To really understand how groups work, it is important to track how they communicate with each other.

BEYOND GROUP IDENTITY: CAPTURING GROUP DYNAMICS

It's easy to forget that the reason language evolved was so we could communicate with other people. To appreciate how a group functions, look at how members of the group interact with one another. When people in the group are talking, are other members of the group listening? When they are working on problems together, do they tend to talk in similar ways?

In the chapter dealing with close relationships, the topic of language style matching, or LSM, was discussed. LSM measures if two people are in synch with one another by looking at how similarly they use stealth words—personal pronouns, articles, auxiliary verbs, and the like. The more similarly two members of a couple use stealth words when talking, e-mailing, or IMing, the more the couple is "clicking" and the more likely the couple will still be together a few months later.

As with couples, all groups can vary in the degree to which they are cohesive, in synch, or clicking. You may have recently had dinner with a group of friends and marveled at how your group was in perfect harmony. Meeting again a week later, the same group may have been completely out of step for no apparent reason. Most of us have had similar ups and downs with group meetings at work, at home, or in online chats. By measuring each person's relative use of stealth words in these interactions, we can begin to get a sense of how well the group is working and even identify where the problems might be.

SMALL WORKING GROUPS:
SOLIDARITY AND PRODUCTIVITY

Imagine that you are thrown into a work group that must come up with a solution to a complex task. As part of a business school exercise, your group must decide if it would be a good investment to buy LuProds Manufacturing Company. LuProds, you learn, has designed a new gear system for bicycles that could revolutionize the bicycle business. No one in your five-person work group knows anything about LuProds or the bicycle business. Over the next four hours, however, your group must write a report that lays out your recommendations backed up with solid information. To add to the pressure, there are ten other groups doing the same task and it is imperative that your group's performance is among the best.

To succeed on a task like this, each group member must take on an independent task. Someone must learn something about the bicycle business, the gear business, the economic history of LuProds, its competitors, the quality of LuProds's management team, and potential other LuProds buyers. The team members must work closely together in a coordinated way to come up with an overall recommendation based on all the information available.

What makes for a good working group? Even within the first few minutes of your group being together, we can begin to predict how it will do on the task. This may not surprise you but the ways the group members use function words with each other is one of the best predictors. Variations of this project have been run in business schools and psychology departments around the world. In two studies, my colleagues and I calculated style matching scores for each person in the group. So, for example, if there were five people in the group, we could determine the degree to which each of the five people matched with the average of everyone else in the group. The average style matching, or LSM, score for each group tapped the degree to which the entire group was talking in similar ways. The more group members talked alike, the more cohesive the group. In other words, higher LSM scores reflected more tightly knit groups.

More important, style matching was related to how well the group performed. If people in a group are using similar function words at similar rates, the team performs better. Even before the groups turned in their answers, our language analyses could make reasonable predictions about the ultimate success of the different groups. At least in controlled laboratory settings, the use of stealth words such as pronouns and prepositions among the people in the group showed that the participants were all on the same page—they all shared common assumptions about the task and what needed to be done.

LARGER REAL-WORLD GROUPS: WIKIPEDIA

Lab studies of group behavior tell us how people might behave in more natural settings. How many times in your life will you be in a group with four twenty-year-olds making a major business decision on a topic you know nothing about over a four-hour period? Does language style matching predict success in actual real-world groups? The answer is in Wikipedia.

Created in 2001, Wikipedia is an online encyclopedia-like information source that has several million articles. Many of the articles are expertly written and have been carefully edited by dozens, sometimes hundreds of people. For the most commonly read articles, an elaborate informal review takes place. Often, a single person will begin an article on a particular topic. If it is a topic of interest, others will visit the site and frequently make changes to the original article. In many ways, a Wikipedia article is really two articles. The casual visitor sees only the final product. However, by clicking on the "discussion" tab, it is possible to find conversations among the various contributors. These interactions are often quite professional, sometimes detailed and thorough, but occasionally downright rude and nasty.

What makes Wikipedia amazing is that it reflects a form of intellectual democracy that actually works. Although many scholars would be loath to admit it, Wikipedia is often the first professional site they visit to learn about a new topic. It is also a rich source of language data for someone interested in how groups work. In fact, it so intrigued one of my graduate students, Yla Tausczik, that she enlisted the help of the University of Texas at Austin's supercomputer team to download all of Wikipedia, including the behind-the-scenes conversations—a nontrivial task, I might add.

For starters, Yla identified about a hundred American cities that had relatively extensive Wikipedia entries. The cities were all midsized, ranging in population from about 500,000 to 1.5 million people. Each city's site had been edited multiple times by at least fifty different people over several years, so that there had been lengthy discussions concerning the entries. In addition to the articles themselves, each entry had gone through a review process. Indeed, all articles are categorized by Wikipedia along a continuum from "stub" (meaning not worthy of even being called an entry) to exemplary.

The degree to which the various editors used similar language in communicating with each other reflected higher-quality articles. Just as in the lab studies, teams of Wikipedia authors and editors who are in synch with each other—as measured by their similar use of stealth words—produce the best, most authoritative articles. Language style matching in the real world reflects better real-world products.

EVEN LARGER REAL-WORLD GROUPS: COMMUNITIES AND CRAIGSLIST

If we can examine the cohesiveness and interconnections of a changing group of editors on Wikipedia, why not look at real communities? Some towns are more tightly knit than others. Most of us have occasionally visited towns or neighborhoods where people appeared to be remarkably similar in their opinions, food preferences, and social behaviors. In others, virtually no one seems to know their neighbors or has a sense of the history or values of their community.

The Wikipedia project hints that it might be possible to assess the connections between people by simply measuring how people in a community use language. Another amazing Internet development has been the growth of the site Craigslist.org. In most U.S. cities, Craigslist allows people to buy, sell, and give away a large number of goods and services.

The ads themselves are free and people can write as much as they like and even include pictures. The demise of many American print newspapers has been attributed, in part, to Craigslist in that people are more likely to sell their cars, rent their houses, or give away their puppies on Craigslist than use paid classified advertisements in their newspaper.

In 2008, my students and I saved copies of all Craigslist ads in thirty different midsize communities across the United States. Because there are so many categories of ads, we only looked at ads for cars, furniture, and roommates. Within each category, we analyzed between six thousand and ten thousand ads and evaluated how people in the different cities used function words. More specifically, we were curious how similarly different communities used pronouns, prepositions, articles, etc.

The results were fascinating. In several of the communities, people tended to write their ads using the same language style as their neighbors. In Portland, people generally wrote in a personal style with a slight negative emotional tone. People in Salt Lake City, on the other hand, were exceptionally upbeat in their ads. Although Craigslist writers in Portland and Salt Lake City may have had distinctive styles, within each city, people were thinking about their ads in the same ways. In contrast, residents of Bakersfield, California, and Greensboro, North Carolina, were much more scattershot in their writing styles—meaning some people may have been very formal in their writing and others very informal. They simply didn't speak with one voice.

Using a method similar to language style matching, we were able to calculate the degree to which residents in any given town used language in similar ways. The findings suggested that the more similar the community's use of language, the more cohesive the city.

As you look at the table that lists the ten most and least linguistically cohesive communities, the difference between them may not be immediately obvious. It's not a matter of north versus south, liberal versus conservative, rich versus poor, or even a function of the towns' racial makeup, age distribution, or migration into or out of the city. Rather, one of the most striking differences between the two lists is that the most cohesive communities have higher and more equal income

RANKING OF COMMUNITIES BY LANGUAGE STYLE MATCHING STATISTICS FOR CRAIGSLIST ADS

MOST LINGUISTICALLY COHESIVE (TOP 10)	LEAST LINGUISTICALLY COHESIVE (BOTTOM 10)
Portland, Oregon	Bakersfield, California
Salt Lake City, Utah	Greensboro, North Carolina
Raleigh, North Carolina	Louisville, Kentucky
Birmingham, Alabama	Oklahoma City, Oklahoma
Rochester, New York	Dayton, Ohio
Hartford, Connecticut	El Paso, Texas
New Orleans, Louisiana	Jacksonville, Florida
Richmond, Virginia	Columbia, South Carolina
Worcester, Massachusetts	Tulsa, Oklahoma
Tucson, Arizona	Albany, New York

Note: Cohesiveness is calculated by the degree to which people in the various communities used function words at comparable levels in their Craigslist ads.

distributions than the least cohesive. Using a statistic called a Gini co-efficient, demographers can determine the degree to which wealth is spread around in any given city, state, or country. Cities where the residents use language in similar ways tend to be communities that are more similar in terms of their incomes. The bigger the split between the rich and poor of a community, the more varied their writing styles for Craigslist ads.

You can see why the Gini statistic is important. In communities where there is a much larger split between the rich and the poor, it's less likely that the different elements of the city will interact. As the range of income within a town becomes smaller, the residents will likely have more in common with one another and should talk more with others. Not coincidentally, they should also have more objects and services that others in the community would want to exchange on Craigslist.

The magic of this project is not about the links between income distributions and social patterns in cities. Rather, it shows how words in the most mundane of places can reveal important information about a community's social ties. All groups, whether families, work groups, companies, or entire cities, leave trails of their social and psychological lives behind in the words their members use in communicating with each other. Words are one of the human-made elements that connect our thoughts and ideas across people. By tracking our words, we get a sense of the social fabric.

GROUP SPOTTING: HOW WORDS REVEAL WHAT A GROUP IS DOING AND WHERE IT IS

Consider what we know so far. Individuals use words—especially pronouns—to signify their sense of belongingness to a wide range of ever-shifting groups. Whereas we-ness measures reflect feelings of group identity, synchrony measures, such as language style matching, tap a shared worldview by the group members.

Taken together, the various findings point to the shared mind-set of most groups. Within any group—whether a family, school, work team, or even a community—people soon start talking alike. In small groups, they discuss the same topics with each other, and in a sense, it isn't too shocking that their function words are similar. But as groups get larger and not everyone necessarily talks with everyone else, it is impressive that the group still maintains its own linguistic style.

Sociolinguists would not be surprised that large groups share similar linguistic styles. There is now a generation of important research tracking how neighborhoods, cities, and entire regions of a country begin to develop their own unique accents. Further, people can usually modulate their accents depending on who they are talking with. If my wife gets a phone call at home, I can usually make a reasonable guess who she is talking to by her cadence, volume, tone, and even accent. If my brain were wired differently, I could probably also hear her function word use and make even better guesses.

Think about the implications of the "contagion" of function word use. If function words really work a bit like accents, our language should vary depending on the group we are in, what the group is likely doing, and perhaps even where the group resides. We may not be aware of it but we likely shift in our use of function words depending on what groups we happen to be in and what the groups happen to be doing.

Taken together, every group has its own linguistic fingerprint. Parts of the fingerprint may reveal how well the group works together and the degree to which its members identify with the group. Other parts of the fingerprint reflect how the group thinks and feels and how emotionally open, formal, detached, and so forth it is. In theory, the language from any group gathering should provide clues to the dynamics of the group and its members.

WORD CATCHING IN PUBLIC PLACES:
THE SOCIAL ECOLOGY OF WORDS

Groups, of course, have different purposes. Sometimes, we are in groups that work on a task, play a game, or just socialize. Different tasks demand different ways of speaking. By analyzing the words that different group tasks demand, we can get a new perspective on the nature of the groups themselves.

Several years ago, my students and I carried digital recorders to various public places. We would slowly walk through restaurants, crowded hallways, post offices, college basketball and young children's soccer games, classrooms, and poolrooms with our recorders held high. The "word catching" project had very few rules other than we had to keep moving the entire time and not hang around any given conversation for more than a few seconds. The goal was simply to catch words in different types of locations. Over the years, we collected additional language samples that included people working in groups and places where strangers were meeting for the first time. One by one, every language sample was transcribed and added to our Word Catcher archive.

"Why bother doing such a screwy project?" many of my friends and colleagues would often ask. I wanted to know if and how people changed the ways they used words depending on the situations they were in. The results were clear: Every context has its own linguistic fingerprint.

Spend a minute and ponder the findings in the "Language of Situations" table. Every general situation is associated with a very different word pattern. When people are seated and talking with others over lunch or dinner, or even seated in a park, they use high rates of I-words, he-she words, past tense, and negations and, at the same time, very low rates of articles. This may sound obscure but it's not. These word patterns suggest storytelling. And, in fact, reading the transcripts, it is obvious that people who are seated and talking with others are telling stories about themselves and others.

In sports settings, the language is more upbeat and lacking in introspection. Whether playing billiards or watching a sporting event, both men and women are immersed in the game and not focused on themselves. They are living in the moment while feeling as though they are part of a group. This is probably the allure of sports—they serve as an escape from the self. There is an interesting parallel with the language of work groups. They, too, use high rates of we-words and low rates of I-words. The big difference is that work groups use far more complex language and tend to express more negative feelings.

People who are talking with others while walking around are personal, upbeat, and superficial. "Hey, how ya doing? I'm going to

THE LANGUAGE OF SITUATIONS

CONTEXT	HIGH-USAGE WORDS	LOW-USAGE WORDS	TRANSLATION
Seated meals, cafés, on a bench in a park	I-words, he-she, past tense, negations	Articles	Telling stories, low in details
Sporting events, playing sports	We-words, short words, impersonal pronouns, present tense	I-words, future tense, conjunctions	In the moment, with the group, the simple life
Working groups	We-words, impersonal pronouns, big words, articles, prepositions, conjunctions, negative emotions	I-words, you-words, he-she, past tense, adverbs	Complex, analytic, serious, with the group
People in motion: hallways, post office	I-words, you-words, verbs, present tense, positive emotions	Articles, prepositions	Brief, superficial, in the moment, and pleasant
Talking with strangers	Adverbs, quantifiers, positive emotions	We-words, impersonal pronouns, past tense, negations	Upbeat, descriptive, but no shared past

Serena's later. Things are going good. Later, dude." No deep analytic thinking here—just maintaining a friendly public face. It's interesting to compare the superficial people in motion with strangers who happen to be waiting for an experiment or are thrown together in a room to simply get to know each other. Like people in motion, strangers talking to each other tend to be upbeat. They are different in being less personal and more vague in their claims.

These same language patterns appear for online chat rooms as well. Chat rooms for strangers trying to meet others use words like our stranger groups. People in chat rooms devoted to sports talk like real people at real sporting events. And chat rooms made up of people who know each other have conversations that use words similar to those among friends at dinner.

To get a sense of how different the language of these contexts is, imagine that we gave our computer hundreds of new transcripts from recordings across similar situations. How well could the computer categorize which language went with which situation? In this example, there are five different contexts or situations, meaning that a computer should correctly assign language samples to the right category 20 percent of the time by chance alone. Our computers do much better, averaging 84 percent correct.

Think about the logic of these findings. *The situations we are in define the words we use.* Imagine spending a weekend with your friends. If you go to a sporting event, you will use one set of words; you then go to a bar and you call forth a different group of words. All of a sudden, you find yourselves in a grocery store and yet another pattern of words is exchanged. The effects are so strong and predictable, one could even claim that the situations you are in *demand* that you talk in a certain way. OK, "demand" is a little strong. Nevertheless, where we are and what we are doing primes us to think and talk in highly specific ways.

On the surface, this may sound trivial. When playing or watching sports, people tend to talk about the game. When eating dinner with friends, most of us talk about shared friends or experiences from the past. Contexts or situations dictate the *topics* of conversation, which undoubtedly influence people's use of stealth or function words. But there is more to it. Function words tell us the *ways* that groups and the people who inhabit them are paying attention to their worlds, relating to others, thinking, and feeling.

The word-catching studies also provide an interesting and almost upside-down way of thinking about stealth words. Most of this chapter and book has been devoted to showing how the words people use reflect *who* they are. These same words can also tell us *where* people are and *what* they are doing. Feed the transcript of a conversation into the right computer and it will tell you about the individuals in the conversation, their relationships, and their situation.

TRACKING THE GEOGRAPHICAL

LOCATION OF GROUPS

This is where things start to get a little creepy. If groups of people tend to talk and write in similar ways, it should be possible to estimate the physical location of the groups. This goes beyond estimating if someone is at the mall, in a park, or eating in a restaurant. By using both content and function words, it is possible to make educated guesses about which particular mall, park, or restaurant the speakers happen to be visiting.

The logic of linguistic tracking is similar to that of identifying accents. Depending on what country you live in, you probably do better than chance in picking out which region a speaker hails from. In the United States, the southern drawl, the midwestern twang, and the New York dialect can often be spotted within a few seconds by listeners. Computerized text analysis programs, of course, don't analyze accents but instead focus on specific words or word patterns that may be common to different geographic regions.

Regional differences in the naming of things exist for a large array of foods, objects, and behaviors. If you want a soft drink in the Northeast, you will likely ask for a soda, in the South you will ask for a Coke (meaning any type of soft drink—not just Coca-Cola), and in the Midwest, a pop. Depending on where you live, you might refer to that green leafy herb in salsa or Vietnamese pho as cilantro, Mexican parsley, Chinese parsley, or coriander. If you don't want the truck in front of you to splash mud on your front windshield, you better hope that it is equipped with mud flaps (in the West), splash guards (in the Midwest), or splash aprons (in the East). And if you are driving in England, hope it has mud flaps (two words), or in Australia, mudflaps (one word). Later, when you go for a row in your canoe, be careful because you don't want it to tip (U.S. East and West) or tump (U.S. South) over.

One can imagine that by cataloging regional names, we could begin to isolate where people are from. All that would be needed would be to wait until speakers or writers mention their words for soft drinks, spices, or how their boats rolled over. Instead of waiting for relatively obscure words or topics to emerge, it might be more efficient to track more common words. Function words, perhaps?

AS WE'VE SEEN, stealth words vary by context. It also happens that they can vary according to the geographical regions. Some regional differences in function word use are well known. For example, if people are talking to several of their friends, they might refer to them as "all of you" if from Seattle, "youse guys" if from New York, "y'all" if from the American South, or even "yat" in Louisiana (as in "Where are you at?").

Even in relatively formal writing, regional differences exist in function word use. Cindy Chung and I had the opportunity to test this idea using thousands of essays people had written in response to the nationally syndicated radio program *This I Believe*. The original version of *This I Believe* ran briefly in the 1950s with journalist and radio commentator Edward R. Murrow. Over the course of a couple of years, Murrow invited some of the cultural leaders of the time to summarize their most important beliefs. The weekly broadcasts of politicians, sports stars, scientists, philosophers, and others captured the imagination of radio listeners. In 2005, Jay Allison and Dan Gediman resurrected the idea for National Public Radio. Rather than relying on celebrities, regular listeners were encouraged to contribute their own *This I Believe* essays. Over a four-year period, over seventy thousand essays were submitted, although only about two hundred were ever read on air. Most of the essays were eventually posted online for the public to read (www.thisibelieve.org).

Working with Allison and Gediman, we analyzed about 37,500 essays. A number of the stories were riveting, some tragic, many funny, most touching and inspirational. Regional differences emerged in terms of the topics of the essays themselves. Stories about sports were most common in the Midwest, racial issues in the South, and science in the Northeast.

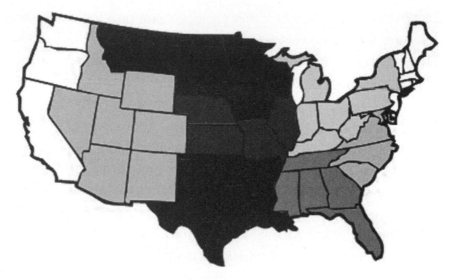

Immediacy Map

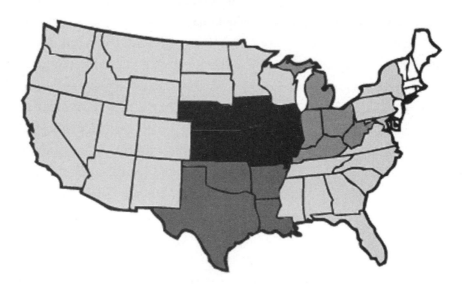

Making Distinctions Map

Relative use of words within an immediacy cluster (I-words, short words, present-tense verbs, nonuse of articles) and making-distinction cluster (exclusive words, negations, causal words, nonuse of inclusive words). Darker regions reflect higher usage. Language samples are based on about 37,500 U.S. This I Believe essays.

Not only did people differ in their topics, but they also differed in terms of their function words. As you can see on the top map, people in the middle of the country tended to use the highest rates of I-words, present-tense verbs, and short words. As you might recall from earlier chapters, this constellation of words reflects psychological immediacy, wherein writers tend to be in the here and now. The darker areas reflect higher rates of immediacy. Contributors from the Northeast and the West were the least personal and social in their writing and the most concrete. These low levels of immediacy reflect a language style of psychological distance and formality.

Recall from earlier chapters that function words often clump together in a way that reflects analytic thinking. People who think analytically often make distinctions between ideas. In making distinctions, it is necessary to use words such as conjunctions (*but, if, or*), negations (*no, not*), and prepositions (*with, over*). In the bottom map, people in the middle of the country make the most distinctions and those in the far Northeast make the fewest.

What accounts for these regional differences? As we have seen with the language style matching, people quickly adjust their speaking styles to others around them. The more time spent conversing, the more individuals begin seeing their worlds in similar ways. As a general rule, my neighbors have the same weather, eat similar foods, share the same community events, and deal with the same schools, tax collectors, stores, and bureaucracies as I do. The people in my community share many of the same issues with those in the next town and, to a certain degree, with those in the neighboring state. But as I travel farther and farther away from home, the weather, food, cultures, and concerns begin to change. As the social and physical environments change, so do the ways people approach their worlds and talk with others.

ALTHOUGH LANGUAGE DIFFERENCES should become more pronounced over greater distances, some variations in language can spring up in neighborhoods separated by only a few blocks where weather, terrain, ethnicity, social class, and every other factor is similar. I grew up in an oil-boom town in West Texas, where most families would move in for about four years before being transferred elsewhere. Even with the constant migration, new neighborhood children would quickly adopt accents and slang consistent with that neighborhood.

Even within schools, researchers have been able to isolate different language patterns among different subgroups. In an important analysis of a Detroit high school in the early 1980s, Penelope Eckert demonstrated that the language of the school's jocks was as distinctive as that of its burnouts. Not unlike most secondary schools in the world, the different tightly knit groups adopted their own language styles in a way that reflected their group's identity.

It's not much of a stretch to imagine that different schools in the same geographical region could develop their own language styles. We have found evidence for this by analyzing over fifty thousand college admissions essays submitted by students who were accepted at the University of Texas at Austin over several years. Working with the school's admissions office, linguist David Beaver and I looked at about two thousand essays from students from nine different high schools surrounding a single large metropolitan area in Texas. The students from the various high schools did equally well in high school and their first year in college and varied only modestly in their social class and ethnic makeup. Nevertheless, the ways they used pronouns, articles, prepositions, and other function words in their essays differed from school to school. In other words, each school had its own linguistic fingerprint.

College admissions essays, like *This I Believe* stories, are unique forms of writing. Most people will write something like them only a few times in their lives—if ever. Usually, the authors sit alone in their rooms (or coffee shops) and reflect on some of the bigger issues in their lives. Their stories reflect their families, their friends and community, and their society. The inner voices that guide their word choices are driven by the ways they think, what they attend to, their emotional states at the time, and their language history.

It is little wonder that self-reflective essays mirror people's sense of place and the groups with which they spend most of their time. Even with relatively crude computer models, we can do much better than chance at estimating which part of the country, what city, and possibly what part of a city a person is from by the ways they use function words in their essays. If we are analyzing transcripts of people in conversations, these same function words provide hints to what people are doing, the situations they are in, and the nature of their connections to the people around them.

If you have paranoid tendencies, know that it is unlikely that a function-word-based predator drone will ever be developed. The words we use have always reflected *who* we are, *where* we are, and *what* we are doing. The who, where, and what have historically been obvious. Prior to the written word, if I were speaking with you, we would both know that I was talking (who), our location (where), and our current actions (what). Only through the fluke of technological advancements have we had a period where the who, where, and what of communicating became opaque. The delicious irony is that with additional advances in technology, we may eventually be able to determine the who, where, and what of communication at levels comparable to our ancestors more than five thousand years ago.

THIS CHAPTER HAS explored how the words people use in groups can reveal something about the groups themselves. Use of we-words by group members often suggests that the members identify with their group. Over time, as people become more comfortable with their group, everyone tends to use we-words more. When groups succeed or are threatened from the outside, group identity increases, with a corresponding increase in the use of we-words.

We-words reflect group identity but not the degree to which a group works well together. It may be possible to increase a team's sense of identity, but that doesn't mean the team will actually perform any better. There may be no *I* in *team* but there is no *we* in *team* either. Language analyses suggest that for groups to work best, they must think alike and pay close attention to the other team members. In all likelihood, language style matching reflects mutual interest and respect among different people in a group.

The definition of a group has been used rather loosely in this chapter. This is OK: I'm a social psychologist. What is particularly intriguing is that similar processes for the use of we-words and language style matching are apparent among dating couples, working laboratory groups, real-world work groups, online communities, and entire schools, communities, and societies. The unifying theme is that all of these groups use language to communicate. Words are the common currency of interaction whether written or spoken.

Finally, just as words of group members reveal information about group processes, they also tell us something about what groups are doing and where they are. In an odd way, function word usage is highly contagious. Whether in couples, small groups, neighborhoods, or communities, people tend to adopt the language styles of the people around them. Our words, especially our function words, inadvertently reveal what we are doing and where we are. Just as our accents, body language, and clothes reveal our social and psychological selves, so do our words.

If you are a private investigator, put away your spyglass. Instead, boot up your computer and start counting words.

CHAPTER 10

Word Sleuthing

I~N STUDYING WORDS~, I have frequently been asked to analyze language to answer questions that I would have never considered. Lawyers, historians, music lovers, political consultants, educators, intelligence agents, and others have occasionally contacted me to see if our language approach could give them a different perspective on a problem they have been thinking about.

This chapter brings together some of the more interesting projects my students and I have been playing with over the years. The topics vary quite a bit. Nevertheless, they showcase different ways words can be analyzed to answer novel questions.

USING WORDS TO IDENTIFY AUTHORS

The phone call I received from the senior partner in a law firm caught me off guard. He was curious if I could analyze an e-mail that had been sent to a member of his firm; let's call her Ms. Livingston. It was quite sensitive, he confided, and it was important that he talk directly with the person who had sent the e-mail. The only problem was that the e-mail had been sent anonymously from an untraceable e-mail address. After I agreed to look at it, he sent me the following e-mail:

> Ms. Livingston:
> I think you should know that David Simpson has perpetuated the idea that you have no credibility among your colleagues. He says you altered depositions and falsified expense reports at your last job in New York. He says this is the reason you left so abruptly.

He has spread these stories to people in various departments, including Billing, Personnel, Public Relations and to those at the executive level. It is uncertain how and when our senior partners will deal with this. But if you start getting the cold shoulder, you will know why.

When I first heard of this, I was surprised, but took what he said at face value. Of course, this was before I learned of his voracious appetite for propagating half-truths, gossip, and outright lies, all in the name of somehow making himself look knowledge-able and "better."

Such a pity. He obviously has talent, but it is all negated by his vile, malicious tongue. All I can think of is a tremendous sense of insecurity. But I digress. I just thought you would like to know.

A friend

After receiving the e-mail, Ms. Livingston turned it over to the law firm. She dismissed the rumor as provably false but was concerned that if David Simpson really was spreading false rumors, it could dam-age her reputation along with that of the firm. I had spent several years developing methods to analyze language and personality but had never been paid to be a word detective.

What kind of person may have written the note? Is "A friend" a male or female and what is his or her approximate age? What is the per-son's link to Ms. Livingston, to David Simpson, and to the firm? Any hints as to the person's personality traits?

In the years since I worked on the case, several new ways of look-ing at words have been developed. One involves comparing the words "A friend" used with those of tens of thousands of regular bloggers. For example, by looking at just the function and emotion words, we can guess that there is a 71 percent chance that the author is female and a 75 percent chance that she is between the ages of thirty-five and forty-five. It is much harder to get a good read on her personality. One analysis suggests that there is a fairly good chance that the author of the e-mail is high in the trait of narcissism—meaning she may be somewhat conceited and manipulative.

Look more closely at the e-mail and other hints emerge. The person is psychologically connected to the firm ("our senior partners") and has knowledge of rumors from across several departments within the firm. The person also is working to impress Ms. Livingston by using a large vocabulary. Particularly interesting is the use of words and phrases such as "voracious appetite," "vile," and "malicious tongue." These are Old Testament words that, in other analyses, were primarily used by people between forty-two and forty-four years of age at the time of the project.

One other important clue was the layout and punctuation. The e-mail was professionally typed with paragraphs of equivalent size. There was only one space between the period and the beginning of the next sentence, which suggests the person learned to type after about 1985—when desktop computers became popular—*or* the person had some background in journalism or publishing before 1985, where the single space after a period was the norm. (My wife, who was in publishing before 1985, explained this to me.)

What happened? When I submitted my report to the senior partner, he was relieved because it precisely matched the person he had suspected—a conscientious women in her early forties with a background in newspapers who had been with the firm for several years. I never learned the final disposition of the case, but I see that Ms. Livingston is now a senior partner with the firm.

WHO WROTE IT? THE ART OF AUTHOR IDENTIFICATION

Deciphering linguistic clues to solve crimes has a rich tradition in criminology. The FBI, various national security agencies, and local police departments around the world occasionally seek the expertise of linguists to help decode ransom notes or written threats, or to assess who might have written legal or other documents.

One of the best-known early forensic linguists is Donald Foster, a professor of English at Vassar College. Using a mixture of computer and deductive skills, along with a broad knowledge of history and literature, Foster has worked with law enforcement agencies on high-profile cases such as the Unabomber, the 2001 anthrax attacks, and the 1997 JonBenét Ramsey murder case. He has also applied his methods to determine the authenticity of some works by Shakespeare and others. Perhaps his most successful venture was in identifying Joe Klein as the author of an anonymously published satirical novel on the Clinton presidency, *Primary Colors*.

Foster has been a controversial figure because several of his high-profile claims about authorship have not panned out. He has also been less than forthcoming about the details of his methods of author identification, something that reflects his training in English rather than statistics and science. Nevertheless, Foster's approach has alerted the literary and forensic worlds to the promise of computer-based methods to identify authors and their work.

FINDING THE TELLS

World-class poker players closely watch and listen to their opponents in attempts to predict the cards they may be holding. Often players will pretend they have a poor set of cards when they have a good set; other times they will bluff by giving the impression they have a winning hand when they don't. Experts look for telling signs of deception—or "tells." Some players avoid looking around the table, others tap their feet, yet others talk more loudly. The ability to decipher tells can give card players a large advantage in high-stakes poker games.

There are various types of tells in people's use of written language as well. Two are particularly good clues in identifying authors: function words and punctuation. This can be seen in looking back at the blogs we collected in 2001 as part of the September 11 project discussed in the last chapter. Recall that we saved about seventy blog entries from each of a thousand people in the two months before and after the 9/11 attacks. Every few years, my students and I revisit LiveJournal.com to see if the same people are still posting. Ten years later, 25 to 30 percent are still active. About 25 percent have erased their accounts. The remainder stopped posting, on average, five years after the attacks, in 2006. Many of the former posters migrated to other systems such as Facebook or Twitter.

Simply reading the last ten years of people's posts provides an intimate picture of their lives. Not unlike Michael Apted's *Seven Up!* documentary series, we have been able to track the unfolding experiences of the bloggers as they grow older. Many of the same issues still drive the authors. Even though some have now married, had children, and started careers, recurring insecurities, motives, and goals keep returning. Those who were happy and upbeat in 2001 tend to be the same optimistic people nine years later. For example, a young father writes in a random blog in 2001 about his favorite hockey team:

> lucky lucky chicken bone. i shall do the happy-cup-dance. we shall win. we shall triumph. and there will be much rejoicing! i just need to get cable first. ok. i wasn't just gonna post about hockey, but yvonne's ready to go. yeah. shut up. you try resisting that sweet, sweet candeh.

And nine years later, you see the same person:

> My first attempt at making salsa was, in my humble opinion, not too shabby. protip: don't use Roma tomatoes. I'm not sure why the hell I thought they'd work out fine, but I was terribly wrong. Ok, not *terribly* just mildly. ah, salsa humor. I'm heading back to the mexi-mart today to pick up the goods to try another batch. Maybe i'll have it done in time for the bbq. Who knows? Since my catharsis, I've been in an amazing headspace.

Obviously, these two writing samples are from the same person. I mean, anyone could spot it immediately.

Really?

Actually, we can see the similarities once we know that they were written by the same person. But what if we read blogs all day and came across the second one several hours after reading the first? In all likelihood, most people wouldn't jump up yelling, "Aha! I have read that writing style earlier . . . yes, from the guy who wrote about hockey." Could language experts or computers make a definitive match? Are language fingerprints as reliable as DNA or real fingerprints? The short answer is no. However, computerized language analyses do a reasonably good job at matching which writing goes with which person.

Imagine we had a large number of blog entries from twenty bloggers. Several years later, we retrieve a handful of new postings from each of the same twenty bloggers. Now imagine sitting on your living room floor with hundreds of pages of posts trying to match each current blog entry with the original posts of the twenty bloggers. All things being equal, anyone should be able to match 5 percent of the blog posts correctly just due to chance alone. Most people would do terribly on this task. It is unlikely that you would match at rates any better than 10–12 percent. The writing style differences are too subtle and there is just too much information.

Computers are more patient and systematic. If we just analyze function words, the computer correctly matches the recent blog posts with the original authors about 29 percent of the time. This is actually impressive given the time lag between the writing of the posts.

But there is more to author identification than function words. Look at the consistency of punctuation. The following woman, for example, continues to use asterisks in the same way nine years apart. This was part of an early 2001 entry:

> Oh.. I have also discovered a shy streak I didn't know I had. I guess you would call it shyness. Somebody made me *blush*. Repeatedly. That is *weird*. I don't blush.

And in 2010:

> We °are° in post-post-punk now, aren't we? The guys in the band
> made a joke about how they just wrote that song yesterday, and
> maybe a quarter of the people in the room didn't get why the rest of
> us were chuckling. weird. °shrug°

Others use punctuation in equally unique but more subtle ways. From
a twenty-seven-year-old male in 2001:

> I mailed memorial gift checks to Immanuel [endowment donation
> in honor of Joan's mother]; and St Anne's - for my favorite account-
> ing professor the Smythe scholarship. Frank & Rebecca brought
> over "Midnight in the Garden of Good & Evil" and a couple home-
> brews. My eyelids want to close so I better . . .

In 2010:

> I didn't quite know what to say thinking, "hmm, mud, what is it . . .
> when I found a mirror I didn't see any other "brown stuff" i brought
> a watermelon and Costco multi-grain chips, Had a couple beers, I
> took Yuengling B & T - dinner was boiled/grilled chicken, okra, slaw,
> "dipping" brownies.

This person is the Alvin Ailey of punctuation. He jumps, swirls,
swoops, and rolls with the full gamut of punctuational possibilities:
[; - . . . & "/. Oddly, when I first read his blog, I didn't even notice his
use of punctuation marks—they just blended into his writing. However, when his blogs were computer analyzed, his use of punctuation
stood out.

Punctuation marks can identify some people better than anything they write. In fact, when looking only at punctuation, computer
programs identified 31 percent of authors correctly—essentially the
same rate as relying on function words. When both function words

and punctuation were used together, the computer correctly paired the original bloggers with writing samples several years later 39 percent of the time.

Punctuation, function words, and content words that are used in everyday writing are all parts of our personal signature. To appreciate this, go to your own e-mail account and spend a few minutes looking at the e-mails you send to and receive from others. Start with the page layout. Some people tend to write very long e-mails, whereas others keep them to a sentence or two. People tend to differ in the length of their paragraphs and sentences. Their greetings and closings vary tremendously as well. Some use emoticons; some never do.

Some of these differences may be psychologically important but most probably aren't. The person who ends most e-mails with "Sincerely" may do this just because they were told to do so when they were younger. Even though these variations may not say anything about your conflicts with your mother when you were an infant, they still mark you. That is, they are part of your general writing style that makes you stand out from everyone else. And that is the interesting story. All of the language features we can measure can help to identify you.

THE CASE OF THE FEDERALIST PAPERS

In 1787 and 1788, a series of eighty-five essays were published in pamphlets and newspapers across the American colonies in an attempt to sway people to support the proposed document that would become the U.S. Constitution. Published anonymously under the name Publius, the papers discussed a wide range of topics, including the role of the presidency, taxation, state versus federal power, etc. Even at the time, many knew that Publius was not a single person but, instead, James Madison (who would become the fourth president), Alexander Hamilton (the first secretary of the treasury), and John Jay (the first chief justice of the Supreme Court).

In the years that followed, the authorship of seventy-four of the essays gradually became known. Madison wrote fifteen, Hamilton fifty-one, Jay five, and Madison and Hamilton jointly wrote three of the articles. The authorship of the remaining eleven was never determined and has been a source of speculation ever since. The first serious attempt to identify the author of the eleven papers was undertaken by historian Douglass Adair as part of his dissertation in 1943. Adair's historical analysis deduced that all eleven anonymous essays had been written by James Madison.

The debate resurfaced in 1964 when statisticians Frederick Mosteller and David Wallace introduced a new way to analyze words. By focusing on a small number of function words, they concluded that Adair was indeed correct because their elegant statistical models pointed to Madison as the likely author. Since then, identifying the anonymous authors of the Federalist Papers has become something of a sport whenever new language analysis methods are developed.

I am proud to announce the New Official Findings. Historians, prepare your quills.

Function Word Analyses

Using similar methods to those of Mosteller and Wallace, we find the same effects. The anonymous eleven cases all use pronouns, prepositions, and other stealth words in ways similar to James Madison. Case closed?

Not so fast. Other statisticians have discovered a small problem that exists with the investigation of our founding fathers' function words. Since Mosteller and Wallace, another technique has been devised that is called cross-validation. The idea is to examine each of the original essays individually as if they were anonymously written. In other words, we pull one of the known essays out of the stack and then develop a computer model based on the remaining essays to try to determine who wrote the essay we pulled out. It's a marvelous method because we are determining results about a question whose answer we already know. If our cross-validation analyses successfully guess who wrote all of the known essay writers, we can place a tremendous amount of trust in our research methods.

Heartbreak city. The cross-validation results suggest that Mosteller and Wallace might have been wrong. About 14 percent of the known essays are not classified correctly based on function words. This is a serious problem. If the computer can't tell us what we already know with extremely high accuracy, we have to be careful in interpreting the results from essays about which we don't know the author.

Punctuation Analyses

Recall that people's use of punctuation can reveal authorship in many cases. Using similar cross-validation analyses on punctuation resulted in disappointing results as well. And using a combination of function words and punctuation to predict authorship produced slightly better results than the function words alone. Interestingly, the function words plus punctuation results hinted that Hamilton wrote three of the eleven anonymous essays.

Going for the Tell: People's Use of Obscure Words

Over the course of my career I have written more papers than I care to admit. Perhaps ten years ago, a colleague thanked me for a review I had written about her research. I was flattered, of course, but a bit puzzled since my review had been written anonymously. "How did you know I was the author of that review?" I blurted out. She just laughed and said one word: *intriguing.*

Intriguing, indeed. I went back to many of my reviews, then articles, and even books. I was shocked by how frequently I used the word *intriguing.* Even this book is littered with intrigue—I just can't help myself. Over the years, I've noticed that most of my colleagues and friends have their own favorite but relatively obscure words that even they aren't familiar with. The words aren't used at high rates but they find their ways into the occasional e-mail, Facebook post, blog, tweet, or article.

Did Madison or Hamilton have tell words in their articles? With a little sleuthing it turns out the answer is yes. In almost half of his papers, Hamilton used the word *readily*; Madison never did. In nine of his fifteen articles, Madison used *consequently*, compared with Hamilton's use of the word three times across his fifty-one papers. Hamilton also had a fondness for *commonly, enough, intended, kind,* and *naturally.* Madison tended to overuse *absolutely, administer, betray, composing, compass, innovation, lies, proceedings,* and *wish.*

If we just examine the use of these fourteen words, the statistics are promising—almost a perfect score for cross-validation. However, the story for the unknown authors comes out quite differently than what the earlier scholars claimed. They suggest that Hamilton actually wrote eight of the anonymous essays and Madison wrote only three.

What is truth in this case? Reading Douglass Adair's delightful account of the controversy surrounding the eleven articles, it is clear that Hamilton and Madison had very different memories of who wrote what. Adair is ultimately more sympathetic to Madison's claims, although the objective evidence to assign authorship is not compelling either way. Like Mosteller and Wallace, I have no in-depth knowledge of the actual case. Nevertheless, historians should know that from a statistical perspective, the case is still open.

WHAT SONG LYRICS SAY ABOUT THE BAND: THE BEATLES

The Beatles were together for about ten years before breaking up in 1970. During their time together, they recorded over two hundred songs and influenced music, politics, fashion, and culture for the next generation. The lead songwriters, John Lennon and Paul McCartney, together or separately wrote 155 songs, and George Harrison penned another 25. Even today, scholars—and the occasional barfly—debate about the relative creativity of the band members, who ultimately influenced whom, and how the band changed over time.

Most of this book is devoted to the words people generate in conversations or write in the form of essays, letters, or electronic media such as blogs, e-mails, etc. Music lyrics, however, tell their own stories about their authors. My good friend and occasional collaborator from New Zealand, Keith Petrie, suggested that a computerized linguistic analysis of the Beatles was long overdue. Once we realized how complicated the topic really was, we invited another music lover and psychologist from Norway, Borge Sivertsen, to join us. What could we learn about the Beatles by analyzing their lyrics? Quite a bit, it turns out.

In many ways, the lyrics of the band reflected the natural aging process one usually sees in all working groups. Recall from the last chapter that as working groups spend time together, their conversations evidence drops in I-words and increases in we-words, with increasing language complexity, including bigger words and more prepositions, articles, and conjunctions. As the group aged together, the Beatles expressed themselves through their lyrics in the same way any group would in their conversations with each other.

In their first four years together, their songs brimmed with optimism, anger, and sexuality. Their thinking was simple, self-absorbed, and very much in the here and now. In the last years of the band, the group's lyrics became more complex, more psychologically distant, and far less positive. Particularly telling was the drop in the use of I-words from almost 14 percent during their first years together to only 7 percent in their last three years. Lyrics also provide a window into the personalities of the various songwriters within a group. Although John Lennon and Paul McCartney had an agreement that all of their songs would include both men as authors, the order of authorship and extensive interviews has provided historians with a solid, albeit not perfect, record about who wrote what. Between the two, Lennon is credited as the primary writer for seventy-eight songs, McCartney for sixty-seven, and another fifteen songs are considered true collaborations where both were closely involved in the lyrics.

In the popular press, John Lennon was generally portrayed as the creative intellectual and McCartney as the melodic, upbeat tunesmith. The analyses of their lyrics paint a different picture. Lennon did use slightly more negative emotion words in his songs than McCartney, but the two were virtually identical in their use of positive emotions, linguistic complexity, and self-reflection. Interestingly, McCartney's songs more often focused on couples—as can be seen in his higher use of we-words—than did Lennon's.

Who was the more creative or varied in his lyric-writing abilities? We can actually test this by seeing how the lyrics from different songs are mathematically similar—both in terms of content as well as linguistic style. Whereas the popular press usually assumed that Lennon was the creative and stylistically variable writer, the numbers clearly support McCartney. Across his career as a Beatle, Paul McCartney proved to be far more flexible and varied both in terms of his writing style and also in the content of his lyrics.

And let's not forget George Harrison, the quiet, spiritual Beatle who wrote about twenty-five songs, especially in the last years of the Beatles. Although somewhat more cognitively complex in his words than either McCartney or Lennon, he was the least flexible in his writing. In other words, both the content and style of his lyrics were more predictable from song to song. These same types of analyses also demonstrated that Harrison was more influenced in his songwriting style by Lennon than by McCartney.

DOES COLLABORATION RESULT IN AVERAGE OR SYNERGISTIC RESULTS?

Collaborations between writers is a funny business. When two people work together, in John Lennon's words, "eyeball to eyeball," do they produce something that is the average of their usual styles or is the result something completely different than either could have written alone? Language analyses can answer this question for both the Beatles and the Federalist Papers. Recall that Lennon and McCartney had very close collaborations on 15 of their 160 songs. Alexander Hamilton and James Madison jointly wrote three Federalist Papers.

Across the various dimensions of language and even punctuation, we can calculate what percentage of the time the collaboration produces an effect that is the average of the two collaborators working on their own. There are three clear hypotheses:

- **Just-like-another-member-of-the-team hypothesis.** Collaborative writing projects produce language that is similar to that produced by a single person writing alone. Sometimes the work will use words like one author and other times like the other author.

- **The average-person hypothesis.** More interesting is that collaborations produce language that is the average of the two writers. If Lennon uses a low rate of we-words and McCartney uses a high rate, it would follow that their collaboration would produce a moderate number of we-words.

- **The synergy hypothesis.** Even more interesting is the idea that when two people work closely together, they create a product unlike either of them would on their own. Their language style will be distinctive in a way such that most people would not recognize who the author was. Wouldn't it be great if the results supported this hypothesis? Come on, statistics, please, please me.

And the winner by a mile is, in fact, the synergy hypothesis. When Lennon and McCartney and when Madison and Hamilton were working together, they produced works that were strikingly different than works produced by the individual writers themselves. When collaborating, the Lennon-McCartney team produced lyrics that were much more positive, while using more I-words, fewer we-words, and much shorter words than either artist normally used on his own. Similarly, when Hamilton and Madison worked together they used much bigger words, more past tense, and fewer auxiliary verbs than either did on their own. In fact, across about seventy-five dimensions of language and punctuation, more than 90 percent of the time collaborations resulted in language that was either higher or lower than the language of the two writers on their own.

Note that collaborations produce quite different language patterns than what the individuals would naturally do on their own. What's not yet known is if collaborative work is generally better than individual products. This is a research question that is begging to be answered.

SUMMING UP: PACKING YOUR AUTHOR IDENTIFICATION TOOL KIT

Author identification is becoming a very hot topic in the computer world. The three methods that we have relied on involve tracking the rate of function word usage, analyzing punctuation and layout, and examining the use of obscure words. Each of these methods does far better than chance in identifying characteristics of an author as well as matching the author's writing to other writing samples.

In terms of understanding the author's personality, we currently know the most about function words. As discussed throughout the book, pronouns, articles, and other stealth words have reliably been linked to the authors' age, sex, social class, personality, and social connections. Less is currently known about punctuation and personality, but I suspect future research will begin demonstrating convincing links. After all, it's hard to imagine that there isn't a difference between the writer who writes at the end of his or her note, "Thanks." versus one who writes, "Thanks!!!!!!!!!"

The least is known about the use of relatively obscure words and their link to personality. If one author uses *intriguing* and another *re-*

markable, does the choice of the word itself say anything about the person?

There are also a number of other exciting methods being developed by labs around the world that are relevant to author identification. One strategy is to look at something called N-grams. These can be pairs of words (or bigrams), three words in a row (or trigrams), etc. Looking at the beginning of this paragraph, the bigram approach would look at the occurrence of "there are," "are also," "also a," and so forth. The idea is that some people naturally use groups of words together in a unique way that identifies who they are.

More elaborate strategies attempt to mathematically predict word order within sentences based on the words the writer has already used. In the beginning of the last paragraph, the odds that it would start with the word *there* might be 1 in 1,000. The odds that the word *are* would be the second word, knowing that the first word is *there*, is perhaps 1 in 20. Knowing "There are," the odds that the third word is *also* . . . you can get the idea. Researchers can determine how unique a person's writing is and how much it deviates from chance on a sentence-by-sentence level. One argument is that every person's way of stringing words together is unique to them. Yet another linguistic fingerprint idea.

Other new methods examine parts of speech, syntax, cohesiveness of sentences and paragraphs—all using increasingly sophisticated mathematical solutions. The time is not too far away where the author of most any extended language sample will be identifiable.

WORDS AS CLUES TO POLITICAL AND HISTORICAL EVENTS

It comes as no news to historians and literary scholars that the primary key to understanding people or works of the past is the study of the written word. Most scholars, however, rely primarily on their own reading of historical works rather than computerized text analyses. This has been changing over the last few years. One area that has been particularly innovative is political science. Partly because of the availability of transcribed speeches, interviews, newspaper and online articles, newscasts, and even letters to the editor, researchers have been able to tap the appeal of political candidates and people's responses to them.

One of the pioneers in the field, Roderick Hart, has published a series of groundbreaking books and articles that help explain how the results of important historical elections—such as the race between Bill Clinton and Bob Dole—were presaged by the ways the candidates used words in their speeches. He also collected hundreds of letters to the editors in newspapers across the United States and was able to track the perceptions of voters. Extending Hart's work, we can begin to reinterpret historical events by analyzing the words of all the historical players who leave behind trails of words.

WHO *ARE* THESE PEOPLE? TRYING TO FIGURE OUT U.S. PRESIDENTS

Watch any news source—television, Internet, newspaper, magazine— and much of the coverage is devoted to understanding the thinking of the current, future, and past presidents. If it's the middle of an election cycle, pundits make predictions about how each of the candidates would perform if elected. If a president has recently been elected or reelected, we want to know what he or she will try to accomplish in the months and years ahead. And even after the president has stepped down, pundits continue to ask, "What was he thinking? Why did he do that?"

In one of the most impressive books on the psychology of politics, *The Political Brain*, researcher Drew Westen argues that the most successful politicians are the ones who can emotionally connect with the electorate. Logic, intelligence, and reason are certainly very fine qualities but when the voter enters the ballot box, it is the social and emotional dimensions of the campaign that usually drive the election.

We resonate with people who seem to be attentive and respectful to others and, at the same time, exhibit their emotions in a genuine way. Social-emotional styles can be detected through body language, tone of voice, and, of course, words. For presidents and presidential candidates, we have ample opportunity to evaluate social-emotional style through speeches, interviews, pictures, and videos of their interacting with their families and others. From a language perspective, presidents leave a stream of words like no other humans.

A fairly simple way to measure social-emotional styles is to count how often personal pronouns and emotion words are used. As a general rule, people who are self-reflective and who are interested in others will use all types of personal pronouns at high rates—including *I*, *we, you, she*, and *they*. Similarly, people are viewed as more emotionally present if they use emotion words—both positive and negative—than if they don't. By analyzing pronouns and emotion words in the speeches of presidents, we can begin to get a sense of their general social-emotional tone.

At most, U.S. presidents give inaugural addresses once every four years. However, most submit a State of the Union message to Congress every year that they are in office. State of the Union messages began with George Washington in 1790. Although Washington and John Adams presented the message in speeches to Congress, Thomas Jefferson changed the tradition by simply submitting a written version. In 1913, Woodrow Wilson reinstated the spoken State of the Union message. However, from 1924 until 1932, the messages returned to written format. Beginning with the inauguration of Franklin Delano Roosevelt (or FDR) in 1933 and up to today, virtually all States of the Union have been presented in speech format to Congress. Despite these variations in presentation style, it is fascinating to see how the emotional tones of the messages have changed from president to president.

As you can see in the graph, several presidents were far more

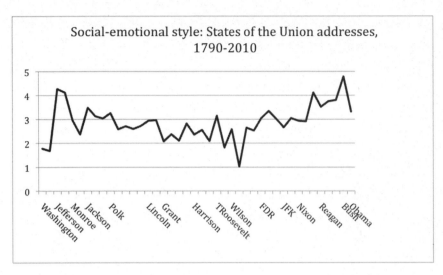

Social-emotional style: States of the Union addresses, 1790-2010

Rate of social-emotional language by U.S. presidents in their annual State of the Union messages delivered to Congress. The numbers have been adjusted to control for written versus spoken presentations.

social-emotional than their predecessors. Thomas Jefferson, Andrew Jackson, Theodore Roosevelt, Jimmy Carter, and George W. Bush used particularly high levels of personal pronouns and emotion words. James Monroe, Warren Harding, and Barack Obama all evidence significantly lower social-emotional ratings than those before them. In fact, it is interesting to see that George W. Bush is unquestionably the most social-emotional president in the history of the office and that Obama is currently the lowest since Richard Nixon.

A State of the Union address is essentially a formal speech that could, in theory, be written by anyone. Its tone may reflect that of the president's administration but it doesn't necessarily tell us about the psychological makeup of the president. Fortunately, a more natural source of a president's language now exists thanks to the popularity of press conferences. Beginning with FDR, press conferences evolved into freewheeling interactions between the press and president that were transcribed and saved.

From a psychologist's perspective, press conferences are glorious. The members of the press variously try to cajole, befriend, challenge, and sometimes outrage the president. The press-president relationship is further complicated because both the press and the president desperately need each other to accomplish their somewhat different goals. Most important, interactions with the press are generally unscripted and allow us to monitor the presidents' thoughts and emotions through the use of words.

Most presidents have only a small number of formal press conferences every year—usually between four and ten—more if there is a national crisis, fewer if they are being publically ridiculed or impeached. In addition to the formal press conferences, presidents often will talk with reporters on random occasions such as after introducing a foreign dignitary or while waiting for their car. Because most meetings with the press are recorded and transcribed, there are usually dozens of natural-language samples available for most presidents since the 1930s.

Interestingly, the ways presidents talk with the press are linguistically quite similar to their State of the Union addresses. As with his State of the Union speeches, George W. Bush emerges as the president whose language is the most social-emotional in press conferences. Since FDR, Nixon has been the lowest by far.

What about Ronald Reagan? Many people consider Reagan one of the most socially adept presidents since FDR. In both speeches and press conferences, Reagan's use of personal and emotional language was always around the average. From the outside, he seemed like a social-emotional person—perhaps a bit like George W. Bush. Closer analyses of Reagan's language suggest that this may be an illusion. Reagan, it seems, stands out more as a storyteller than a social-emotional leader. Recall from earlier chapters that stories or narratives require the use of social words together with past-tense verbs. Combining these two dimensions, Reagan's score on storytelling is *far and away* higher than any other modern president's.

The Ronald Reagan findings provide a little more insight into the different personalities of presumably sociable or personable people. No matter what their politics, most people who spent any time with George W. Bush felt that he was socially engaged. In social gatherings, he was genuinely interested in other people and readily expressed his own emotions. Whether accurately or not, most walked away with a sense of knowing him.

The biographies of Reagan paint a very different picture. Indeed, Reagan's official biographer, Edmund Morris, eventually gave up on a traditional biography because he couldn't get Reagan to open up in a personal or emotional way about himself. Reagan loved to tell stories of all kinds, but according to Morris, he had a "benign lack of interest in individual human beings." After working on an in-depth two-part television series on Reagan in 1998, the series editor Adriana Bosch reported, "Reagan was not a man given to introspection . . . As his son Ron told us, 'No one ever figured him out, and he never figured himself out.'"

Although outsiders may naively think that Bush and Reagan were social-emotional men, the language findings help to burrow under these impressions.

WHAT IS *I* SAYING?: THE MISSING PRONOUNS OF BARACK OBAMA

One hopes that you have been taking notes in reading this book. If you have, please refer to the many ways that the first-person singular pronoun *I* is used. Maybe you have skipped or forgotten these earlier chapters but feel as though you can take the Advanced Placement Test on I-word usage. And you can. Please go to the following website and take the one-minute *I* exam: www.SecretLifeOfPronouns.com/itest. It might be a good idea for those who have taken notes to do so as well.

The ten-item I-test has now been completed by well over two thousand people and demonstrates that very few people know who uses the word *I*. In fact, Ph.D.s in linguistics do about the same on the test as high school graduates, averaging around five correct answers out of ten. If you didn't do well on the exam, you are in very good company.

The word *I* is the prototypical stealth word. It is the most commonly used word in spoken English and we rarely register it when it is used by us or other people. Because people think that I-words must reflect self-confidence or arrogance, they assume that people who are self-confident must use I-words all the time.

Obama is a perfect case study. Within days of his election in 2008, pundits—especially those who didn't support him—started noting that he used the word *I* all the time. Various media outlets reported that Obama's press conferences, speeches, and informal interviews were teeming with I-words. A long list of noteworthy news analysts such as George Will, English scholars including Stanley Fish, and even occasional presidential speechwriters such as Peggy Noonan pointed out Obama's incessant use of I-words. Some of their articles on the topic were published in highly respected outlets that usually have diligent fact-checkers—the *Washington Post*, the *New York Times*.

The only problem is that no one bothered to count Obama's use of I-words or compare them with anyone else's. As you can see in the graph on the next page, Obama has distinguished himself as the *lowest* I-word user of any of the modern presidents. Analyses of his speeches reveal the same pattern. When Obama talks, he tends to avoid pronouns in general and I-words in particular.

If Barack Obama uses fewer I-words than any president in memory, why do very smart people think just the opposite? The problem may lie in the ways we naturally process information. First, as we have found with the I-test, most people believe that those who are the most self-confident use I-words at much higher rates than insecure or humble people. If we think that someone is arrogant, our brains will be searching for evidence to confirm our beliefs. Whenever the presumed arrogant person uses the word *I*, our brains take note—ahhh, additional

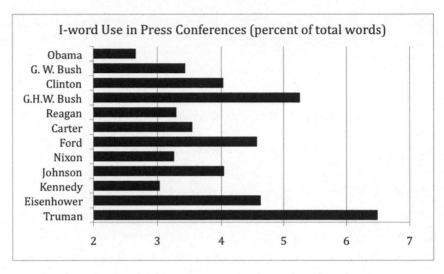

Use of first-person singular pronouns in press conferences as a function of total words.

proof that the person is arrogant. It is not coincidental that the commentators who have crowed the loudest about Obama's obnoxious use of I-words are people who do not share his political views.

There is another story as well. Obama's impressively low use of I-words says something about him: He *is* self-confident. In an interview on National Public Radio's *Weekend Edition* on August 8, 2009, Dan Balz and Haynes Johnson were asked about their book, *The Battle for America 2008: The Story of an Extraordinary Election.* Looking back over his distinguished political reporting career studying presidents since Eisenhower, Johnson noted that Obama is "the single most self-confident of all the presidents" he had ever seen.

Obama's use of pronouns supports Johnson's view. Since his election, Obama has remained consistent in using relatively few I-words compared to other modern U.S. presidents. Contrary to pronouncements by media experts, Obama is neither "inordinately fond" of first-person singular pronouns (as George Will wrote) nor exhibiting "the full emergence of a note of . . . imperial possession" (to quote Stanley

Fish). Instead, Obama's language suggests self-assurance and, at the same time, an emotional distance.

AVERTING YOUR I'S FOR ATTACKS AND WARS

I-words track where people pay attention. If people are self-focused, insecure, or self-effacing, they tend to use first-person singular pronouns at high rates. If confident, focused on a task of some kind, or lying, their rates of using I-words drop. Rarely do we get samples of real-world spoken language from people on a daily basis over several years to be able to track fluctuations in their attentional focus and thinking patterns. Recent U.S. presidents, especially George W. Bush, have proven to be an exception. Unlike most of his predecessors, Bush met with the press an extraordinary number of times. During his first four-year term in office, at least 360 separate press conferences or press gatherings were transcribed and posted on the WhiteHouse.gov website. By analyzing his use of I-words in his answers to questions, we could determine how he was thinking in light of ongoing political and social events.

Bush's presidency will likely be fodder for historical analyses for generations. The prodigal son of the forty-first president, he was generally thought to be a warm and charming man but without a clear vision of what he wanted to accomplish as president. Bush's tenure as president was more tumultuous than most. Nine months into his presidency, operatives working with Osama bin Laden attacked the World Trade Center and Pentagon, killing over three thousand people. Less than a month later, on October 7, 2001, Bush directed an attack that toppled the government of Afghanistan in a futile hunt for bin Laden. In his most controversial act as president, Bush turned his sights on Iraq and, arguing that the country harbored weapons of mass destruction, launched a full-scale invasion in March 2003. No weapons of mass destruction were ever found and the United States and its allies continue the occupation of Iraq to this day. His second term in office, which will not be discussed here, also had its problems, including the destruction of New Orleans from Hurricane Katrina, the mounting turmoil in occupied Iraq, and the beginning of the global economic meltdown.

Overlaying the actions of Bush was his personality. Many considered him to be relatively transparent, sometimes exhibiting boyish delight, petulance, defensiveness, and compassion. In reading the transcripts of his press conferences, the different sides of his personality often emerge even when he was responding to a single question. No matter what your political persuasion, the transcripts reveal a man both warm and charming and, occasionally, arrogant and mean.

Three interconnected events defined his first term. The first was the 9/11 attacks. As noted in the last chapter, within a matter of days he went from being tolerated to being adored by the American population. The second defining event, which the world did not directly witness, was his decision to invade Iraq. And the third was the actual invasion in March 2003. The graph on the next page charts Bush's use of I-words in his press conferences on a monthly basis. Each month, he typically spoke to the press six to eight times, uttering around a thousand words during each press conference. As is apparent, his use of I-words dropped during his first three months in office. In fact, this happens with most new presidents (although not Barack Obama). Starting the job is generally an intimidating experience that takes a few weeks to get used to.

The first dramatic drop in I-word use occurred immediately after the 9/11 attacks. Bush, like the majority of Americans, curtailed his use of *I*'s and increased in his use of we-words. The effect of the attacks on him was large, and over the next few months, his attention was focused on a number of pressing matters—the invasion of Afghanistan, the anthrax attacks, and attempting to reorient the government to deal with terrorism. You will note that after November 2001, his use of I-words gradually increases most months.

The second substantial drop in I-word usage occurred in

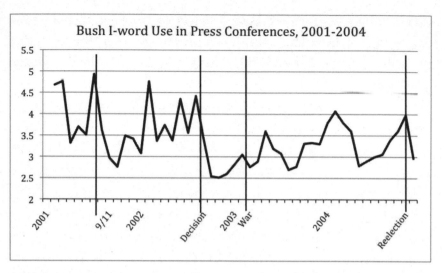

George W. Bush's use of I-words across 360 press meetings during the first term of his presidency (based on percentage of total words). The vertical lines represent the following: 9/11 = September 11 attacks; Decision = probable final decision to go to war in Iraq (October 2002); War = invasion of Iraq (March 2003); Reelection = November 2004.

mid-September 2002. According to White House scholars, the Bush administration had long been troubled by Iraq and its leader Saddam Hussein. In addition, some within the White House felt that Hussein was behind the September 11 attacks and/or was intent on building a nuclear arsenal. In June 2002, some in the Bush administration began to suggest a new approach to foreign policy. Part of the Bush Doctrine, as some referred to it, was that the United States was justified in pre-emptively attacking a country with hostile intent.

Through the summer of 2002, secret plans were drawn up about a possible invasion. In late September, the Bush administration asked Congress for authority to go to war with Iraq. This was couched as a bargaining tool and would only be done as a last resort if Iraq failed to allow inspectors full access to the country to ferret out weapons of mass destruction. Congress voted in support of the request on October 16. In a nationally televised speech that night, Bush made it clear that he hoped that war would be avoided. In an article by *New Yorker* writer and Berkeley journalism professor Mark Danner, British documents eventually surfaced proving that, with the final blessing of the U.S. Congress, war was a virtual certainty.

Imagine you are a leader and you know you are going to attack another country. To be effective, you have to keep your plans completely secret. You can't let anything slip about troop movements, rescaling vast parts of the country's economy, or letting your enemies know what your plans might be. You must be wary about what you say. Not only must you be deceptive, you have to pay attention to every facet of government to coordinate the clandestine war effort. To accomplish all of this, an effective leader must act—and not sit around contemplating his or her feelings.

Drops in I-words are a powerful tell among people who are about to carry out a threat. We have found similar patterns in Truman's language prior to dropping the atomic bombs on Japan in World War II and in Hitler's speeches prior to his invasion of Poland in 1939.

The idea that the language of leaders can predict the outbreak of wars has been suggested by others as well. The Belgian psychologist Robert Hogenraad has studied how leaders mention themes of power and affiliation in their speeches. When references to affiliation and friendship are commonplace and comments about power, aggression, and mastery are low, the outlook for the country is usually good. However, if themes of power and aggression start to rise with a corresponding drop in words associated with nurturance and relationships, watch out. High power/low affiliation themes among leaders is a reliable predictor of wars. Conflicts in Northern Ireland, the former Yugoslavia, Georgia and Russia, and various hotspots in the Middle East all were presaged by language shifts by the countries' leaders.

One final observation. It's interesting that Bush's I-words never changed substantially once the war started. They temporarily went up a bit coinciding with his "Mission Accomplished" speech in May 2003, when he felt that the war was over. Subsequent drops in I-word use in the summers of 2003 and 2004 reflect his increasing focus on the war and, in 2004, his defensiveness with the press for its questioning his decisions about it.

THE POWER OF WORDS TO RETHINK HISTORY

I've tried to give a taste of the exciting possibilities that word analysis can bring to the study of politics and history. Wherever there is a word trail—no matter what language—computer text analysis methods can help interpret the psychology of the authors. Some of the studies in this area have practical applications. Other work is simply fun to do.

For example, my students, colleagues, and I have worked with several federal agencies to better understand the psychology of leaders of groups such as al-Qaeda to try to understand the relationships between their public messages and their sometimes-brutal actions. Can we understand their appeal by studying their language or the language of their followers? We have used these same methods to better understand extremist groups in the United States, ranging from far-right-wing neo-Nazis to far-left-wing Weathermen. In general, we are finding the violent groups have a very different linguistic fingerprint than nonviolent ones. Further, as they evolve from being nonviolent to increasingly violent, their language shifts accordingly.

We have also turned our language tools to the study of powerful, often despotic leaders of the past and present. For example, how have leaders such as Mao, Hitler, Castro, and others changed in their language use as they themselves changed from revolutionaries, to dictators, to sometimes-respected leaders in their countries? How has their language predicted changes in their countries and how have events changed their language?

Most important, language analyses can shed light on historical events in new ways. We've seen some possibilities with the Federalist Papers, relationships among poets and scholars, and even the Beatles. The historical questions that can be answered are limited only by the availability of language samples and the researchers' imaginations. For example, did the Australian explorer Henry Hellyer really commit suicide or might he have been murdered? (Probably suicide based on his language in his diaries.) Did St. Paul really write all the letters attributed to him in the Bible? (Nope—not a chance.) Has Lady Gaga had an affair with Tom Cruise? (No idea. Hope not.)

Now it's your turn.

USING PEOPLE'S WORDS TO PREDICT THEIR BEHAVIORS IN THE FUTURE

Can word analyses tell us if someone will eventually be a good president, a good spouse, a good employee or student? In fact, we do these calculations in our heads all the time. If a student writes to me and wants to work in my lab, I read her e-mail, her résumé, and her plans. Her words—which reflect her accomplishments, hopes for the future, and personality—will be the basis of my decision. People who rely on online dating sites may ultimately decide who their spouse will be based on his or her word use. And yes, we weigh political candidates' faces and body language, but we also evaluate their platforms and plans, which are expressed in language.

Although we listen to and think about people's words before voting for, hiring, or marrying them, it is impressive how frequently we err in our judgments. Would a language analysis program do a better job? Or would it help us in making better decisions? The jury is still out, but some interesting examples can be found among students planning to go to college and prisoners planning to find a normal life.

USING WORDS IN COLLEGE ADMISSIONS ESSAYS TO PREDICT COLLEGE GRADES

My linguist friend David Beaver and I were sitting in a bar talking about pronouns. (How many bar stories have you heard start off that way?) Wouldn't it be great if there was some simple relationship between word use and how people later behave in life? We started to challenge each other about possible language samples we could get that could be linked to important real-world behaviors. And then I remembered Gary Lavergne.

Several years earlier, I had met Gary, the chief researcher in the University of Texas at Austin's admissions office. Gary was not your usual statistician. He has published a series of nonfiction thrillers on mass murderers and, most recently, a book on the history of school desegregation in Texas. He was also interested in what factors predicted who would succeed in college. The University of Texas always has one of the largest student bodies of any campus in the United States. Although the school enrolls over seven thousand new first-year college students each year, the admission standards are surprisingly competitive. Part of the application process involves students writing two general essays.

Could the function words students use in their admissions essays predict their college grades? This was an appealing question for both David and me and, as it turned out, for Gary as well. To be clear, this was not a strategy to invent a new way to evaluate college essays to determine who should be admitted. Rather, we first wanted to learn if word use was related to academic performance and, if it was, whether we could influence the students to become better writers and thinkers in college.

We eventually analyzed over fifty thousand essays from twenty-five thousand students who had enrolled over a four-year period. The results were straightforward. Word use was indeed related to students' grades over all four years of college. The word categories most strongly related to making good grades were:

- High rates of articles and concrete nouns
- High rates of big words
- Low rates of auxiliary and other verbs (especially present tense)
- Low rates of personal and impersonal pronouns

This constellation of words should look familiar to you. You might recall from earlier chapters that people differ in the degree to which they are categorical versus dynamic thinkers. A categorical thinker is someone who tends to focus on objects, things, and categories. The opposite end of this dimension are people who are more dynamic in their thinking. When thinking dynamically, people are describing action and changes. Often, dynamic thinkers devote much of their thinking to other people (which explains their high use of pronouns).

Does this mean that categorical thinkers are simply smarter than dynamic thinkers? Not at all. However, the American educational system is designed to test people concerning the ways they categorize objects and events.

Look at these two examples of college admissions essays that display categorical versus dynamic thinking. (The actual content of these essays has been changed considerably while keeping the rate of articles, nouns, large words, verbs, and pronouns intact.)

The categorical thinker
The concept of choice has played a prominent role in Western philosophy. One's personality is polished to a more defined state by both conscious and unconscious considerations. The ultimate aim of liberty cannot be reached without a thorough control over the choices one makes. The divorce of my parents made me lead a double life. My partial withdrawal from reality had severe negative effects, including the inability to understand other viewpoints . . .

Notice how the writer's sentences methodically define and categorize thoughts and experiences. The writing is structured and largely impersonal but, at the same time, ponderous. Compare the categorical thinker with a more dynamic one.

The dynamic thinker

I looked over at my brother, who was much older and wiser, only to see him crying. Before I knew it, I was crying too. I didn't really know why, but if my brother thought it was bad, it was bad. Everyone moves, but it was the magnitude of my journey, a seven-hundred-mile trip from a small farming village to one of the biggest cities in America. It was going to be challenging but also an opportunity to grow. It involved giving up everything that is important to young children; family, friends, school.

The dynamic writer is far more personal and works to tell a story. The language is more informal and simple, using shorter words. Every sentence has multiple verbs, which has the effect of making the story more alive.

Although both of these students came to college with virtually identical high school records and received liberal arts degrees, the categorical thinker had a much higher grade-point average every year in college. It wasn't because the categorical thinker was a better writer. Rather, a categorical thinking style is more congruent with what we reward in college. Most exams, for example, ask students to break down complex problems into their component parts. At the same time, very few courses ask students to discuss ongoing events or to tell their own stories.

Most universities will never use word counting programs to decide who to admit to college. Once students discovered such a system was operative, their admissions essays would be a jumble of big words and articles, and practically verb-free. Instead, findings such as these point to ways we might think about training our students in high school and earlier. To the degree that categorical thinking is encouraged and rewarded in our educational systems, students should be explicitly trained in doing it.

Another argument is that we should explore whether dynamic thinking should be encouraged at the college level. Telling stories and tracking changes in people's lives are skills that can serve people well. It also raises the question about how successful people are in the years after college. Is it possible that dynamic thinkers are better adjusted or happier? And finally, how flexible is thinking style? It is entirely possible that all of us occasionally need to think categorically and, at other times, dynamically.

USING WORDS TO PREDICT A BETTER LIFE AFTER PRISON

Drug and alcohol abuse takes a massive toll on society. One way that many states have attempted to curb and treat abuse is by establishing therapeutic communities—which are essentially treatment prisons where people are given the opportunity to undergo intensive drug and alcohol rehabilitation over several months after they have been convicted of a drug-related crime. If the participants successfully complete the program and stay drug- or alcohol-free for a specified time after they are released, their records are usually expunged. Most therapeutic communities require intensive group therapy along with writing exercises.

One of my former graduate students, Anne Vano, conducted an ambitious project to learn if the ways women wrote within a treatment facility might predict their lives once they were released from prison. Working with a single therapeutic community, Anne collected and transcribed writing samples from about 120 women. The writing samples she focused on were essays that the women wrote within about a week of their being released. The essays were expected to be personal and heartfelt. In the months afterward, Anne worked with the warden's office to collect follow-up information, such as the women's abilities to maintain jobs and whether or not they violated their parole or were re-arrested.

The stories the women wrote were powerful by any measure. They often described instances of being the victims of physical and

sexual abuse and, at the same time, detailed their own deplorable behaviors toward others, such as their children. They often expressed
great anxiety about their leaving the prison to return to an uncertain
home life.

After leaving the prison, 15 percent of the 120 women were ar-
rested and another 10 percent jumped parole four months after the
program was completed. About 65 percent were holding down a
steady job.

Interestingly, the way the women wrote in their final essay modestly predicted whether they were functioning effectively four months
later. The two language dimensions that were most closely associated
with therapeutic success were:

- a high social-emotional style, which includes use of personal
  pronouns and emotion words
- a high rate of positive emotion words

The tasks for the women on leaving the therapeutic community
were to integrate into new jobs and into a functioning social network.
Categorical and dynamic thinking were simply irrelevant dimensions
for these women. To survive in their worlds outside prison they needed
to be aware of others and themselves. It appears that the social-emotional
and optimistic styles they exhibited in their writings were skills that
could serve them well on the outside.

IT'S HARD TO imagine two studies more different than the college
admissions and therapeutic community projects. Categorical thinking
predicts better college grades for one group; social-emotional language
predicts lower re-arrest rates in another. Different aspects of language
are linked to different parts of our lives.

What I love about these two studies—and, in fact, all of the projects in this book—is that stealth words rearrange themselves in differ-

ent configurations to predict a broad array of behaviors. For example, using language associated with high social-emotional style can help keep you out of prison and contribute to your being elected president and maybe provide some of the skills needed to write successful top-selling love songs.

Depending on the context, using I-words at high rates may signal insecurity, honesty, and depression proneness but also that you aren't planning on declaring war any time in the near future. Using I-words at low rates, on the other hand, may get you into college and boost your grade-point average but may hurt your chances of making close friends.

It's important to return to a theme that has bubbled up several times. The words related to social and psychological states are reflections of those states—not causes. They are telling us what is going on inside people's heads. The people who use high rates of personal pronouns and emotion words just prior to their release from prison are approaching their writing topic in a social-emotional way. It's unknown if the treatment program they were immersed in actually pushed them to think social-emotionally. It is also impossible to know if the words in their writing samples directly affected their behaviors once they were released. And it's even more unlikely that if they had forced themselves to use these words in their essays (thinking it might be good for them) it would have influenced their lives outside the prison gates at all.

We are standing on the threshold of a new world. Think of the many applications that the computer analysis of function words has opened up. By analyzing inaugural speeches or ancestral diaries, we are able to know the influential writers or speakers of our past. We can also start to answer some of the burning psychological questions we have in our everyday lives. We can gain insight into how our online dating prospects view us, distinguish which rap artists are honest about being true gangsters, diagnose if our therapists are just as depressed as we are, or expose which of our colleagues secretly think they are highest in status.

Function words can help us know our worlds just a little better. From author identification that can help in catching criminals or in identifying historical authors, to understanding the thinking of presidents or tyrants, to predicting how people might behave in the future, function words are clues about the human psyche. Most promising, however, is that by looking at our own function words, we can begin to understand ourselves better.

A Handy Guide
for Spotting and Interpreting
Function Words in the Wild

DIFFERENT FUNCTION WORDS can signal different psychological states. Pronouns, articles, prepositions, verbs, and emotion words provide different information about how people are thinking, feeling, and connecting with others. Feel free to tear out this Word Guide for use in all future settings where people are using language.

ATTENTIONAL FOCUS: PRONOUNS, VERB TENSE

Language tracks our focus of attention. We talk and write about objects, events, and people that are on our minds. A good rule of thumb is that people who pay a great deal of attention to other people tend to use personal pronouns at high rates. People who obsess about the past use past-tense verbs. Turning this observation upside down, by counting instances of pronoun and verb tense use, we can guess what naturally grabs people's attention.

PERSONAL PRONOUNS

We probably spend more time thinking and talking about other people than anything else. If another person makes us exuberantly happy, furiously angry, or deeply sad, we often can't stop thinking about him or her. We will often drop his or her name in our conversations with others, tossing in numerous pronouns as we refer to the person. Consequently, if the speaker is thinking and talking about a friend, expect high rates of third-person singular pronouns. If worried about communists, right-wing radio hosts, or bureaucrats, words such as *they* and *them* will be more frequent than average.

The word *I* is no different. If people are self-conscious, their attention flips to themselves briefly but at higher rates than people who are not self-conscious. For example, people use the word *I* more when completing a questionnaire in front of a mirror than if no mirror is present. If their attention is drawn to themselves because they are sick, feeling pain, or deeply depressed, they also use *I* more. In contrast, people who are immersed in a task tend to use I-words at very low levels.

VERB TENSE

Whereas personal pronouns provide information about the subject of attention, verb tense can tell us how people are thinking about time. Not surprisingly, when people think about the past, they use the past tense; when thinking about the future, they tend to use the future tense. More interesting is when people flip between tenses. For example, people suffering from post-traumatic stress disorder (or PTSD) often have flashbacks of horrific events that they may have experienced months or years in the past. Here, a Vietnam veteran describes a terrifying night that occurred decades earlier:

> We had used bulldozers to build . . . bunkers . . . to protect us from
> sporadic shelling. I could not sleep in the bunker (it was like a
> crypt). This night . . . we were getting incoming [mortar fire and]
> our platoon sergeant cracked, rolled himself up in the corner of the
> bunker and hysterically cried. I went outside to the top of the berm
> after the shelling stopped and waited. Shit. It was dark again. As we
> all sat there, sporadic ground fire would open up from time to time,
> and we would all send some rounds down . . . Maybe an hour later,
> I'm on top of the berm, looking out, and I feel his presence again. I

keep staring, trying to see movement, but it's too dark. I get up, run over to . . . ask for flares. I go back up top, staring, waiting for the illumination, none comes. I know he's out there again and not alone . . . Obviously, I made it okay. I just can't remember what happened next.

Notice how the author flips from the past tense to the present tense. The sergeant, the shelling, the gunfire all happened in the past. "Maybe an hour later, I'm on top of the berm . . ." The soldier is back in Vietnam and right in the middle of it. His verbs tell us how his mind is working—and that Vietnam continues to be an ongoing experience in his life.

SOCIAL RELATIONSHIPS AND EMOTIONS: PRONOUNS, ARTICLES, EMOTION WORDS

Language in its most basic function is necessary for communication. Style words provide information about social processes that are integral to understanding others. They provide clues about who has more status, whether a group is working well together, if someone is being deceptive, and the quality of a close relationship

STATUS AND POWER

In virtually all groups of primates, the first order of business is to establish dominance and status. We humans, of course, are much more refined in the ways we approach this task. We usually don't make threats on meeting others. Instead, we change our posture, our tone of voice, and the ways we use words. As discussed in chapter 7, status is quickly signaled by the use of pronouns—especially first- and second-person pronouns such as *I*, *we*, and *you*. Contrary to what most people think, high-status people tend to use *we* and *you* at high rates compared to lower-status individuals. And low-status individuals overuse *I*.

HONESTY AND DECEPTION

We also use function words differently when being honest than when lying. When telling the truth, we tend to "own" what we say. That is, truth-tellers are more likely to use words like *I* and *my*. When lying, we distance ourselves from what we are saying. President Bill Clinton's claim that he didn't have sexual relations "with that woman" is a startling example. "That" woman is certainly more distant than, say, "my woman" or simply "Monica." We also think and talk in more complex ways when being truthful. As seen in chapter 6, lying is hard work. If we are having to invent a story that isn't true, we avoid certain conjunctions (such as *but* and *or*), prepositions (*except, without*), and negations (*not, never*).

STRANGERS AND FRIENDS

People who are good friends and have a long history use language with each other in ways that are quite different from two strangers. Some language markers are obvious—people who like one another use the first-person plural (*we, us,* and *our*) more than strangers. They also use more positive and negative emotion words. People with a shared background are more likely to use the specific article *the*, as in "the chair," since both have probably talked about that same damned chair for years. Strangers will initially talk about "a chair" or maybe "that chair," especially in the early phase of their relationship.

THINKING STYLES: CONJUNCTIONS, PREPOSITIONS, NOUNS, VERBS, AND CAUSAL WORDS

You discover that your best friend's spouse is having an affair. Should you tell your friend? Why or why not?

Questions such as this force people to think about complex topics that don't have easy answers. People's answers generally require a certain degree of logic, reasoning, and causal thinking. Unanticipated complex questions also require people to work through a problem. They often begin answering in one way and then adopt a different perspective to evaluate if their thinking makes sense. As people write about complex issues, their style words provide clues to the ways they are thinking in general.

Although there are dozens of ways to analyze thinking styles, three are particularly well suited to language analysis.

COMPLEX VERSUS SIMPLE THINKING

So your best friend's spouse is having an affair. Ask a dozen people what they would do and you will get twelve different responses. However, some answers will reveal a much more complicated way of thinking:

> **Complex thinker:** First, what is the history of their relationship? If the couple has some preexisting agreement about extramarital relationships, then nothing needs to be said. What are the costs to my friend, the spouse, and to me for either talking about it or keeping it secret? If it had been the other way and it was my spouse that was having an affair, would I want to know from my friend? Unless the friend's spouse is intentionally trying to hurt my friend, I would probably not say anything. But I really need more information to answer this question.
>
> **Simple thinker:** What happens in Vegas stays in Vegas. That's my motto. What will happen with my friend will happen. I'll keep my nose out of things. Out of sight, out of mind. Know what I mean?

Although the complex and simple thinker come to the same conclusion, the complex thinker weighs different options and looks at the problem from multiple angles. In addition, the complex thinker relies on reasoning, logic, and even emotional awareness. Note the language differences as well. Complex thinking generally involves bigger words, longer sentences, and more complicated sentences, often involving prepositions (*with, of, to*). Prepositions, by the way, are glorious language markers. They help to situate an idea in time and space.

Most important, a complex thinker makes distinctions. "The friend's spouse had an affair but it is now over" is more complex than just "The spouse had an affair." To make a distinction, speakers must tell us what is in a category and what is not in the category: "It's this but not that." In order to make distinctions, it is useful to draw on a set of words that we call exclusive words. Examples of exclusive words include *except, but, without, unless*, and a number of related prepositions and conjunctions.

And don't forget if-then phrases, which lie at the heart of logical thinking. IF a person uses the word *if*, THEN, by definition, that person is making distinctions.

CAUSAL VERSUS NONCAUSAL THINKING

What are your thoughts about waking up with one of your legs amputated? I've asked hundreds of college students this question and the answers are mesmerizing. Some claim that it would be so devastating that they would consider suicide. Others shrug their shoulders and report that it wouldn't change their life much at all. Yet others focus on why they walked between the cars and what made one of the cars roll backward.

All humans naturally engage in causal thinking. However, some of us engage in it more than others. Some people, for example, are obsessed with knowing why bad things have happened to them. Why did I walk between those cars? Why did I have to lose my leg? In a stunning series of studies, psychologists Camille Wortman and Roxanne Silver asked thousands of people how they have dealt with major upheavals in their lives—incest, death of a child, death of a spouse. In general, those who have a simple causal explanation of a terrible event cope quite well. Another group simply doesn't look for a causal explanation and, they, too, cope well. The one group that has the most difficulty is made up of people who desperately seek answers to why the event occurred. They frequently ask, "Why did this happen?" and "Why me?" but never find an answer.

In most circumstances, causal thinking can be invaluable. If you can find a satisfactory reason for an event, you can better deal with similar events in the future. However, if you are unable to find an answer to your question, continued searching may only bring you frustration and unhappiness.

Capturing causal thinking in language is straightforward. Recall from high school English that conjunctions are words that link words or phrases—words such as *or, and, but*. Some conjunctions are specifically designed to express causal thinking: words such as *because, hence, therefore, since*. Although not officially function words, there are also a large number of nouns and verbs that signal causation as well, such as *cause, effect, reason, rationale, impel, control*. The more people naturally use these words in writing and speaking, the more they search for and think about causes.

DYNAMIC VERSUS CATEGORICAL THINKING

In chapter 2, people were asked to describe a picture of two people. Two of the descriptions were:

> PERSON 1: In the aforementioned picture an elderly woman is about to speak to a middle aged woman who looks condescending and calculating.
>
> PERSON 2: I see an old woman looking back on her years remembering how it was to be beautiful and young.

Whereas the first person, a male, describes the women in fairly direct and concrete terms, the second person, a female, paints a more dynamic picture that begins to construct a story. The more categorical-thinking male sees the world in terms of objects, events, and particular people. Categorical thinking demands the use of specific or concrete nouns.

And with specific nouns comes the need for articles. The first person used three articles: *the* aforementioned picture, *an* elderly woman, and *a* middle-aged woman. The second person used only one—*an* old woman.

You can see the differences in categorical and dynamic thinking in everyday life as well. John McCain and Barack Obama, as they were running for president in the fall of 2008, revealed themselves to be strikingly different in their thinking styles. Through his debates, interviews, and even speeches, McCain used articles at very high rates. Obama, on the other hand, used articles at rates lower than McCain and, indeed, any other serious candidates in the presidential race. In mid-October, the two men settled into their final debate with each other. Both were asked to explain why America's educational system was the most expensive in the world but was not viewed as very strong among the industrialized nations.

> MCCAIN: Well, it's **the** civil rights issue of **the** twenty-first century. There's no doubt that we have achieved equal access to schools in America after **a** long and difficult and terrible struggle. But what is **the** advantage in **a** low-income area of sending **a** child to **a** failed school and that being your only choice? So choice and competition amongst schools is one of **the** key elements that's already been proven in places in like New Orleans and New York City and other places.

> OBAMA: This probably has more to do with our economic future than anything and that means it also has **a** national security implication, because there's never been **a** nation on earth that saw its economy decline and continued to maintain its primacy as **a** military power. So we've got to get our education system right. Now, typically, what's happened is that there's been **a** debate between more money or reform, and I think we need both. In some cases, we are going to have to invest.

In using almost twice as many articles in answering the question, McCain breaks down the problem into its components. Education, in his thinking, is a civil rights issue, part of a struggle, that is not fixed by sending a low-income child to a bad school. It is this and that but not that. Obama, on the other hand, frames his answer in a more dynamic way—it is linked to the changing past and future. Whereas McCain thinks concretely about the problem, Obama is more abstract, relying on broader ongoing and ever-changing principles, such as economic future, educational systems, money or reform, and investment.

In looking back over the thinking styles—complex versus simple, causal versus noncausal, and dynamic versus categorical—no single style is naturally better or more productive than another. Sometimes complex, causal, and dynamic thinking styles can help people get through the day; sometimes these same styles can be a problem. In reality, all of us bounce around in our thinking styles depending on what we are thinking about. Just because Obama is abstract in answering a question about education, it doesn't tell us how he thinks about his decision to smoke a cigarette or take aspirin for a headache.

Notes

In addition to the extensive comments and feedback from Cindy Chung, Sam Gosling, and Ruth Pennebaker, a number of other people read all or parts of the manuscript, including David Beaver, Molly Ireland, Jeff Hancock, Maureen O'Sullivan, Rich Slatcher, and Yla Tausczik. Thank you all.

PREFACE

ix   Estimates of the number of words in the average person's vocabulary range from thirty thousand to a hundred thousand. Part of the problem is in the definition of a word. For example, do you count singular and plural? Different spellings of the same word? How about a word that you might use that isn't in the dictionary, such as "fancify" (as in, to make something fancy)? For a discussion of the number of function words, see Chung and Pennebaker (2007).

x   One of the most exciting breakthroughs in language analysis is the recent release of the Google Books corpus. In a stunning article by Jean-Baptiste Michel and his colleagues in the journal *Science*, the authors analyzed the words from over five million books, or 4 percent of all the books that have ever been printed. Focusing on language use over the last two hundred years, the authors were able to examine a wide range of historical trends. For example, how frequently has Freud or Darwin been mentioned? How long does fame last? How has language been evolving?

   I urge you to try out Google Labs' program Books Ngram Viewer at ngrams .googlelabs.com/. The study of history will never be the same.

xi   Some of the best popular books on language that combine a rich knowledge of language with basic social and psychological questions include Goffman's *Forms of Talk*, Lakoff and Johnson's *Metaphors We Live By*, George Miller's *The Science of Words*, Pinker's *The Language Instinct*, Tannen's *You Just Don't Understand*, and Wierzbicka's *Understanding Cultures Through Their Key Words*.

CHAPTER 1: DISCOVERING THE SECRET LIFE OF THE MOST
FORGETTABLE WORDS

3   The website Analyzewords.com is one of several experimental sites that we have
been developing. This one was the result of a collaboration among Chris Wilson, a
writer at Slate.com; my daughter, Teal Pennebaker, who is a world-class expert on
social media; and my longtime computer guru and collaborator Roger Booth. The
program analyzes the recent history of anyone's Twitter posts. Using algorithms we
have developed over several years of studying language and personality, we are able
to estimate personality profiles by language use. As with all experimental systems,
please don't take the results too seriously.

4   The expressive writing research has a rich history. The basic idea is that if people
are asked to write about a traumatic experience for fifteen to twenty minutes a day
for three or four consecutive days, they later show improvements in physical and
mental health compared to others who have been asked to write about superficial
topics. To get a better sense of the literature, see my popular book *Opening Up* as
well as articles by Frattaroli (2006) and Pennebaker and Chung (2011). For a list of
articles, including many that you can read for free, go to the publications link on my
website, www.psy.utexas.edu/pennebaker.

6   For technical information about the development of the LIWC program, see the
articles associated with Linguistic Inquiry and Word Count on the publications link
of my website, www.psy.utexas.edu/pennebaker. The LIWC program is commercially
available from www.liwc.net. All profits from the sales of the program are returned to
the University of Texas at Austin graduate program in the Department of Psychology.
      LIWC is by no means the only text analysis program around. Dozens of different
programs are now available. Programs that are particularly useful for people interested in language and psychology include:
      Art Graesser's Coh-Metrix program (cohmetrix.memphis.edu), which calculates
the degree to which any groups of texts are readable and coherent.
      Rod Hart's DICTION program (www.dictionsoftware.com) was designed to
capture the verbal tone of messages, with particular focus on political speeches.
      Tom Landauer's Latent Semantic Analysis (lsa.colorado.edu) is a suite of pro-
grams that allows people to compare the similarity of any texts with other texts.
      Mike Scott's Wordsmith program (www.lexically.net) is a wonderful all-purpose
word analysis tool. Although not tailored for advanced psychological analyses, it is a
nice word counting system.

10–12   The findings concerning positive emotions, negative emotions, and change in
cognitive words were first published in Pennebaker, Mayne, and Francis in 1997. See
also Moore and Brody (2009) and Graham, Glaser, Loving, Malarkey, Stowell, and
Kiecolt-Glaser (2009).

12–13   The findings on pronouns and changing perspectives were based on an article by Sherlock Campbell and me, published in 2003.

13   One of the more interesting discoveries about expressive writing was reported in an important paper by Youngsuk Kim. In her expressive writing project, bilingual Korean-English and Spanish-English students wrote either in their native language, second language, or both. Youngsuk had all participants wear a portable tape recorder for two days prior to writing and, again, a month after the writing experiment. Compared to people who did not write, participants who wrote about emotional upheavals spent more time with others, talked more, and laughed more. Although the effects were modest, those who wrote in both their native and learned languages tended to benefit the most.

14   Cheryl Hughes and Martha Francis were the first two students to earn doctoral degrees in psychology at Southern Methodist University. The results of Hughes's attempts to change people's thinking by influencing their word choice were the basis of her doctoral dissertation in 1994. More recently, Yi-Tai Seih, Cindy Chung, and I asked people to write in either the first person (as if they were simply describing their experience), second person (as if they were talking into a mirror), or third person (as if they were watching themselves in a movie) in their expressive writing. In another study, people were asked to change perspectives from essay to essay. To our surprise, people reported that writing in any perspective was helpful, as was switching perspectives. Our current thinking is that enforced perspective switching is probably good for some people and not others. Not the kind of groundbreaking conclusion we were looking for.

CHAPTER 2: IGNORING THE CONTENT, CELEBRATING THE STYLE

19   The drawing is from the *Thematic Apperception Test* by Henry A. Murray, Card 12F, Cambridge, MA, Harvard University Press.

20   Throughout this book, I include quotations from people who have been in my studies or classes, from text on the Internet, or even from conversations or e-mails from friends or family members. In all cases, all identifying information has been removed or altered.

22   In this book, the terms *style, function,* and *stealth words* are used interchangeably. They have many other names as well—*junk words, particles,* and *closed-class words.* Linguists tend to disagree about the precise definitions of each of these overlapping terms.

26   The table of function word usage rate is based on analyses from our own data representing language samples from over two thousand conversations, two hundred novels, twenty thousand blogs, and thousands of college student and adult writing samples. For more information, see Pennebaker, Chung, Ireland, Gonzales, and Booth (2007).

28   Political campaigns are wonderful to analyze. Presidential candidates are under the spotlight most every day, whether giving speeches, doing interviews, or simply

talking with people on the street. Most of their words are transcribed, making it easy for text analysis experts to track language over the course of the campaign. For some analyses of the 2004 presidential election, see an article by Rich Slatcher, Cindy Chung, Lori Stone, and me. You might also be interested in a site that David Beaver (a linguist from the University of Texas), Art Graesser (cognitive scientist, University of Memphis), Jeff Hancock (communications expert, Cornell), and I have created devoted to political issues, www.wordwatchers.wordpress.com.

29   One of the finest books that discuss the roles of the brain and language is George Miller's *The Science of Words*. It is the perfect introduction to the topic for someone without a great deal of background in the area.

31   The story of Phineas Gage is discussed in George Miller's book. Alexander Luria described Pavlov's experiences with his dogs in his classic 1973 book.

32–34   Knowing what pronouns and other words refer to within a given communication based on previous shared knowledge is called common ground. It is so central to communication that it has been studied across various fields and has been written about extensively in psycholinguistics by Herb Clark as a theory of common ground, in linguistics by David Beaver as presupposition theory, and in the cognitive sciences by Phil McCarthy and his colleagues as givenness/newness.

35–36   Unfortunately, the cross-language research is not covered in any detail in this book. My former student Nairán Ramírez-Esparza is discovering some remarkable changes in the ways people think as they switch from English to Spanish and vice versa. For example, bilingual speakers feel that they are more outgoing when speaking English and more reserved when speaking Spanish even though their behaviors show the opposite. Working with Cindy Chung and others, Nairán finds that the ways people think about a topic in Spanish are subtly different than the ways they think about it in English. See also work by Kashima and Kashima (1998).

   I'm pretty certain that there is a legal requirement for anyone who writes about language to mention the Whorf Hypothesis (or, if you are an anthropologist, the Sapir-Whorf Hypothesis). In line with these regulations, the extreme version of the Whorf Hypothesis is that one's language and vocabulary dictates one's perception. So, for example, if I didn't have a word for the color orange, I wouldn't be able to perceive the color. Due to an interesting historical movement in psychology and linguistics, the Whorf Hypothesis was roundly dismissed, beginning in the 1960s. New and more interesting versions of the hypothesis keep returning. The research of Nairán, Lera Boroditsky, and many others is now showing that, in some cases, our language can direct our attention, thinking, and memory.

CHAPTER 3: THE WORDS OF SEX, AGE, AND POWER
40–44   The best summary of our research on sex differences and language is a paper by Matt Newman, Carla Groom, Lori Handelman, and me published in 2008.

41 When people sit in front of a mirror and complete a questionnaire, they use more words like *I* and *me* than when the mirror is not present (Davis and Brock, 1975). The nature of self-focus among women has been demonstrated in a series of studies by Barbara Frederickson, Tomi-Ann Roberts, and their colleagues. An interesting take on people's stereotypes of the ways pronouns work has been shown by Wendi Gardner and her colleagues.

45 Ask any group of people in any culture and they will agree that women talk far more than men. A group of my former students Matthias Mehl, Simine Vazire, Nairán Ramírez, Rich Slatcher, and I ran six experiments in the United States and Mexico where we asked almost four hundred college students to wear a digital tape recorder for two to four days. Everything they said was later transcribed. Surprisingly, across all studies men and women spoke almost exactly the same number of words per day. It is very rare for a study that found absolutely nothing to be published, but the premier journal *Science* did so in 2007.

46–47 The blog project where we identified authors was conducted by Shlomo Argamon, Moshe Kopel, Jonathan Schler, and me in papers that came out in 2007 and 2009.

49–51 The script paper by Molly Ireland and me is currently under review.

57–60 In addition to the Pennebaker, Groom, Loew, and Dabbs article, see recent work by Jon Maner's lab as well as by Robert Josephs and his colleagues dealing with testosterone and behavior.

60–63 As we get older, our personalities change. Richard Robins and his colleagues have shown higher self-esteem, John Loehlin and Nick Martin reported increases in emotional stability, and Seider et al. (2009) found greater use of relational pronouns with increasing age. Much of this section is based on an article by Pennebaker and Stone (2003).

67 In the last twenty years, research on social class and physical health has ballooned within the United States. Some excellent articles on the topic include papers by Edith Chen, Karen Matthews, and Thomas Boyce as well as a classic by Nancy Adler and her colleagues.

68–70 There have been virtually no scientifically sound studies tracking natural language use in the home among people of differing social classes. The Hart and Risley study is promising, as is an earlier one by Brandis and Henderson in 1970.

CHAPTER 4: PERSONALITY: FINDING THE PERSON WITHIN
76–82 Most of the initial work on personality and language was the result of a collaboration with Laura King. You can see the actual analyses by reading the Pennebaker

and King (1999) paper. A number of people have expanded on this work, especially in how language is related to self-reported personality. Two great projects have been published, one by Francois Mairesse and colleagues and another by Tal Yarkoni. Psychologists Lisa Fast and David Funder, as well as Matthias Mehl, Sam Gosling, and I, have published on word use and personality. See also the creative work of Jon Oberlander, Alastair Gill, and Scott Nowson.

85–90   Cindy Chung's insight into the Meaning Extraction Method, or MEM, is now being used by labs around the world. It essentially allows researchers to extract themes from text automatically. One of the slickest applications is in pulling out themes written in different languages. For example, we can have the computer analyze thousands of blogs in, say, Finnish. Using the MEM, we can pull out several themes that are popular in Finnish blogs. All we have to do at the end of the project is to find someone who speaks Finnish so that he or she can tell us what we have discovered. The first MEM paper was by Chung and Pennebaker (2008).

97   Some of the criticisms of the TAT mirror those about the Rorschach. For example, the traditional judge-based method of grading essays is subjective. Two people could look at the same writing sample and come away with very different interpretations. Another problem is that when you ask the same person to write a story about the same picture on two occasions, they usually think up a new story to tell, often with different themes. Traditional personality researchers want tests that provide the same results on different occasions. Unfortunately, people are too inventive—they like to create new stories, especially if they have to tell them to the same people.

99   The bin Laden project was published by Pennebaker and Chung (2008). Cindy Chung, Art Graesser, Jeff Hancock, David Beaver, and I have all been immersed in a broader endeavor to learn how leaders change in their rhetoric over time. Hitler, Mao, Castro, as well as less extreme western leaders share changes in language use prior to going to wars, after being attacked, and as their regimes begin to fail.

100   To learn more about other text analysis methods, refer back to the notes for page 6 of the book.

CHAPTER 5: EMOTION DETECTION

106   Many people have argued that emotions affect the ways we think. Barbara Fredrickson, for example, has proposed a broaden-and-build model of positive emotions. Her studies suggest that when people are happy, they are able to pull back, see a broader perspective, and build new ideas. Thomas Borkovec has found that people who are sad or depressed tend to focus their negative feelings on past events, whereas people who are anxious are more worried about future events. Recently, Charles Carver and Eddie Harmon-Jones have provided compelling evidence to suggest that the emotion of anger activates brain areas associated with approach—much like posi-

tive emotions. Feelings of sadness or anxiety are linked to brain areas typically associated with avoidance.

108–110   The links between depression and self-focused attention have been independently discovered by several labs over the last thirty years. Walter Weintraub, one of the founding fathers of word analysis, was the first to report it in his 1981 book on verbal behavior. Tom Pysczynski and Jeff Greenberg developed a general theory of self-focus as a cause of depression. In addition to the suicidal poet project by Shannon Stirman and me published in 2001, a paper by Rude, Gortner, and Pennebaker (2004) found depressed college students used more I-words in their essays about their college experience than non-depressed students. See also recent work by Kaufman and Sexton on self-focus among suicidal poets.

110–114   The Giuliani project reference is Pennebaker and Lay (2002).

115   Dan Wegner's research on thought suppression is ingenious on several levels. Drawing on Tolstoy's childhood experience, Wegner asked students to *not* think of a white bear for as little as a minute or two. In doing so, he found that they actually started thinking of bears at high rates. More striking, when students were told that they no longer had to suppress their white bear thoughts, many students reported thinking of white bears at even higher rates. Wegner's early studies led him to develop a series of important theories about how the mind monitors information.

117–121   A number of investigators are now using blogs and other social media to track the emotional states of large communities of people. For example, Peter Dodds and Christopher Danforth have done this to track happiness, as has Adam Kramer; Bob Kraut, a pioneer of Internet research in psychology, has examined bulletin message boards to track emotional support in online communities; Elizabeth Lyons, Matthias Mehl, and I have analyzed blogs by pro-anorexics to assess their emotional profiles; Markus Wolf, Cindy Chung, and Hans Kordy have analyzed e-mails by psychotherapy patients to their therapists.

122   Over the years, my students and I have studied several large upheavals. Most of this work has attempted to understand how large-scale emotional events unfold over time. To read more about them, see the papers on the Texas A&M bonfire disaster (Gortner and Pennebaker, 2003); the death of Princess Diana (Stone and Pennebaker, 2002); the Loma Prieta earthquake and the Persian Gulf War (Pennebaker and Harber, 1993); and September 11, 2001 (Cohn, Mehl, and Pennebaker, 2004; Mehl and Pennebaker, 2003).

122–123   My colleague Darren Newtson and I traveled around Oregon and Washington for about a month after Mount St. Helens erupted. In towns that had experienced a great deal of damage, we randomly interviewed people by going door-to-door and by making random phone calls. One of the more interesting findings was that the more damage that had been done to a community, the more the residents wanted to talk. Those communities that were close to the volcano but that escaped damage were the most suspicious of outsiders and were least likely to agree to be interviewed. See my earlier book *Opening Up* for a more detailed account.

123   A particularly promising development in social psychology concerns "affective forecasting." According to its founders, Dan Gilbert, Tim Wilson, and others, people are remarkably bad at guessing how they will react to a future event. In general, people predict that they will be more distressed about a traumatic experience than they actually would be.

124   Societies frequently adopt well-intentioned interventions that don't work. In addition to CISD, abstinence-only sex education and D.A.R.E. have generally caused more problems than they solved. See Timothy D. Wilson's book *Redirect*.

125   Cindy Chung's dissertation involved tracking 186 bloggers on a blog community devoted to dieting for one year.

126   Are secrets always toxic? Actually, no. In fact, secrets may be bad but telling others can sometimes be worse. For a wonderful summary of the psychology of secrets, see Anita Kelly's book and articles.

126–127   The story of Laura was first described in my book *Opening Up*.

127   People have a powerful urge to talk about emotional events. Bernard Rimé and his colleagues find that people across all cultures typically confide in others for virtually all types of emotional events. One of my favorite findings is that if you have an emotional experience and you tell someone about it *and* you ask your friend to keep it secret, your friend will tell two or three others about it. Even hearing about a secret is an emotional event that the listener needs to share.

CHAPTER 6: LYING WORDS
131   The research on the physiology of confession involved people talking about the most traumatic experience of their lives into a tape recorder. All potential identifying information from the story has been changed. From an article by Pennebaker, Hughes, and O'Heeron (1987).

134   For anyone seeking a discussion of self-deception in English literature, I recommend the writer and scholar Jim Magnuson. His wisdom on this and other topics has been invaluable to me in our discussions over the years.

140   Somewhere between self-deception, deception, and marketing is the concept of "spin." In the political world, *spin* is defined as the art of glossing over the truth. Indeed, after an important debate or speech, political operatives will often meet with

members of the press to spin the speech of their own candidate to make it sound even better than it was and spin the opponent's words to sound worse. In fact, a cutting-edge computational linguist at Queen's University in Canada, David Skillicorn, has developed a model to identify spin based on linguistic features associated with deception (research.cs.queensu.ca/home/skill/election/election.html).

140–141   In his *Introductory Lectures on Psychoanalysis*, Freud devotes a surprising amount of time to slips of the tongue, or, as he refers to them, parapraxes. In retrospect, you can understand why he used parapraxes as a way to introduce his general theory. Everyday slips of the tongue are common and reveal certain truths about what people are really thinking.

142–143   I'm indebted to Melanie Greenberg for allowing me to reanalyze her language data.

144–146   A fascinating account of the Stephen Glass case is available at www.rickm cginnis.com/articles/Glassindex.htm. For the analyses, I only examined thirty-nine of his forty-one stories (one was co-written by someone else and the other was made up exclusively of published quotes).

Somehow relevant to this discussion is a wonderful quote by author Mary McCarthy. In 1979, she was interviewed by the television host Dick Cavett about the author Lillian Hellman, who had a reputation for fabricating some of her stories. When asked about Hellman's work, McCarthy snorted, "Every word she writes is a lie, including *and* and *the*." Hellman subsequently filed a defamation suit against McCarthy, which was dropped after Hellman's death in 1984.

149   There are several other fascinating papers that are worth mentioning in the literature on high-stakes, real-world deception detection using computerized text analysis. For example, David Skillicorn and his colleagues, as well as Max Louwerse, Gun Semin, and their colleagues, along with other labs around the world have examined the e-mails between Enron employees during the decade leading up to the company's bankruptcy in 2001 due to its fraudulent accounting activities. In addition, David Larcker and Anastasia Zakolyukina used computerized text analysis to classify deceptive versus truthful chief executives in their quarterly earnings conference calls.

152–153   The project by Denise Huddle and me has not yet been submitted for publication. One additional finding is particularly noteworthy. Recall that I-words signal innocence. Closer inspection indicated that it wasn't all I-words. In fact, the more that defendants used the actual word *I* (and *I'll*, *I'm*, *I'd*, etc.), the more likely they were to be innocent. In fact, use of the word *me* was used more by the truly guilty.

155   The dating project is by Toma, Hancock, and Ellison (2008).

165   Discrepancy or modal verbs identify words that make a distinction between an ideal and a real state. "I *should* be eating vegetables" indicates that I'm not eating

them (reality) but the ideal person would be. Columbia University psychologist Tory Higgins has developed an elaborate theory around the self-discrepancy idea that has implications for goals, motivations, and mental health. The ideal-real discrepancy is also inherent in Robert Wicklund's work on self-awareness.

167   I love performatives. Not only are they psychologically interesting but they are at the center of some eye-opening debates in philosophy. Check out the work of the philosopher John Searle and also John L. Austin.

168   Although not discussed here, another verbal feature of deception is the use of words such as *um* or *er*. A recent article by Joanne Arciuli and her colleagues is worth reading. Also, see Michael Erard's book *Um*.

CHAPTER 7. THE LANGUAGE OF STATUS, POWER, AND LEADERSHIP
176   Recall that pronouns tell us where people are paying attention. Many of the pronoun effects we see with humans match the gaze finding among nonhuman primates. For a delightful analysis of status hierarchies in chimpanzees, see the work of Frans De Waal. In humans, visual cues to dominance have been discussed by Jack Dovidio and his colleagues.

188–189   John Dean, personal communications, August 30, 2002.

190   I'm indebted to Ethan Burris and his colleagues for allowing us to reanalyze their data for this project.

192   The leadership literature has grown increasingly complex. To get a flavor of some of the directions, see the pioneering work of Fred Fiedler. A summary of research dealing with leadership among women and men is best captured by Alice Eagly and her colleagues. David Waldman and his group have done a nice job of examining leadership attributes.

194   Another example of language shifts across languages and cultures was discovered by Doug Sofer as part of his dissertation. He found that the use of the first-person singular in letters to the presidents of the South American country Colombia between 1944 and 1958 differed by social class. As you might guess, the lower the social class of the author, the higher their use of I-words. See also the seminal work of Howard Giles on accommodation theory, a framework for understanding when people shift in their language to match their interaction partners.

194   Thanks to George Theodoridis for his observations on Ancient Greek language (personal communication, November 6, 2009).

195   Note that there are other language dimensions that we find to be linked to status. Although the effects are modest, people with lower status tend to use the fol-

lowing word categories more: negations, impersonal pronouns, tentative words, swear words.

CHAPTER 8: THE LANGUAGE OF LOVE

197–198   The IM interaction was part of the Slatcher and Pennebaker (2006) project. The on-air fight between Elisabeth Hasselbeck and Rosie O'Donnell that follows had been brewing for several months. O'Donnell had already announced that she was leaving the show in three weeks. The overall interaction between the two women evidenced a language style matching (or LSM) score of .94—which is exceedingly high.

202–204   The research on the mirror neuron system continues to be controversial. There is an increasing number of studies that demonstrate highly specialized brain activity in Broca's area that reflects behavioral mimicking. The primary objection about the mirror neuron approach is that no consistent theory or model explains how it works or how it is related to cognitive activity. Particularly interesting papers are available by Rizzolatti and Craighero (2004), Kimberly Montgomery and her colleagues (2009), and Kotz et al. (2010).

207   The LSM project dealing with liars was conducted by Hancock, Curry, Goorha, and Woodworth (2008). For a report on additional text analyses of the same data, see Duran, Hall, McCarthy, and McNamara (2010).

208   Despite the intuitive appeal of multitasking, the evidence is clear that it is not an effective technique to accomplish even moderately complex tasks. A particularly convincing case of the downside of multitasking has been published by Ophir, Nass, and Wagner (2009).

211   The speed-dating project had a complicated history. Paul Eastwick, a faculty member at Texas A&M, visited our department in the spring of 2010 to describe some speed-dating research he had been doing with a colleague of his, Eli Finkel, who is at Northwestern. Molly Ireland was fascinated by his talk and asked if he would be interested in applying the LSM methodology to the speed-dating transcripts. Within a few days, Molly's analyses yielded the remarkable finding that LSM in speed-dating conversations was a powerful predictor of later dates. Molly then added the speed-dating analyses to Richard Slatcher's IM project (see p. 212) and, in record time, submitted the paper to a top journal, where it was accepted and published. The resulting paper is Ireland, Slatcher, Eastwick, Scissors, Finkel, and Pennebaker (2011).

212–215   The IM project was initially published as Slatcher and Pennebaker (2006) and then, with the reanalyses of the data, as Ireland, Slatcher, et al. (2011).

216   John Gottman's research on relationships has a number of practical applications for making good marriages. In addition to his books and articles, *New York Times*

writer Tara Parker-Pope has written a balanced book on marriage and relationships that relies on some of the most recent research.

218–223   The analyses of Elizabeth Barrett and Robert Browning, Sylvia Plath and Ted Hughes, and Sigmund Freud and Carl Jung were part of a paper published by Molly Ireland and me in 2010.

CHAPTER 9: SEEING GROUPS, COMPANIES, AND COMMUNITIES
THROUGH THEIR WORDS

228   Several studies have tracked language use and its relationship with successful marriages. Not surprisingly, use of pronouns, especially we-words, between the couples is a reliable predictor. See the work of Seider and colleagues (2009) and of Rachel Simmons, Peter Gordon, and Diane Chambless (2005).

229   The project linking pronoun use among couples and heart failure was conducted by Rohrbaugh and colleagues.

The Sexton and Helmreich project focused only on flight simulation studies. Later analyses by Brian Sexton found links between low we-word use and human error in the cockpit voice recordings of planes that had crashed (personal communication, April 20, 2010). See also the work of Foushee and Helmreich.

232   One of the more interesting approaches to studying natural interactions was pioneered by Bill Ickes, a social psychologist at the University of Texas at Arlington. In a typical study, pairs of students are instructed to visit Ickes's research lab to participate in a conversation. After both complete questionnaires and a consent form to be videotaped, the experimenter tries to begin filming and then "discovers" that his camera is broken. The experimenter leaves the lab, claiming he's going to find a technician. The students remain in the lab and usually begin talking with one another.

What they don't know is that another hidden camera is taping their interaction. Later, the students are told about the hidden camera and are asked to rate their interaction on a minute-by-minute basis. Ickes is able to see how the two people were thinking about each other as their conversation unfolded. Bill has kindly allowed us to analyze some of his interactions. I strongly recommend his recent book, *Strangers in a Strange Lab*.

And while we are talking about real-world approaches to studying the behavior of people, I insist that you check out the work of Sandy Pentland and Roz Piccard, who are at MIT's Media Laboratory. Together and separately, the two have devised a striking number of methods that track how people see and emotionally react to their worlds as they go about daily life.

232–235   One way to think about the increase in we-words over time is that the longer people talk with others, the more their identities become fused. Bill Swann and his colleagues have been conducting a number of imaginative projects tracking identity fusion. For example, making people more aware of their own group increases the likelihood that they will endorse fighting and dying for it.

233 The national defense project was run by Andrew Scholand, Yla Tausczik, and me and funded by Sandia National Laboratory. The research tracking twenty professional therapists over three years was conducted by Susan Odom and Stephanie Rude. The findings are reported in Odom's dissertation, which was completed in 2006.

234–235 Drops in suicide rates following terrorist attacks have been reported by Emad Salib and his colleagues. Additional findings about language and psychological changes following the subway bombings in Madrid in 2004 have been reported by Itziar Fernandez, Dario Paez, and me. The language changes in written essays among New Orleans residents after Hurricane Katrina were collected by Sandy Hartman.

238–239 A former graduate student of mine, Amy Gonzales, conducted a complex laboratory experiment where groups of students had to work together either in face-to-face groups or in online groups. The details are reported in Gonzales, Hancock, and Pennebaker (2010). A second project, which was described earlier, was run with business school students by Ethan Burris and his colleagues. The two lab studies are consistent with some fascinating real-world projects conducted by Paul Taylor and his colleagues. For example, Taylor found higher LSM levels in the transcripts of successful hostage negotiations between police and hostage-takers in the UK relative to unsuccessful hostage negotiations.

240–243 The Craigslist project is part of a larger study focusing on measures of community cohesiveness. The primary team members include Cindy Chung, Yla Tausczik, and me. We are indebted to Mark Hayward for his help in providing the relevant Gini statistics.

243–247 The word-catching research is based on an archive of tape recordings I have collected between 1990 and 2010. They include the anlayses of 1,162 conversational files of people in the real world having natural conversations. Discriminant analyses (for you statistics fans out there) show that cross-validation classifications are accurate at 80 to 84 percent for anywhere from five to seven settings, where 16 to 20 percent is chance.

248 One of my favorite language maps tracks the usage of the words *pop*, *soda*, and *Coke* as generic names for soft drinks. Check out www.popvssoda.com.

248–253 One of the giants in the world of sociolinguistics is William Labov from the University of Pennsylvania. Labov has pioneered ways to track how word usage and accents change across regions and time. Some of his early work, for example, examined language differences within blocks and neighborhoods of large cities. Later, he began to focus on much broader trends across the United States.

Due in large part to Labov's influence, the University of Pennsylvania has taken an important lead in advancing our knowledge of social communication and language use. It houses the Linguistic Data Consortium, or LDC (www.ldc.upenn.edu), which houses one of the largest text archives in the world. In addition, Mark Liberman—a particularly thoughtful linguist—has created Language Log, a highly influential blog site (languagelog.ldc.upenn.edu).

249–251   The *This I Believe* project has been growing in multiple directions. Cindy Chung, Jason Rentfrow, and I have been developing detailed maps of language use across the United States based on both function words and content words.

251–252   A particularly hot approach to text analysis examines how people use emotion words in their blogs, tweets, or other communications. Although sentiment analysis focuses only on people's use of positive and negative emotion words, it can provide a general overview of the happiness of cities, regions, or entire countries. For a discussion, see the work of Adam Kramer, Jason Rentfrow, and also Alex Wright's article in the *New York Times*. Also, check out a truly wonderful book by Eric Weiner, *The Geography of Bliss*, on one man's attempt to understand why some countries are happier than others.

252   In deducing the linguistic fingerprint of the Texas high schools, discriminant analyses showed that we could accurately classify students at a 19 to 20 percent rate, where 11 percent was chance.

CHAPTER 10: WORD SLEUTHING

258–261   Matching blog entries to specific authors can be done in a number of ways. In the chapter, we try to match blogs written today with those written many years ago by the same authors. This is much harder than matching blogs written by authors at about the same time. In fact, think back to the example of the twenty bloggers. Imagine we have, say, ten blog entries on consecutive days from each of the twenty people. We pull out one of the ten entries for each person and put this into a separate stack. The goal is to match the twenty "orphan" entries with the twenty bloggers by reading the nine blog entries of known authorship. Our computer does a much better job at guessing which orphan entry goes with which blogger. The overall hit rate is closer to 58 percent (where 5 percent is chance).

262–265   In addition to the work of Adair and of Mosteller and Wallace dealing with the Federalist Papers, be sure to see recent articles by Patric Juola (2006) and by Jeff Collins and his colleagues (2004).

265   Pardon me for a minute while I have a little chat with the twenty people on Earth who really, really want to know the methods for analyzing the Federalist Papers. The cross-validation approach is based on discriminant analyses assuming equal group

size. The original function-word assignment method, which assigned all unknown texts to Madison, correctly classifed 92.4 percent of the original essays and 86.4 percent for cross-validation. The numbers for function words plus punctuation were 98.5 percent and 84.8 percent. Analyses based on the fourteen "tell" words used a binary procedure (was the word used or not within an essay) and yielded both classification and cross-validation accuracies of 98.5 percent. The one assignment error was for essay forty-one, which is attributed to Madison. The tell-word analyses estimated that Hamilton was the author of 49, 52 through 57, and 63, and that Madison was the author of 50, 51, and 62.

Whereas Hamilton claimed credit for all eleven of the unknown manuscripts, he reported that three additional ones were jointly written by Madison and himself. Madison's later recollection was that he (Madison) had written them with some supplemental comments by Hamilton. All linguistic analyses show that the jointly written papers were completely different from either Hamilton's or Madison's solo-authored pamphlets. Given this, I tend to side with Hamilton's accounts of the authorship issue rather than with Madison's.

265–267   A recent project by Terry Pettijohn and Donald Sacco (2009) analyzed the lyrics of number one *Billboard* songs between 1955 and 2003. They discovered that during economic downturns, people preferred lyrics that were more complex, social, and future oriented.

268   There are several ways to determine if collaborations result in average or synergistic language use. Consider how John Lennon and Paul McCartney used present-tense verbs in their lyrics. For their individually written songs, Lennon consistently used more than McCartney (15.8 percent versus 13.7 percent). According to the average-person hypothesis, their collaboration should have resulted in songs that ranged between 13.7 and 15.8 percent present-tense verbs. In fact, the Lennon-McCartney eyeball-to-eyeball collaborations resulted in songs with 17.6 percent present-tense verbs. In this case, Lennon was somewhere between McCartney and Lennon-McCartney—the average writer. We can calculate the percentage of time that Lennon, McCartney, and Lennon-McCartney produced songs that were in the middle of the other two linguistically. The author who was statistically the average person for the Beatles was: 50.6 percent for Lennon, 36.1 percent for McCartney, and 13.3 percent for Lennon-McCartney. The statistically average author for the Federalist Papers was: 39.5 percent for Hamilton, 53.9 percent for Madison, and 6.6 percent for Hamilton-Madison. In other words, when collaborating Lennon-McCartney and Hamilton-Madison were far more extreme than either author on his own.

270   N-gram analyses have been used to characterize authors. For example, Art Graesser and his colleagues have also developed speech-act classifiers that assess the first three words in a sentence to determine what type of sentence is being uttered (e.g., "Are you here?" "Here you are!" "You are here."). Their speech-act classifier can be used to determine the relative status of two interactants.

270–271   Another way to think about language use is to listen to how presidents create stories about themselves. Dan McAdams has spent much of his career analyzing the stories people tell to get a better sense of their personality. His most recent work is a fascinating analysis of George W. Bush.

272   Perhaps the best source for presidential documents is through the American Presidency Project, directed by Gerhard Peters at the University of California at Santa Barbara. Peters and his collaborators are bringing together one of the largest archives of presidential documents, including speeches, interviews, press conferences, and much more. For more information, go to www.presidency.ucsb.edu/.

273   The figure is based on summing the standardized scores (z-scores) for personal pronouns and total emotion word use. To make all the numbers positive values, a constant of 3.0 was added to the resultant z-scores.

274   Although Franklin Roosevelt's press conferences have been transcribed, they have also been heavily edited. FDR had arrangements with press members so that large blocks would be off the record. In terms of social-emotional language, his was the lowest of any modern president. However, because his language records are so heavily edited, they have not been included in the press conference corpus.

275   Bosch quote from the 2000 program notes of the PBS documentary series *Reagan*. www.pbs.org/wgbh/amex/reagan/filmmore/description.html

275–277   The Obama missing-*I* case was originally reported on Mark Liberman's blog, the Language Log, at http://languagelog.ldc.upenn.edu/nll/?p=1651. The I-word press conference data includes thirty-five press conferences or meetings of Obama from his inauguration in January 2009 through May 2010. Note that Mark Liberman, the founder of the Language Log blog, reported comparable findings in his analysis of Obama's speeches.

276   The quotations about Obama's use of I-words were written by George Will in the *Washington Post*, June 7, 2009, and by Stanley Fish in the *New York Times*, June 7, 2009.

281   An increasing number of researchers are trying to determine if it is possible to predict terrorism, extremism, and violent behavior through language analysis. Allison Smith, who now works for the Department of Homeland Security, has analyzed both violent and nonviolent extremist groups around the world and found that the ways they express themselves are quite different. For example, those groups that make the most references to in-group affiliations and power or dominance are the ones most likely to engage in violent behaviors.

283   On the southeast tip of Australia is Tasmania, an Australian island the size of England. One of Tasmania's first and, arguably, most famous explorers was Henry

Hellyer. To read an interesting account of how and why he died, see a recent analysis of his letters and journals by Jenna Baddeley, Gwyneth R. Daniel, and me.

284–287 The research on the admissions essays comes with several caveats. In general, traditional academic markers such as college board scores and high school rank are correlated with college grades at levels higher than our language measures (multiple Rs for traditional measures = .435; for language alone = .233; for both = .455, based on an N of 23,794).

APPENDIX: A HANDY GUIDE FOR SPOTTING AND INTERPRETING
FUNCTION WORDS IN THE WILD
292 I'm indebted to Claude M. Chemtob for providing a large number of transcripts from people suffering from PTSD.

Bibliography and References

Adair, D. (1944). The authorship of the disputed Federalist Papers. *William and Mary Quarterly, 1*, 97–122. (Available at www.jstor.org/stable/1921883.)

Adler, N. E., Boyce, T., Chesney, M. A., Cohen, S., Folkman, S., Kahn, R. L., & Syme, S. L. (1994). "Socioeconomic status and health: The challenge of the gradient." *American Psychologist, 49*, 15–24.

Allport, G. W. (1961). *Pattern and growth in personality.* New York: Holt, Rinehart & Winston.

Arciuli, J., Mallard, D., & Villar, G. (2010). "Um, I can tell you're lying": Linguistic markers of deception versus truth-telling in speech. *Applied Psycholinguistics, 31*, 397–411.

Argamon, S., Koppel, M., Pennebaker, J. W., & Schler, J. (2007). Mining the blogosphere: Age, gender and the varieties of self-expression. *First Monday, 12* (peer-reviewed journal on the Internet). http://firstmonday.org/issues/issue12_9/argamon/index.html.

———. (2009). Automatically profiling the author of an anonymous text. In *Communications of the Association for Computing Machinery (CACM), 52*, 119–123.

Austin, J. L. (1962). *How to do things with words.* Cambridge, Mass.: Harvard University Press.

Baddeley, J. L, Daniel, G. R., & Pennebaker, J. W. (In press). How Henry Hellyer's language use foretold his suicide. *Death Studies.*

Balz, Dan, & Johnson, Haynes. (2009). *The battle for America 2008: The story of an extraordinary election.* New York: Viking.

Beaver, D. I. (2001). *Presupposition and assertion in dynamic semantics.* Stanford, CA: CSLI Publications.

Beaver, D., & Zeevat, H. (2007). Accommodation. In Ramchand, G. & Reiss, C. (eds.) *Oxford handbook of linguistic interfaces*, New York: Oxford University Press.

Berry, D. S., Pennebaker, J. W., Mueller, J. S., & Hiller, W. S. (1997). Linguistic bases of social perception. *Personality and Social Psychology Bulletin, 23*, 526–37.

Biber, D. (1988). *Variation across speech and writing.* Cambridge: Cambridge University Press.

Boals, A., & Klein, K. (2005). Word use in emotional narratives about failed romantic relationships and subsequent mental health. *Journal of Language and Social Psychology, 24,* 252–68.

Bond, G. D., & Lee, A. Y. (2005). Language of lies in prison: Linguistic classification of prisoners' truthful and deceptive natural language. *Applied Cognitive Psychology, 19,* 313–29.

Borkovec, T. D. (2002). Life in the future versus life in the present. *Clinical Psychology: Science and Practice, 9,* 76–80.

Boroditsky, L. (2001). Does language shape thought? Mandarin and English speakers' conception of time. *Cognitive Psychology, 43,* 1–22.

———. (2010). Lost in Translation. *Wall Street Journal.* July 24.

Bosson, J. K., Swann Jr., W. B., & Pennebaker, J. W. (2000). Stalking the perfect measure of implicit self-esteem: The blind men and the elephant revisited? *Journal of Personality and Social Psychology, 79,* 631–43.

Brandis, W., & Henderson, D. (1970). *Social class, language, and communication.* London: Routledge.

Brown, R. (1968). *Words and things: An introduction to language.* New York: Free Press.

Burgoon, J. K., Stern, L. A., & Dillman, L. (1995). *Interpersonal adaptation: Dyadic interaction patterns.* New York: Cambridge University Press.

Burgoon, J. K., and Qin, T. (2006). The dynamic nature of deceptive verbal communication. *Journal of Language and Social Psychology, 25,* 76–96.

Burris, E., Rodgers, M., Mannix, E., Hendron, M., and Oldroyd, M. (2009). Playing favorites: The influence of leaders' inner circle on group processes and performance. *Personality and Social Psychology Bulletin, 35,* 1244–57.

Campbell, R. S., & Pennebaker, J. W. (2003). The secret life of pronouns: Flexibility in writing style and physical health. *Psychological Science, 14,* 60–65.

Carroll, L. (1865). *Alice in wonderland.* Gutenberg Press, ftp://sunsite.unc.edu/pub/docs/books/gutenberg/etext97/alice30h.zip.

Carstensen, L. L. (2009). *A long bright future.* New York: Random House.

Carver, C. S., & Harmon-Jones, E. (2009). Anger is an approach-related affect: Evidence and implications. *Psychological Bulletin, 135,* 183–204.

Chen, E., Matthews, K. A., and Boyce, W. T. (2002). Socioeconomic differences in children's health: How and why do these relationships change with age? *Psychological Bulletin, 128,* 295–329.

Chung, C. K. (2009). Predicting weight loss in blogs using computerized text analysis. *Dissertation Abstracts International: Section B: The Sciences and Engineering, 70*(9-B), 5893.

Chung, C. K., Jones, C., Liu, A., & Pennebaker, J. W. (2008). Predicting success and failure in weight loss blogs through natural language use. *Proceedings of the 2008 International Conference on Weblogs and Social Media,* 180–81.

Chung, C. K., & Pennebaker, J. W. (2007). The psychological functions of function words. In Fiedler, K. (ed.), *Social communication,* 343–59. New York: Psychology Press.

———. (2008). Revealing dimensions of thinking in open-ended self-descriptions: An automated meaning extraction method for natural language. *Journal of Research in Personality, 42,* 96–132.

————. (In press). Linguistic Inquiry and Word Count (LIWC): pronounced "Luke" . . . and other useful facts. In McCarthy, P., & Boonthum, C. (eds.), *Applied natural language processing and content analysis: Identification, investigation, and resolution,* Hershey, Pennsylvania: IGI Global.

Chung, C. K., Rentfrow, P. J., & Pennebaker, J. W. (2011). *Geographical variations in beliefs: Validation of "This I Believe" themes.* Talk presented at the 2011 Annual Meeting for the Society of Personality and Social Psychology, San Antonio, TX.

Cialdini, R. B., Borden, R.J., Thorne, A., Walker, M.R., Freeman, S., & Sloan, L. R. (1976). Basking in reflected glory: Three (football) field studies. *Journal of Personality and Social Psychology, 34,* 366–75.

Clark, H. H. (1996). *Using language.* Cambridge, UK: Cambridge University Press.

Clark, H. H., & Brennan, S. E. (1991). Grounding in communication. In Resnick, L. B., Levine, J. M., & Teasley, S. D. (eds.), *Perspectives on socially shared cognition,* 127–49. Washington, D.C.: American Psychological Association.

Cohn, M. A., Mehl, M. R., & Pennebaker, J. W. (2004). Linguistic markers of psychological change surrounding September 11, 2001. *Psychological Science, 15,* 687–93.

Collins, J., Kaufer, D., Vlachos, P., Butler, B., & Ishizaki, S. (2004). Detecting collaborations in text: Comparing the authors' rhetorical language choices in the Federalist Papers. *Computers and the Humanities, 38,* 15–36.

Damasio, A. R. (1995). *Descartes' error: Emotion, reason and the human brain.* New York: HarperCollins.

Danner, Mark. (2005). The secret way to war. *New York Review of Books.* June 9. www.nybooks.com/articles/archives/2005/jun/09/the-secret-way-to-war/

Davis, D., and Brock, T. C. (1975). Use of first person pronouns as a function of increased objective self-awareness and performance feedback. *Journal of Experimental Social Psychology, 11,* 381–88.

Davison, K. P., Pennebaker, J. W., & Dickerson, S. S. (2000). Who talks? The social psychology of illness support groups. *American Psychologist, 55,* 205–17.

De Waal, F. (2000). *Chimpanzee politics,* rev. ed. Baltimore: Johns Hopkins University Press.

Dickens, C. (1843). *A Christmas carol.* London: Elliot Stock.

Dodds, P. S., & Danforth, C. M. (2009). Measuring the happiness of large-scale written expression: Songs, blogs, and presidents. *Journal of Happiness Studies, 11,* 441–56.

Dovidio, J. F., & Ellyson, S. L. (1985). Patterns of visual dominance behaviors in humans. In Dovidio, J. F., & Ellyson, J. F. (eds.), *Power, dominance, and nonverbal behavior,* New York: Springer-Verlag.

Duran, N. D., Hall, C., McCarthy, P. M., & McNamara, D. S. (2010). The linguistic correlates of conversational deception: Comparing natural language processing technologies. *Applied Psycholinguistics, 31,* 439–62.

Eagly, A. H., Johannesen-Schmidt, M. C., & van Engen, M. L. (2003). Transformational, transactional, and laissez-faire leadership styles: A meta-analysis comparing women and men. *Psychological Bulletin, 129,* 569–91.

Eastwick, P. W., Saigal, S. D., & Finkel, E. J. (In press). Smooth operating: A Structural Analysis of Social Behavior (SASB) perspective on initial romantic encounters. *Social Psychological and Personality Science.*

Eckert, P. (2000). *Linguistic variation as social practice.* Oxford: Blackwell.

Ekman, P., O'Sullivan, M., & Frank, M.G. (1999). A few can catch a liar. *Psychological Science, 10,* 263–66.

Erard, M. (2007). *Um: Slips, stumbles, and verbal blunders, and what they mean.* New York: Random House.

Fast, L. A., & Funder, D. C. (2008). Personality as manifest in word use: Correlations with self-report, acquaintance-report, and behavior. *Journal of Personality and Social Psychology, 94,* 334–46.

Fernandez, I., Paez, D., & Pennebaker, J.W. (2009). Comparison of expressive writing after the terrorist attacks of September 11th and March 11th. *International Journal of Clinical and Health Psychology, 9,* 89–103.

Fiedler, F. E. (1967). A theory of leadership effectiveness. New York: McGraw-Hill.

Fiedler, K., & Semin, G. R. (1992). Attribution and language as a socio-cognitive environment. In Semin, G. R., & Fiedler, K., (eds.), *Language, interaction, and social cognition,* 58–78. Thousand Oaks, CA: Sage Publications, Inc.

Finkel, E. J., Eastwick, P. W., & Matthews, J. (2007). Speed-dating as an invaluable tool for studying romantic attraction: A methodological primer. *Personal Relationships, 14,* 149–166.

Foltz, P. W. (1996). Latent semantic analysis for text-based research. *Behavior Research Methods, Instruments and Computers, 28,* 197–202.

Foster, D. W. (2000). *Author unknown: On the trail of anonymous.* New York: Henry Holt.

Foushee, H. C., & Helmreich, R. L. (1988). Group interaction and flight crew performance. In Wiener, E. L., & Nagel, D. C. (eds.), *Human Factors in Aviation,* pp. 189–225, San Diego: Academic Press.

Francis, W. N., & Kucera, H. (1982). *Frequency analyses of English usage: Lexicon and grammar.* Boston: Houghton Mifflin.

François, M., & Walker, M. (2010). Towards personality-based user adaptation: Psychologically informed stylistic language generation. *User Modeling and User-Adapted Interaction, 20,* 227–78.

François, M., Walker, M., Mehl, M. R., & Moore, R. (2007). Using linguistic cues for the automatic recognition of personality in conversation and text. *Journal of Artificial Intelligence Research, 30,* 457–500.

Frattaroli, J. (2006). Experimental disclosure and its moderators: A meta-analysis. *Psychological Bulletin, 132,* 823–65.

Fredrickson, B. L. (2005). The broaden-and-build theory of positive emotions. In Huppert, F. A., Baylis, N., & Keverne, B. (eds.), *The science of well-being,* 217–38. New York: Oxford University Press.

Fredrickson, B. L., Roberts, T.-A., Noll, S. M., Quinn, D. M., & Twenge, J. M. (1998). That swimsuit becomes you: Sex differences in self-objectification, restrained eating, and math performance. *Journal of Personality and Social Psychology, 75,* 269–84.

Freud, S. (1901). *Psychopathology of everyday life.* New York: Basic Books.

———. (1920/1977). *Introductory lectures on psychoanalysis.* Translated by James Strachey. New York: Norton.

Galinsky, A. D., Magee, J. C., Gruenfeld, D. H., Liljenquist, K. A., & Whitson, J. A. (2008). Power reduces the press of the situation: implications for creativity, conformity, and dissonance. *Journal of Personality and Social Psychology, 95*, 1450–66.

Galinsky, A. D., Magee, J. C., Inesi, M. E., & Gruenfeld, D. H. (2006). Perspectives not taken. *Psychological Science, 17*, 1068–74.

Gardner, W. L., Gabriel, S., & Lee, A. Y. (1999). "I" value freedom, but "we" value relationships: Self-construal priming mirrors cultural differences in judgment. *Psychological Science, 10*, 321–26.

Gilbert, D. T. (2006). *Stumbling on happiness.* New York: Alfred A. Knopf.

Giles, H., Coupland, J., & Coupland, N. (1991). *Contexts of accommodation: Developments in applied sociolinguistics.* New York: Cambridge University Press.

Gill, A. J., Nowson, S., and Oberlander, J. (2009). What are they blogging about? Personality, topic and motivation in blogs. *Proceedings of the Third International AAAI Conference on Weblogs and Social Media*, Menlo Park, CA, 18–25. San Jose, CA.

Gill, A. J., Oberlander, J., & Austin, E. (2006). The perception of e-mail personality at zero-acquaintace. *Personality and Individual Differences, 40*, 497–507.

Goffman, E. (1981). *Forms of talk.* Philadelphia: University of Pennsylvania Press.

Gonzales, A. L., Hancock, J. T., & Pennebaker, J. W. (2010). Language indicators of social dynamics in small groups. *Communications Research, 37*, 3–19.

Gortner, E. M., and Pennebaker, J. W. (2003). The archival anatomy of a disaster: Media coverage and community-wide health effects of the Texas A&M Bonfire Tragedy. *Journal of Social and Clinical Psychology, 22*, 580–603.

Gosling, S. D. (2008). *Snoop: What your stuff says about you.* New York: Basic.

Gottman, J. M., and Levenson, R.W. (2002). A two-factor model for predicting when a couple will divorce: Exploratory analyses using 14-year longitudinal data. *Family Process, 41*, 83–96.

Gottman, J. M. (1995). *Why marriages succeed or fail.* New York: Simon and Schuster.

Gottschalk, L. A., & Gleser, G. C. (1969). *The measurement of psychological states through the content analysis of verbal behavior.* Berkeley: University of California Press.

Graesser, A. C., Han, L., Jeon, M., Myers, J., Kaltner, J., Cai, Z., McCarthy, P., Shala, L., Louwerse, M., Hu, X., Rus, V., McNamara, D., Hancock, J., Chung, C., & Pennebaker, J. (2009). Cohesion and classification of speech acts in Arabic discourse. Presented at the nineteenth annual meeting of the Society for Text and Discourse, Rotterdam, the Netherlands, July.

Graesser, A. C., & Petschonek, S. L. (2005). Automated systems that analyze text and discourse: QUAID, Coh-Metrix, and AutoTutor. In Lenderking, W. R., & Revicki, D. (eds.), *Advancing health outcomes research methods and clinical applications*, McLean, VA: Degnon Associates.

Graesser, A. C., McNamara, D. S., Louwerse, M. M., & Cai, Z. (2004). Coh-Metrix: Analysis of text on cohesion and language. *Behavior Research Methods, Instruments and Computers, 36*, 193–202.

Graham, H. E., Glaser, R., Loving, T. J., Malarkey, W. B., Stowell, J. R., & Kiecolt-

Glaser, J. K. (2009). Cognitive word use during marital conflict and increases in proinflammatory cytokines. *Health Psychology, 28,* 621–30.

Graybeal, A., Seagal, J. D., & Pennebaker, J. W. (2002). The role of story-making in disclosure writing: The psychometrics of narrative. *Psychology and Health, 17,* 571–81.

Greenberg, M. A., Stone, A. A., & Wortman, C. B. (1996). Health and psychological effects of emotional disclosure: A test of the inhibition-confrontation approach. *Journal of Personality and Social Psychology, 71,* 588–602.

Groom, C. J., & Pennebaker, J. W. (2005). The language of love: Sex, sexual orientation, and language use in online personal advertisements. *Sex Roles, 52,* 447–61.

Halfaker, A., Kittur, A., Kraut, R., & Riedl, J. (2009). A jury of your peers: Quality, experience, and ownership in Wikipedia. Paper presented at ACM Annual Meeting, October 25–27. doi.acm.org/10.1145/1641309.1641332

Hall, J. A., Coats, E. J., & Smith LeBeau, L. (2005). Nonverbal behavior and the vertical dimension of social relations: A meta-analysis. *Psychological Bulletin, 131,* 898–924.

Hancock, J. T., Beaver, D. I., Chung, C. K., Frazee, J., Pennebaker, J. W., Graesser, A., & Cai, Z. (2010). Social language processing: A framework for analyzing the communication of terrorists and authoritarian regimes. *Behavioral Sciences of Terrorism and Political Aggression, 2,* 108–32.

Hancock, J. T., Curry, L. E., Goorha, S., & Woodworth, M. (2008). On lying and being lied to: A linguistic analysis of deception in computer-mediated communication. *Discourse Processes, 45,* 1–23.

Hart, B., & Risley, T. (2003). The early catastrophe: The 30 million word gap. *American Educator, 27,* 4–9.

Hart, R. P. (2001). *Campaign talk: Why elections are good for us.* Princeton, NJ: Princeton University Press.

———. (2000). *DICTION 5.0: The text analysis program.* Thousand Oaks, CA: Sage-Scolari.

Hart, R. P., Jarvis, S. E., Jennings, W. P., & Smith-Howell, D. (2005). *Political keywords: Using language that uses us.* New York: Oxford University Press.

Higgins, E. T. (1987). Self-discrepancy: A theory relating self and affect. *Psychological Review, 94,* 319–40.

Hogenraad, R. (2005). What the words of war can tell us about the risk of war. *Peace and Conflict: Journal of Peace Psychology, 11,* 137–51.

Holleran, S. E., Whitehead, J., Schmader, T., & Mehl, M. R. (In press). Talking shop and shooting the breeze: A study of workplace conversation and job disengagement among STEM faculty. *Social Psychology and Personality Science.*

Hoyt, T., & Yeater, E. A. (2009). Factors affecting women's verbal immediacy to sexually risky situations. *Journal of Language and Social Psychology, 28,* 312–19.

Hughes, C. F. (1994). Effects of expressing negative and positive emotions and insight on health and adjustment to college. *Dissertation Abstracts International: Section B: The Sciences and Engineering, 54,* 3899.

Ickes, W. (2009). *Strangers in a strange lab: How personality shapes our initial encounters with others.* New York: Oxford.

Ireland, M. E., & Pennebaker, J. W. (2010). Language style matching in writing: Synchrony in essays, correspondence, and poetry. *Journal of Personality and Social Psychology*, 99, 549–71.

———. (2011). *Men imitate life, women underestimate it: Sex differences in scriptwriters' portrayal of naturalistic dialogue.* Manuscript under review.

Ireland, M. E., Slatcher, R. B., Eastwick, P. W., Scissors, L. E., Finkel, E. J., & Pennebaker, J. W. (2011). Language style matching predicts relationship formation and stability. *Psychological Science*, 22, 39–44.

James, W. (1890). *The principles of psychology*, vol 1. New York: Henry Holt.

Jamison, K. R. (1993). *Touched with fire: Manic-depressive illness and the artistic temperament.* New York: Free Press.

Josephs, R. A., Sellers, J. G., Newman, M. L., & Mehta, P. H. (2006). The mismatch effect: When testosterone and status are at odds. *Journal of Personality and Social Psychology*, 90, no. 6, 999–1013.

Juola, P. (2006). Authorship attribution. *Foundation and Trends in Informational Retrieval*, 1, 233–332.

Kacewicz, E., Pennebaker, J. W., Davis, M., Jeon, M., & Graesser, A. C. (2011) Pronoun use reflects standings in social hierarchies. Submitted for publication.

Kahn, J. H., Tobin, R. M., Massey, A. E., & Anderson, J. A. (2007). Measuring emotional expression with the Linguistic Inquiry and Word Count. *The American Journal of Psychology*, 120, 263–86.

Kashima, E., & Kashima, Y. (1998). Culture and language: The case of cultural dimensions in personal pronoun use. *Journal of Cross-Cultural Psychology*, 29, 461–86.

Kaufman, J. C., & Sexton, J. D. (2006). Why doesn't the writing cure help poets? *Review of General Psychology*, 10, 268–82.

Kelly, A. (2002). *The psychology of secrets.* New York: Kluwer Academic/Plenum Publishers.

Kelly, A., & Macready, D. (2009). Why disclosing to a confidante can be good (or bad) for us. In Afifi, T. D., & Afifi, W. D. (eds.), *Uncertainty, information management, and disclosure decisions: Theories and applications*, (384–402). New York: Routledge/Taylor and Francis Group.

Keltner, D., Gruenfeld, D. H., & Anderson, C. (2003). Power, approach, and inhibition. *Psychological Review*, 110, 265–84.

Kim, Y. (2008). Effects of expressive writing among bilinguals: Exploring psychological well-being and social behaviour. *British Journal of Health Psychology*, 13, 43–47.

King, S. (2000). *On writing: A memoir of the craft.* New York: Scribner.

Kittur, A., & Kraut, R. E. (2010). Beyond Wikipedia: Coordination and conflict in online production groups. In *CSCW 2010: Proceedings of the ACM Conference on Computer-Supported Cooperative Work*, 215–24. New York: ACM Press.

Knapp, M. L., Hart, R. P., & Dennis, H. S. (1974). An exploration of deception as a communication construct. *Human Communication Research*, 1, 15–29.

Koppel, M., Schler, J., & Zigdon, K. (2005). Determining an author's native language by mining a text for errors (short paper), *Proceedings of KDD*, Chicago IL, August.

Kotz, S. A., D'Ausilio, A., Raettig, T., Begliomini, C., Craighero, L., Fabbri-Destro, M., Zingales, C., Haggard, P., & Fadiga, L. (2010). Lexicality drives audio-motor transformations in Broca's area. *Brain and Language, 112*, 3–11.

Kramer, A. D. I. (2010). An unobtrusive model of "gross national happiness." *Proceedings from CHI, 2010,* 287–90. New York: ACM Press.

Labov, W. (2001). *Principles of linguistic change,* vol. 2: *Social factors.* Oxford: Blackwell.

Lakoff, G., & Johnson, M. (1981). *Metaphors we live by.* Chicago, IL: University of Chicago Press.

Lakoff, R. (1975). *Language and woman's place.* New York: Harper and Row.

Landauer, T. K., Foltz, P. W., & Laham, D. (1998). Introduction to latent semantic analysis. *Discourse Processes, 25,* 259–84.

Larcker, D. F., & Zakolyukina, A. A. (2010). Detecting deceptive discussions in conference calls. Stanford GSB Research Paper No. 2060; Rock Center for Corporate Governance Working Paper no. 83.

Lavergne, Gary M. (2010). *Before Brown: Heman Marion Sweatt, Thurgood Marshall, and the long road to justice.* Austin: University of Texas Press.

———. (2006). *Bad boy: The true story of Kenneth Allen McDuff, the most notorius serial killer in Texas history.* New York: St. Martin's.

Lepore, S. J., & Smyth, J. M. (2002). *The writing cure: How expressive writing promotes health and emotional well-being.* Washington, D.C.: American Psychological Association.

Levertov, Denise. (1962). The ache of marriage. *Poems, 1960–1967* by Denise Levertov. New York: New Directions.

Little, A., & Skillicorn, D. B. (2010). Patterns of word use for deception detection in testimony. *Annals of Information Systems, 9,* 25–40.

Loehlin, J. C., & Martin, N. G. (2001). Age changes in personality traits and their heritabilities during the adult years: Evidence from Australian twin registry samples. *Personality and Individual Differences, 30,* 1147–60.

Louwerse, M. M., Lin, K., Drescher, A., & Semin, G. (In press). Linguistic cues predict fraudulent events in a corporate social network. *Proceedings of the 32nd Annual Conference of the Cognitive Science Society.*

Luria, A. R. (1973). *The working brain.* New York: Penguin.

Lyons, E. J., Mehl, M. R., & Pennebaker, J. W. (2006). Linguistic self-presentation in anorexia: Differences between pro-anorexia and recovering anorexia Internet language use. *Journal of Psychosomatic Research, 60,* 253–56.

Maass, A., Karasawa, M., Politi, F., & Suga, S. (2006). Do verbs and adjectives play different roles in different cultures? A cross-linguistic analysis of person representation. *Journal of Personality and Social Psychology, 90,* 734–50.

Mairesse, F., Walker, M. A., Mehl, M. R., & Moore, R. K. (2007). Using linguistic cues for the automatic recognition of personality in conversation and text. *Journal of Artificial Intelligence Research, 30,* 457–500.

Maner, J. K., Miller, S. L., Schmidt, N. B., and Eckel, L. A. (2008). Submitting to defeat: Social anxiety, dominance threat, and decrements in testosterone. *Psychological Science, 19,* 764–68.

Martindale, C. (1990). *A clockwork muse: The predictability of artistic change.* New York: Basic.

McAdams, D. P. (2011). *George W. Bush and the redemptive dream: A psychological portrait.* New York: Oxford University Press.

McCarthy, P. M., Dufty, D., Hempelman, C., Cai, Z., Graesser, A.C., & McNamara, D. S. (In press). Evaluating giveness/newness. In *Applied natural language processing and content analysis: Identification, investigation, and resolution,* eds. P. M. McCarthy and Boonthum, C. Hershey, PA: IGI Global.

McCarthy, P. M., Myers, J. C., Briner, S. W., Graesser, A. C., & McNamara, D. S. (2009). Are three words all we need? A psychological and computational study of genre recognition. *Journal for Language Technology and Computational Linguistics, 1,* 23–57.

McClelland, D. C. (1979). Inhibited power motivation and high blood pressure in men. *Journal of Abnormal Psychology, 88,* 182–90.

Mehl, M. R., Gosling, S. D., & Pennebaker, J. W. (2006). Personality in its natural habitat: Manifestations and implicit folk theories of personality in daily life. *Journal of Personality and Social Psychology, 90,* 862–77.

Mehl, M. R., & Pennebaker, J. W. (2003). The social dynamics of a cultural upheaval: Social interactions surrounding September 11, 2001. *Psychological Science, 14,* 579–85.

———. (2003). The sounds of social life: A psychometric analysis of students' daily social environments and conversations. *Journal of Personality and Social Psycho-lolgy, 84,* 857–70.

Mehl, M. R., Vazire, S., Ramírez-Esparza, N., Slatcher, R. B., & Pennebaker, J. W. (2007). Are women really more talkative than men? *Science, 317,* 82.

Mergenthaler, E. (1996). Emotion-abstraction patterns in verbatim protocols: A new way of describing psychotherapeutic processes. *Journal of Consulting and Clinical Psychology, 64,* 1306–15.

Michel, J-B., Shen, Y. K., Aiden, A. P., Veres, A., Gray, M. K., the Google Books Team, Pickett, J. P., Hoiberg, D., Clancy, D., Norvig, J., Pinker, S., Nowak, M. A., & Aiden, E. L. (2010). Quantitative analysis of culture using millions of digitized books. *Science,* 1199644, published online, December 16, 2010.

Miller, G. A. (1995). *The science of words.* New York: Scientific American Library.

Montgomery, K. J., Seeherman, K. R., & Haxby, J. V. (2009). The well-tempered social brain. *Psychological Science, 20,* 1211–13.

Moore, S. D., & Brody, L. R. (2009). Linguistic predictors of mindfulness in written self-disclosure narratives. *Journal of Language and Social Psychology, 28,* 281–96.

Morris, Edmund. (1999). *Dutch: A memoir of Ronald Reagan.* New York: Random House.

———. (2005). Conservative compassion. *New York Times,* August 17, 2005. www.nytimes.com/2005/08/17/opinion/17morris.html

Mosteller, F., & Wallace, D. L. (1984). *Applied Bayesian and classical inference: The case of the Federalist Papers.* New York: Springer-Verlag.

Newman, M. L., Groom, C. J., Handelman, L. D., & Pennebaker, J. W. (2008). Gender differences in language use: An analysis of 14,000 text samples. *Discourse Processes*, *45*, 211–46.

Newman, M. L., Pennebaker, J. W., Berry, D. S., & Richards, J. M. (2003). Lying words: Predicting deception from linguistic styles. *Personality and Social Psychology Bulletin*, *29*, 665–75.

Niederhoffer, K. G., & Pennebaker, J. W. (2002). Linguistic style matching in social interaction. *Journal of Language and Social Psychology*, *21*, 337–60.

Nisbett, R. E. (2003). *The geography of thought: How Asians and westerners think differently.* New York: Free Press.

Nixon, R. M. (1974). *Submission of recorded presidential conversations to the committee on the judiciary of the house of representatives.* Washington, D.C.: Government Printing Office.

Oberlander, J., & Gill, A. J. (2006). Language with character: A stratified corpus comparison of individual differences in e-mail communication. *Discourse Processes*, *42*, 239–70.

Odom, S. D. (2006). *A qualitative and linguistic analysis of an Authority Issues Training.* Doctoral dissertation, University of Texas at Austin.

Ophir, E., Nass, C. I., & Wagner, A. D. (2009). Cognitive control in media multitaskers. *Proceedings of the National Academy of Sciences*, *106*, 15583–87.

Parker-Pope, T. (2010). *For better: The science of a good marriage.* New York: Dutton.

Pennebaker, J. W. (1997). *Opening up: The healing power of expressing emotions*, rev. ed. New York: Guilford Press.

———. (2009). What is "I" saying? The Language Log, guest post, August 9. langua gelog.ldc.upenn.edu/nll/?p=1651

Pennebaker, J. W., Booth, R. J., & Francis, M. E. (2007). *Linguistic Inquiry and Word Count: LIWC (2007).* Austin, TX: LIWC (www.liwc.net).

Pennebaker, J. W., & Chung, C. K. (2008). Computerized text analysis of al-Qaeda transcripts. In Krippendorff, K., and Bock, M. A. (eds.), *A content analysis reader*, 453–65. Thousand Oaks, CA: Sage.

———. (In press). Expressive writing and its links to mental and physical health. In Friedman, H. S. (ed.), *Oxford handbook of health psychology*, New York: Oxford University Press.

Pennebaker, J. W., Chung, C. K., Ireland, M., Gonzales, A., & Booth, R. J. (2007). *The development and psychometric properties of LIWC 2007.* Software manual. Austin, TX: LIWC.net.

Pennebaker, J. W., & Gonzales, A. (2008). Making history: Social and psychological processes underlying collective memory. In Wertsch, J. V., & Boyer, P. (eds.), *Collective memory*, 110–29. New York: Cambridge University Press.

Pennebaker, J. W., Groom, C. J., Loew, D., & Dabbs, J. (2004). Testosterone as a social inhibitor: Two case studies of the effect of testosterone treatment on language. *Journal of Abnormal Psychology*, *113*, 172–75.

Pennebaker, J. W., and Harber, K. D. (1993). A social stage model of collective coping: The Loma Prieta earthquake and the Persian Gulf War. *Journal of Social Issues*, *49*, 125–45.

Pennebaker, J. W., Hughes, C. F., & O'Heeron, R. C. (1987). The psychophysiology of confession: Linking inhibitory and psychosomatic processes. *Journal of Personality and Social Psychology, 52,* 781–93.

Pennebaker, J. W., & Ireland, M. (2008). Analyzing words to understand literature. In Auracher, J., & van Peer, W. (eds.), *New beginnings in literary studies,* 24–48. Newcastle, UK: Cambridge Scholars Publishing.

Pennebaker, J. W., & King, L.A. (1999). Linguistic styles: Language use as an individual difference. *Journal of Personality and Social Psychology, 77,* 1296–1312.

Pennebaker, J. W., & Lay, T. C. (2002). Language use and personality during crises: Analyses of Mayor Rudolph Giuliani's press conferences. *Journal of Research in Personality, 36,* 271–82.

Pennebaker, J. W., Mayne, T. J., & Francis, M. E. (1997). Linguistic predictors of adaptive bereavement. *Journal of Personality and Social Psychology, 72,* 863–71.

Pennebaker, J. W., Mehl, M. R., & Niederhoffer, K. G. (2003). Psychological aspects of natural language use: Our words, our selves. *Annual Review of Psychology, 54,* 547–77.

Pennebaker, J. W., & Stone, L. D. (2003). Words of wisdom: Language use over the lifespan. *Journal of Personality and Social Psychology, 85,* 291–301.

Pentland, A. (2008). *Honest signals: How they shape our world.* Cambridge, MA: MIT Press.

Perdue, C. W., Dovidio, J. F., Gurtman, M. B., & Tyler, B. (1990). Us and them: Social categorization and the process of intergroup bias. *Journal of Personality and Social Psychology, 59,* 475–86.

Petrie, K. J., Pennebaker, J. W., & Sivertsen, B. (2008). Things we said today: A linguistic analysis of the Beatles. *Psychology of Aesthetics, Creativity, and the Arts, 2,* 197–202.

Pettijohn II, T. F., & Sacco Jr., D. F., (2009). The language of lyrics: An analysis of popular *Billboard* songs across conditions of social and economic threat. *Journal of Language and Social Psychology, 28,* 297–311.

Picard, R. W. (2010). Emotion research by the people, for the people. *Emotion Review, 2,* 250–54.

Pinker, S. (1991). Rules of language. *Science, 253,* 530–35.

———. (1994). *The language instinct.* New York, NY: William Morrow & Company.

———. (2007). *The stuff of thought: Language as a window into human nature.* New York: Penguin.

Plath, Sylvia. (1953). Mad girl's lovesong. In *The collected poems of Sylvia Plath,* 1981. New York: Harper & Row.

Pysczynski, T., & Greenberg, J. (1987). Self-regulatory preservation and the self-focusing style: A self-awareness theory of reactive depression. *Psychological Bulletin, 102,* 122–38.

Ramírez-Esparza, N., Chung, C. K., Kacewicz, E., & Pennebaker, J. W. (2008). The psychology of word use in depression forums in English and in Spanish: Testing two text analytic approaches. *Proceedings of the 2008 International Conference on Weblogs and Social Media,* 102–8.

Ramírez-Esparza, N., Chung, C. K., Sierra-Otero, G., & Pennebaker, J. W. (In press). Cross-cultural constructions of self-schemas: Americans and Mexicans. *Journal of Cross-Cultural Psychology.*

Ramírez-Esparza, N., Gosling, S. D., Benet-Martínez, V., Potter, J., & Pennebaker, J.W. (2006). Do bilinguals have two personalities? A special case of frame switching. *Journal of Research in Personality, 40,* 99–120.

Ramírez-Esparza, N., Mehl, M. R., & Pennebaker, J. W. (2009). Are Mexicans more or less sociable than Americans? Insights from a naturalistic observational study. *Journal of Research in Personality, 43,* 1–7.

Rentfrow, P. J., Gosling, S. D., & Potter, J. (2008). A theory of the emergence, persistence, and expression of geographic variation in psychological characteristics. *Perspectives on Psychological Science, 3,* 339–69.

Rentfrow, P. J., Mellander, C., Florida, R. (2009). Happy states of America: A state-level analysis of psychological, economic, and social well-being. *Journal of Research in Personality, 43,* 1073–82.

Rimé, B., Paez, D., Kanyangara, P., & Yzerbyt, V. (2011). The social sharing of emotions in interpersonal and in collective situations: Common psychosocial consequences. In Nykliček, I., Vingerhoets, A., & Zeelenberg, M. (eds.), *Emotion regulation and well-being,* 147–63. New York: Springer Science + Business Media.

Rizzolatti, G., & Craighero, L. (2004). The mirror-neuron system. *Annual Review of Neuroscience, 27,* 169–92.

Robins, R. W., Tracy, J. L., Trzesniewski, K., Potter, J., & Gosling, S. D. (2001). Personality correlates of self-esteem *Journal of Research in Personality, 35,* 463–82.

Rohrbaugh, M. J., Mehl, M. R., Shoham, V., Reilly, E. S., & Ewy, G. A. (2008). Prognostic significance of spouse "we" talk in couples coping with heart failure. *Journal of Consulting and Clinical Psychology, 76,* 781–89.

Rosenberg, S. D., & Tucker, G. J. (1978). Verbal behavior and schizophrenia: The semantic dimension. *Archives of General Psychiatry, 36,* 1331–37.

Rude, S. S., Gortner, E. M., & Pennebaker, J. W. (2004). Language use of depressed and depression-vulnerable college students. *Cognition and Emotion, 18,* 1121–33.

Salib, E. (2003). Effect of 11 September 2001 on suicide and homicide in England and Wales. *British Journal of Psychiatry, 183,* 207–12.

Salib, E., & Cortina-Borja, M. (2009). Effect of 7 July 2005 terrorist attacks in London on suicide in England and Wales. *British Journal of Psychiatry, 194,* 80–85.

Scholand, A. J., Tausczik, Y. R., & Pennebaker, J. W. (2010). Linguistic analysis of workplace computer-mediated communication. *Proceedings of Computer Supported Cooperative Work 2010.*

Scott, M. (2010). *WordSmith Tools v.5.* Liverpool: Lexical Analysis Software.

Searle, J. (1989). How performatives work. *Linguistics and Philosophy, 12,* 535–58.

Seider, B. H., Hirschberger, G., Nelson, K. L., & Levenson, R. W. (2009). We can work it out: Age differences in relational pronouns, physiology, and behavior in marital conflict. *Psychology and Aging, 24,* 604–13.

Seih, Y., Chung, C. K., & Pennebaker, J. W. (In press). Experimental manipulations of perspective taking and perspective switching in expressive writing. *Cognition and Emotion.*

Semin, G. R., & Fiedler, K. (1988). The cognitive functions of linguistic categories in describing persons: Social cognition and language. *Journal of Personality and Social Psychology, 54,* 558–68.

Semin, G. R., Rubini, M., & Fiedler, K. (1995). The answer is in the question: The effect of verb causality on the locus of explanation. *Personality and Social Psychology Bulletin, 21,* 834–41.

Sexton, J. B., & Helmreich, R. L. (2000). Analyzing cockpit communications: The links between language, performance, and workload. *Human Performance in Extreme Environments, 5,* 63–68.

Silver, R. C., & Wortman, C. B. (2007). The stage theory of grief. *JAMA: The Journal of the American Medical Association, 297,* 2692.

Simmons, R. A., Chambless, D. L., & Gordon, P. C. (2008). How do hostile and emotionally overinvolved relatives view relationships? What relatives' pronoun use tells us. *Family Process, 47,* 405–19.

Simmons, R. A., Gordon, P. C., & Chambless, D. (2005). Pronoun use in marital interaction: What do "you" and "I" say about marital health? *Psychological Science, 16,* 932–36.

Skillicorn, D. B. (2008). *Knowledge discovery for counterterrorism and law enforcement.* Toronto: CRC Press.

Slatcher, R. B., Chung, C. K., Pennebaker, J. W., & Stone, L. D. (2007). Winning words: Individual differences in linguistic style among U.S. presidential and vice presidential candidates. *Journal of Research in Personality, 41,* 63–75.

Slatcher, R. B., & Pennebaker, J. W. (2006). How do I love thee? Let me count the words: The social effects of expressive writing. *Psychological Science, 17,* 660–64.

Smith, A. G. (2008). The implicit motives of terrorist groups: How the needs for affiliation and power translate into death and destruction. *Political Psychology, 29,* 55–75.

Sofer, D. O. (2003). *El Pueblo and La Rosca [electronic resource]: A political dialogue in Colombia, 1944–58.* Austin, Texas: University of Texas Libraries.

Spera, S. P., Buhrfeind, E. D., & Pennebaker, J. W. (1994). Expressive writing and coping with job loss. *Academy of Management Journal, 37,* 722–33.

Stirman, S. W., & Pennebaker, J. W. (2001). Word use in the poetry of suicidal and non-suicidal poets. *Psychosomatic Medicine, 63,* 517–22.

Stone, L. D., & Pennebaker, J. W. (2002). Trauma in real time: Talking and avoiding online conversations about the death of Princess Diana. *Basic and Applied Social Psychology, 24,* 172–82.

Stone, P. J., Dunphy, D. C., & Smith, M. S. (1966). *The General inquirer: A computer approach to content analysis.* Cambridge, MA: MIT Press.

Swann Jr., W. B., Gómez, A., Huici, C., Morales, F., & Hixon, J. G. (2010). Identity fusion and self-sacrifice: Arousal as catalyst of pro-group fighting, dying and helping behavior. *Journal of Personality and Social Psychology, 99,* 824–41.

Tannen, D. (1990). *You just don't understand.* New York: William Morrow & Company.

Tausczik, Y. R., & Pennebaker, J. W. (2009). Leadership in informal groups: A linguistic investigation of Wikipedia. Presented at the annual meeting of Group Processes and Intergroup Relations, Society for Personality and Social Psychology, Las Vegas, NV, January.

———. (2010). The psychological meaning of words: LIWC and computerized text analysis methods. *Journal of Language and Social Psychology, 29,* 24–54.

———. (2011). Predicting the quality of online mathematics contributions from users' reputations. *Proceedings of the 2011 Conference for the Computer Human Interaction Society (CHI 2011).*

Tavris, C., & Aronson, E. (2007). *Mistakes were made (but not by me): Why we justify foolish beliefs, bad decisions, and hurtful acts.* Orlando, FL: Harcourt.

Taylor, P. J., & Thomas, S. (2008). Linguistic style matching and negotiation outcome. *Negotiation and Conflict Management Research, 1,* 263–81.

Toma, C. L., Hancock, J. T., & Ellison, N. B. (2008). Separating fact from fiction: An examination of deceptive self-presentation in online dating profiles. *Personality and Social Psychology Bulletin, 34,* 1023–36.

Trivers, R. L. (2011). *Deceit and self-deception.* New York: Basic Books.

Vano, A. M. (2001). *Linguistic predictors of treatment success among female substance abusers.* Unpublished doctoral dissertation, University of Texas at Austin.

Vano, A. M., & Pennebaker, J. W., (1997). Emotional vocabulary in bilingual Hispanic children: Adjustment and behavioral effects. *Journal of Language and Social Psychology, 16,* 191–200.

Vrij, A., & Mann, S. (2006). Criteria-Based Content Analysis: An empirical test of its underlying processes. *Psychology, Crime and Law, 12,* 337–49.

Waldman, D. A., Ramirez, G. G., House, R. J., & Puranam, P. (2001). Does leadership matter? CEO leadership attributes and profitability under conditions of perceived environmental uncertainty. *Academy of Management Journal, 44,* 134–43.

Wegner, D. M. (1989). *White bears and other unwanted thoughts: Suppression, obsession, and the psychology of mental control.* New York: Viking/Penguin.

Weiner, E. (2008). *The geography of bliss: One grump's search for the happiest places in the world.* New York: Twelve.

Weintraub, W. (1981). *Verbal behavior: Adaptation and psychopathology.* New York: Springer.

———. (1989). *Verbal behavior in everyday life.* New York: Springer.

Weston, D. (2007). *The political brain: The role of emotion in deciding the fate of the nation.* New York: Public Affairs.

Wicklund, R. A. (1975). Objective self-awareness. *Advances in Experimental Social Psychology, 8,* 233–75.

Wierzbicka, A. (1997). *Understanding cultures through their key words.* New York: Oxford University Press.

Wilson, Timothy D. (2002). *Strangers to ourselves: Discovering the adaptive unconscious.* Cambridge, MA: Belknap Press.

Wilson, Timothy D. (2011). *Redirect: The surprising new science of psychological change.* New York: Little, Brown.

Winter, D. G. (1998). A motivational analysis of the Clinton first term and the 1996 presidential campaign. *The Leadership Quarterly, 9,* 367–76.

Winter, D. G., & McClelland, D. C. (1978). Thematic analysis: An empirically derived measure of the effects of liberal arts education. *Journal of Educational Psychology*, *70*, 8–16.

Wolf, M., Chung, C. K., & Kordy, H. (2010). Inpatient treatment to online aftercare: E-mailing themes as a function of therapeutic outcomes. *Psychotherapy Research*, *20*, 71–85.

———. (2010). MEM's search for meaning: A rejoinder. *Psychotherapy Research*, *20*, 93–99.

Wolf, M., Horn, A. B., Mehl, M. R., Haug, S., Pennebaker, J. W., & Kordy, H. (2008). Computergestützte quantitative Textanalyse: Äquivalenz und Robustheit der deutschen Version des Linguistic Inquiry and Word Count [Computer-aided quantitative text analysis: Equivalence and robustness of the German adaption of the Linguistic Inquiry and Word Count]. *Diagnostica*, *54*, 85–98.

Woods, K. M. (2007). *Iraqi Perspectives Project: Saddam and terrorism: Emerging insights from captured Iraqi documents*, vols. 1. Institute for Defense Analysis, Alexandria, VA. www.fas.org/irp/eprint/iraqi/index.html

Wright, A. (2009). Mining the web for feelings, not facts. *New York Times*, August 23. www.nytimes.com/2009/08/24/technology/internet/24emotion.html

Yarkoni, T. (2010). Personality in 100,000 words: A large-scale analysis of personality and word use among bloggers. *Journal of Research in Personality*, *44*, 363–73.

Zhou, L., Burgoon, J. K., Nunamaker, J. F., & Twitchell, D. (2004). Automating linguistics-based cues for detecting deception in text-based asynchronous computer-mediated communications. *Group Decision and Negotiation*, *13*, 81–106.

Zijlstra, H., van Meerveld, T., van Middendorp, H., Pennebaker, J. W., & Geenen, R. (2004). De Nederlandse versie van de Linguistic Inquiry and Word Count (LIWC), een gecomputeriseerd tekstanalyseprogramma [Dutch version of the Linguistic Inquiry and Word Count (LIWC), a computerized text analysis program]. *Gedrag & Gezondheid*, *32*, 273–83.

Index

Note: page references in italics refer to tables or figures.

A NOTE ON THE AUTHOR

JAMES W. PENNEBAKER is the Regents Centennial Professor of
Liberal Arts and Chair of the Department of Psychology at the University of Texas at Austin. In addition to being an avid researcher and
teacher, he enjoys running, movies, pronouns, auxiliary verbs, and arti-
chokes. He and his wife, Ruth Pennebaker, who is a respected author,
live in Austin. Their daughter, Teal, lives in Washington, D.C., and their
son, Nick, lives in Austin.

You can analyze your own language using his websites, www.Secret
LifeOfPronouns.com and www.analyzewords.com.